THE SPIRIT OF ADV

towards a better world…

Colin Mortlock.

Lessons learned from a life of
challenge and discovery

Colin Mortlock

Outdoor Integrity
Publishing

An Outdoor Integrity Publishing Book

Published by Outdoor Integrity Publishing Limited
22 Underley Hill,
Kendal, LA9 5EX
T: +44 (0)1539 723172

www.soaadventure.org

ISBN 978-1-907362-00-2

British Library Cataloguing-in-Publication data
A catalogue record for this book is available from the British Library

Cover design by Steve Scott — Lavahouse Associates
Set in Bembo.
Design and Typesetting by Jacqui Hill and Georgie Lowry — Lavahouse Associates
Assisted by Fiona Exon — IOL

Printed in GB by Absolute Digital Print, on stock from FSC accredited sources

To Annette

A painting taken from Annette's 1998 Pyrenean Expedition Diary.

This was what she wrote:

The flower of the expedition, Callianthemum Anemonoides. A brilliant white filling the crevice in rocky ground close to the snow line. Bright as only white flowers can be in dark places.

Introduction to the Author

I shall not attempt to write an account of the life of Colin Mortlock, as he shares his personal experiences in this book beautifully. I do believe, however that his contributions to adventure, education and values have progressed practical education in the UK and internationally, beyond adventure outdoors into something deeper and more worthwhile concerning human nature and existence.

I first met Colin in 2003 when he gave a lecture on some of the concepts explored in this book. I had been studying development training at masters level and Colin's two previous books the *The Adventure Alternative* and *Beyond Adventure* frequently cropped up in debate as did his contributions to Outdoor Education. Colin held the influential post of Director for the Centre for Outdoor Education at Charlotte Mason College from 1975 to 1992. I wanted to know what motivated him, what made him make some of the decisions he took back in the early sixties when he taught at Royal Wolverhampton and Manchester Grammar Schools. I felt I had to know more about him.

Colin studied at Keble College, Oxford leaving with a 2:1 in Modern History, despite attending only three lectures! It was at this stage in his life that climbing became an obsession. He became president of the Oxford University Mountaineering Club and continued to climb seriously for the next fifteen years.

In 1965 Colin became principal of Oxford's outdoor centre, The Woodlands, situated in South Wales. The centre quickly became recognised for the highest standards of adventure and innovation. When we recently talked together in Colin's conservatory, one of the messages that came across was how creative and balanced were his courses for young teenagers. It seemed to me also that, Colin had raised the bar in terms of the capabilities of young people to adventure and survive in a wide range of outdoor environments and conditions. His thinking and actions at that time were both visionary and brave. They were to be repeated from Ambleside with his later work with primary schoolchildren, students, teachers and a large community project.

It is obvious that during a lifetime dedicated to outdoor education, adventure and a search for the 'truth' in all things, Colin has consistently questioned himself and his actions. I cannot begin to understand the tenacity and drive required to undertake such expeditions as his solo kayak trip in Alaska and his pioneering expeditions for groups of children and young people. I believe this is what makes Colin different. He does not write from an academic or conceptual standpoint. He writes from experiences, and invites the reader to join him in his struggles to begin to understand their values. In this book especially the reader is witness to a fascinating account of a lifetime of increasingly mature reflection.

As one of those readers I have been inspired by the values he has discovered – not just as a fellow traveller who loves adventure and wild Nature but in my work. In my previous post, on reading the proof of the book, I determined to use these values as the basis for all courses at what is the largest outdoor centre in Europe. To that end Colin came and talked to staff. Like the author I have no doubt that, in a frenetic and materialistic modern world, where decisions are often taken according to power, money and status, the values he projects could not be more important. I believe these core values should underpin not only courses using wild Nature for developing human potential but should underpin our individual lives.

Colin is a private man with an impressive career both in education and personal adventure, I am convinced that he has followed strongly in the footsteps of Outward Bound's Kurt Hahn. His quest to influence people to think critically about the value of wilderness experiences, the world that they live in and their actions has inspired many over the years. They include young people, students and teachers, friends and colleagues and those who have heard his lectures around the world. His beliefs will survive him and continue to shape many generations to come.

A dear friend, someone who has had a profound and positive impact upon my life, I am honoured to know Colin and love him dearly.

Thank you Colin – you make me want to be a better person.

Tracy A Dixon

Contents

i	Introduction (Part 1)	xi
ii	Introduction (Part 2)	xv
1	School Days	1
2	The Instinct for Adventure	7
3	Underlying Wisdom	13
4	Who Am I?	17
5	Where Am I Going?	27
6	If Only...	31
7	How Do I Get There?	37
8	Values and Virtues	41
	Honesty	50
	Awareness	55
	Respect	61
	Compassion	63
	Determination	66
	Patience	68
	Self discipline	71
	Self reliance	73
	Concentration	75
	Altruism	77
	Empathy	79
	Friendliness	81
	Kindness	84
	Gentleness	86
	Gratitude	88
	Tolerance	91
	Forgiveness	93
	Justice	95
	Creativity	98
	Responsibility	101
	Humility	103
	Purity	106
	Simplicity	109
	Vitality	111
	Courage	113
	Humour	116
9	Wisdom	127
10	Specific Wisdoms	133
	Action - Reflection	135

	A Sense of Awe and Wonder	137
	The Search for Truth	141
	Singular Universal	144
	Heroes & Heroines	148
11	**Wisdoms From Nature**	153
	Uncertainty	155
	Energy	159
	Balance	161
	Unity	163
12	Act According to Conscience	165
13	Transcendent Experiences	171
14	The Search for Beauty	181
15	Music	187
16	Mystery and God	193
17	Love	201
18	Friendship	213
19	Truth and Living in the Moment	219
20	Natural Examinations	225
21	Looking Back	234
22	Towards a Better World	239
23	Epilogue	245
24	Postscript	249
	Appendices	253
	A. Annette	253
	B. Author Background	257
	Acknowledgements	261
	Information on Authors Quoted	262
	Current Authors Quoted	267
	Bibliography	268
	Endnotes	279
	Index	283
	Comments On The Book (pre-publication)	292

i

Introduction

"The unconsidered life is not worth living...a life well lived is one which has goals and integrity...which is chosen and directed by the one who lives it, to the fullest extent possible."

Socrates

In 2002 life seemed good. Annette, my wife, and I had completed three one-month trekking expeditions in the mountains of Europe. We had both retired from education and seemed in excellent health. By spring 2003 Annette was dead from bowel cancer. Shattered, I moved from the Lake District to live remotely in North West Scotland. I read about and reflected upon death. I tried to understand what it meant. Eventually, knowing that putting pen to paper can often clarify one's thoughts, I wrote to myself.

Although I did not realise this at the time, it was to be the beginning of this book.

Now in my seventies, and after a lifetime of work and play in wild Nature, I have glimmerings of understanding as to who I am, where I am going and how I get there. What I have discovered is both profound and wonderful. It is of special importance in this excessively materialistic age, where more than any religion previously, the great God of consumerism has swept the planet.

Please come with me on this journey. It has taken a lifetime of experience and much of the last four years, with help from others, to put this book together. My life has been a search for the truth of what life is about. The great truths are beyond words, but words can help us to increase our awareness of the magic of Adventure and Love, Beauty and Wisdom.

You may find this journey unconventional if not challenging. Some of the ideas too may seem strange but try and keep an open mind. If I come across as self-centred it is almost inevitable. I can only speak from my own experiences. My conscience, however, is clear. I know that to begin to understand who I am I have to move beyond egoism. I now also realise that the path through life has to be one of humility rather than arrogance.

There are three interwoven strands:

Personal experiences	–	*autobiography*
Reflections on those experiences	–	*values and philosophy*
Quotations	–	*wisdom of the ages*

Please do not ask me in which section you would find this book in the library!

Life is, or should be, a search to begin to understand your own uniqueness and how best to live your life. Your uniqueness is matched by your sameness with everyone else. This includes the fact that we are all essentially natural. By that I mean we come into the world through a wonderful natural process. In whatever way we choose to live our lives we are inevitably affected by natural processes such as instincts. We then depart, or return to Nature, through the natural process of death. Wild Nature holds crucial answers as to how to live our lives.

I do not intend for the book to be prescriptive. Rather I hope it becomes, or provides, a basis for discussion and stimulates people to think about the issues raised. Life must always be an individual journey yet, as the book reveals, I now believe there is an underlying unity. There is huge potential for hearts to meet across all borders of time and space.

Most importantly enjoy the book. If you are confused at times, then remember I am no different. Just find inspiration to intensify your own search to understand the magic of your own existence.

ii

Introduction

Several friends, in commenting on the drafts for the book, were in favour of publication but said they had a serious reservation. This was simple and stark: "Was it not too late?" I knew immediately what they meant. Momentarily I was tempted to reply: "Yes, I agree, and here at least is one reason why I am thankful to be in old age." Sanity quickly took hold, thank goodness. Unless I have hope both for the future of the planet and the human race, then I would rather be dead.

There is little doubt in my mind, however, that Armageddon could be imminent. In no way would I be surprised if the human race was to disappear within fifty years. It would almost be poetic justice in terms of human responsibility, for the innumerable other species of life that it has already destroyed.

We happen to be at a most crucial (and exciting!) time in the history of civilisation. A time perhaps, when we are on the cusp of beginning to pay for all the accumulated human vices generally, and man's rampant greed in particular. To have any hope of a bright future I sense the human race – both *individually* and *collectively* – is going to have to make a massive effort. Even then, I suspect, it will need a large slice of luck.

The following quotations aptly express some of my strongest feelings about the human world in which we live.

"The present state of the world calls for a moral and spiritual revolution, revolution in the name of personality, of man, of every single person. This revolution should restore the hierarchy of values, now quite shattered, and place the value of human personality above the idols of production, technics, the state, the race or nationality."
— Nicholai Berdyaev

"We try to evade the question (of existence) with property, prestige, power, production, fun, and, ultimately, by trying to forget that we – that I – exist. No matter how often he thinks of God or goes to church, or how much he believes in religious ideas, if he, the whole man, is deaf to the question of existence, if he does not have an answer to it, he is marking time, and he lives and dies like one of the million things he produces."
— Erich Fromm

"The evolution of consciousness has given us not only the Cheops Pyramid, the Brandenburg Concertos, and the Theory of Relativity, but also the burning of witches, the holocaust and the bombing of Hiroshima. But that same evolution of consciousness gives us the potential to live peacefully and in harmony with the natural world in the future. Our evolution continues to offer us freedom of choice. We can consciously alter our behaviour by changing our values and attitudes to regain the spirituality and ecological awareness we have lost."
— Fritjof Capra

"How do we find meaning, value and connection in a society that is dislocated and in many ways dysfunctional? We have lost our sense of community or belonging to any-thing much beyond our own individual circumstance. We have become voyeurs, vacuously gazing at reality TV shows and sitcoms while exhibitionists and ever-new 'celebrities' grab their shot at fifteen minutes of fame.

Technology has radically altered our existence in so many ways. Everything happens faster, while we struggle to keep up, ever desperate to be ahead of the game. In isolation we scan the internet, and email or text our friends, as a substitute for real connection. We inform ourselves about the soaring crime rate, the effects of drugs and alcohol abuse, domestic violence, the horrors of war, the scandalous antics of corrupt businessmen and their friends, the politicians.

We digest the endless details of humankind's abuse and exploitation, while our polluted planet heats up around us. Ice caps melt, ancient rainforests disappear, the population explodes and animal species hurtle towards extinction. I am mad to have any expectation that it could be anything otherwise. But somehow I still cling to the notion that there is some kind of intelligence, sanity, goodness, compassion, or hope, somewhere on this planet."
— Annie Lennox, 2007

1

School Days

Our attitude to life and the life we lead is inevitably shaped to some degree by our experiences. The following school episodes, I now realise, were of significance in my journey.

That particular Friday morning school assembly remains a vivid memory. The expected moment finally came as the headmaster announced to the 800-strong boys' grammar school that he had a special notice to give out: unless the boy or boys who had played the practical joke on one of the staff a week ago came to see him in his office by twelve noon, then the matter would be put in the hands of the police.

It had seemed a long, albeit interesting, week for the two culprits. Tension in the school had been building all week, and my history master in his lessons constantly boomed at me, "I know you are guilty! Why don't you confess?"

My friend Roy and I had taken a strong dislike to the elderly spinster head of English, who had about a dozen boys who were her special favourites in our class. When we heard she was to have a party for them at her home on the Friday evening, we decided that we would arrange for taxis to take them home. This hardly seems very amusing but the reality certainly made us smile as we discreetly watched events. She happened to live in the middle of a high-class estate of small bungalows and narrow avenues on the edge of town. The thirty-five taxis eventually, and with some difficulty, finally congregated in the area. A deputation of four drivers marched up to the house and knocked. Her face was a picture as she was informed that her taxis had arrived. It took some time for the grumbling taxi drivers to reluctantly accept that she had not ordered their presence.

Come Monday morning back at school and Roy and I were informed that she wished to see us at morning break. One of her favourites had obviously ratted on us. To my shame I told her she must have been mistaken. Not accustomed to lying, I was simply trying to prolong the fun of the situation!

At noon precisely on the deadline Friday we knocked on the headmaster's door. Punishment inevitably followed. We were suspended from school for a fortnight and told to go and see all of the taxi firms. It was emphasised that we were fortunate not to have been expelled. The headmaster had only two weeks previously written glowing references for us for Oxford and Cambridge! About half of the taxi drivers demanded payment; most of them found it funny but emphasised it was not to be repeated. We later learned that most of the staff had also found it amusing.

At secondary school I had lived for sport. Lessons, apart from those on physical geography, were something to be endured. Academic teachers, unless too formidable, were to be tormented. My main sport in summer was cricket, and I dreamed that one day I would play for the country. Derbyshire had a great tradition for providing fast bowlers for England. The other opening fast bowler in our Derbyshire boys' team, by name of Harold Rhodes, did indeed eventually play for England. As I took more wickets than he did in those days my dream seemed possible.

I found great satisfaction in intimidating opening batsmen by sheer speed, though I must stress that, in those more civilised times, there was no thought of aiming at the batsmen. Accomplished at fast bowling I was typically a very poor batsman, who would go in as last man. In one county match when batting against a fast bowler I received a nasty high bouncer. The mouth was not the best place to receive such a delivery. Experience is a wonderful, if sometimes painful, way to learn what it is like to be on the receiving end.

By the time of the sixth form I was mortified to discover that I eventually was not even in the school 1st team at cricket. I had not been taught the arts of outswingers and inswingers and speed alone was deemed insufficient. With hindsight it was a blessing in disguise as I looked elsewhere for physical challenge.

Reading in the library one day, I came across 'Let's Go Climbing' by Colin Kirkus. His unbridled enthusiasm was impossible to resist. A Saturday bike ride with a school friend and I stood beneath Black Rocks in Derbyshire. The gritstone edge was always less than thirty metres in height but the walls, cracks and chimneys looked steep and often intimidating. Careful study of the simple guide led us to the choice of a 'very difficult' crack. I led the first two pitches, and brought up my friend. The third pitch – a short vertical crack – proved daunting. I got stuck halfway up and became frightened. The ground looked a long way below and protection was minimal. My mother's clothes line certainly did not inspire confidence. More by luck than skill I managed to retreat without falling off. Back on the ground I felt both chastened yet fascinated. The young man devoted to normal sports – cricket, tennis, basketball and gymnastics in particular – was becoming hooked on a new, more exciting and more dangerous game.

The other particularly important memory (in terms of later trying to begin to understand the mystery of human existence) was at Gardom's Edge, again in Derbyshire. I had skipped school, hitched to the Peak District from Derby and climbed all day solo. As I sat on a large prow of rock and watched the sunset, the rock around me became bathed in a glorious pink light. The beauty of those moments has remained etched in my memory.

One day in the summer of 1953 the Irish ferry en route from Stranraer to Larne is sunk in a storm with the loss of all passengers. On that same day, as a member of the sixth-form geography field trip to the Isle of Arran, I wait impatiently at Ardrossan, the ferry point west of Glasgow, for the boat trip across to Brodick. We are told that due to high winds the start is to be delayed for several hours. Once en route I find I cannot stand the retching and smell of seasickness down below. I retreat up to the deck and eventually move to the stern, hands locked firmly to the rails. I am alone in a wild, wild scene. The air is full of spray, waves crash over the bow and sweep along the decks towards me. The boat plunges and rises in dramatic fashion – a toy in the hands of the sea. I find this adventure exhilarating, although I am a little relieved when we finally arrive at Brodick.

The next day our school party begins to walk north up Glen Rosa aiming for the pass at the head of the valley, and eventually down Glen Sannox to Lochranza. Very quickly I find I am well ahead of everybody. It is a bright and breezy day and to the east, Goat Fell (847m and the highest peak of the island) towers over the valley. Its appeal is irresistible. I leave the track and set off for the summit. It is much further than it appears and takes what seems an age before I scramble up its rocky crest. To someone so young and unfamiliar with such places the view is awe inspiring. I seem to be in the sky, the white-flecked sea a very long way below, and other peaks filling the skyline to the north and west. Magnificent!

I do not stay long. Guilt is beginning to surface. I go down the north side of the peak and as quickly as I can along the ridge towards the pass. I can eventually see a group of black dots. On my arrival the geography master, not to put too fine a point on it, is furious. I apologise profusely but intuitively sense it has been well worth it.

Early November 1953. I am up at Keble College for a week trying to obtain a place to read modern history. A week of examinations and informal interviews leave me under no illusion. I know I am not an academic. I feel like a fish out of water amidst the Oxford spires. That my small town grammar school has no tradition of sending pupils to Oxford, and the weather being consistently gloomy does not help my mood. Tomorrow, after the final formal interview, I can thankfully escape and return home to the Midlands.

Next morning my turn eventually comes to go through the large oak door. Inside is impressive, the equivalent of a boardroom. The largest oval wooden table I have ever seen seems to fill the room. Around the table are large comfortable chairs filled with what appear to be mostly old men, many of whom are smoking pipes. The candidate's chair is very small and insignificant. As I sit down I too feel small and insignificant – not helped by a memory of being certain that I was too unintelligent to even go into the school sixth form. I hope my expression does not show my feelings. "What am I doing here?"

The interview begins with questions which I have long forgotten. The same may be said of my replies. The word 'desultory' springs to mind. Then comes a question which wakes me up completely: "I see that you are a climber. What do you think of the recent first ascent of Everest by a British expedition?" I immediately reply that I totally disagree with the ascent. There is a distinct hush to the proceedings. Then, from somewhere at the far end of the table, through the smoky haze, comes a somewhat icy voice, asking me if I would care to explain my remark. Again I do not hesitate and explain that I am an Eric Shipton small expedition believer.[1] To climb any mountain by military means – large-scale expedition and a military strategy – I feel is unacceptable.

On my return home I am even more convinced Oxford is not for me.

The following January there arrives at home a small brown envelope. The postmark is Oxford and I open it knowing I have been rejected. Not for the first or last time in my life I have got it wrong. I have been accepted even if my mediæval Latin has to be 'substantially improved'. The impossible has happened.

I do not propose to comment in detail on these schoolboy experiences. Nevertheless I will introduce the reader to a key wisdom which I was to come across only much later in life:

The quality of an experience needs to be balanced by the quality of the reflection upon that experience.

With considerable hindsight, I will ask myself, what was the real importance of these experiences in the light of the next fifty years or so of my life?

In four of the five experiences there is a large adventure element. Adventure in the natural world was to become both my work and my recreation.

Anti-social adventure – the practical joke in particular – whilst due to boredom with lessons, inevitably and fortunately, substantially declined. In another, mostly less provocative sense, it has remained and will continue to remain. Since Oxford I have sought to discover the truth of anything and somehow have generally managed to say and act concerning what I believe to be true. In Britain especially, such individuals tend to be unpopular and it often becomes a lonely furrow to plough.

With reference to the cricket, I had an early experience of the importance of the word *awareness*. Only by taking a cricket ball in my mouth did I become painfully conscious of what it can be like to face a fast bowler.

The final word I wish to mention here is beauty.[2] That red sunset was probably the start to an increasing awareness of the immense potential of beauty as an antidote to living in an increasingly ugly and dangerous modern world.

2

The Instinct For Adventure

1 965 and it is eleven years since I left school. Still a climber, but now with increasing enthusiasm for white-water kayaking, I am about to begin my third job. This is the post of Warden or Principal of the Woodlands Outdoor Centre, belonging to the City of Oxford Local Education Authority, and situated in Glasbury on Wye in South Wales. This would be a new challenge for me. After a year teaching PE in Wolverhampton and then PE and social studies at Manchester Grammar School, the decision to make such a distinct change in profession had caused some soul searching. No matter how demanding teaching might be – and it was always busy because I developed extensive programmes in adventure activities – I still had long holidays. These allowed me to adventure and expedition abroad, especially in the summer. The Alps and Norway had become a delightful habit!

Running an Outdoor Centre, on the other hand, meant accepting there were now no long holidays. In addition, being a new Centre, would demand I suspected, great energy from all staff. Knowledge of Outward Bound schools had confirmed this suspicion. I decided I would make the move – the delight of having a new job concerned with the outdoors and adventure full time was distinctly attractive. I was also very conscious that I could not face either my conscience or Annette, my wife, if I did not accept becoming a responsible member of society. Living a life totally dominated by my climbing and canoeing was, put in the kindest way, selfish or self-centred. I knew young people loved adventure, and I loved 'teaching' it.

As I drove south to the Centre my view seemed straightforward: South Wales was a far less adventurous area than North Wales or the Lakes – the hills and crags were distinctly smaller. This was probably good for the youngsters but not for my spare time, although the canoeing seemed to have potential. As far as the young people were concerned, I was sure some of the boys would like adventure and a minority of girls likewise. I was also prejudiced that pupils from Oxford, like the rest of the south of England, would be markedly 'softer' than those from the North, with which I was more familiar. Fortunately I kept these thoughts to myself. Looking back now it seems almost predetermined that the school pupils from Oxford were going to teach me a magnificent lesson over a very memorable six years.

The board of Governors had made it clear to me that the aims of the Outdoor Centre were Field Studies, Gracious Living and Adventure Activities. We quickly discovered that most pupils had no experience of the adventure activities on offer and most came in the first place to get away from school (Courses were in term time).

A programme was designed to provide all the adventure activities during the first week (climbing, caving, map-reading, hill-walking, camping, canoeing and an assault course). For the second week pupils selected a specialist activity taken from their experience of the first week. Those who weren't keen on any of these joined a Field Studies group. The activity selected was then pursued for five days, culminating in an expedition under canvas. These expeditions took place throughout Wales.

With regard to the aim of 'gracious living', the Course and staff would dress formally for the evening meal. Otherwise the emphasis was on informality along with politeness. The idea was that the Centre was more (hopefully) like 'home' than school. Out of doors informality was retained. For example christian names were de rigueur for staff and pupils.

As far as all staff were concerned the approach was that of a 'mini' outward bound course. Facing adventurous challenges, pupils were expected to give of their best.

Staff met every morning, along with the accompanying teachers, to monitor the progress of each pupil. By the Course end a full written review of the performance of each of them was given to the school. These reports were generally regarded as valuable, by the school, the pupil, and parents.

Within a few months the option of Field Studies in the second week was removed. What happened was that on most Courses there was nearly always a group who did not wish to specialise in any of the adventure activities on offer. Through feedback at the end of Courses we discovered that Field Studies was often unpopular. The reason was fascinating – the pupils doing this subject felt strongly that they were missing out on the adventures involving the rest of the Course. So was born a General Adventure Group, and eventually a number of unconventional activities were incorporated into the programme, such as gorge walking and 'dinghying' down rapids. Both of these activities were to become of worldwide popularity for both education and tourism.

Six years later, when I moved north to a new post in the Lake District, I reviewed what I had learned. The first realisation was that there was an *instinct for adventure*. In other words all young people loved adventure, doing something challenging and exciting in a natural environment. The challenge for staff was twofold. The first was always to provide an effective safety framework. The second was to successfully match the type and level of adventure activity with an individual's skills, fitness and adventure threshold.

The second major point was that the young people from Oxford generally responded *magnificently* to the challenges of the Course. Whilst every pupil and every Course was different, responses by pupils were, on the whole, admirable. What I am referring to here is the use of some of those virtues which make being human so worthwhile: determination; self-discipline (especially in the control of fear); empathy (in the sense of encouraging the least able in a group); humour; vitality and hard work.

Adventure activities in general range from being fun and fairly gentle to extremely challenging. A single example follows to illustrate the latter: In winter the river Wye was often in spate with rapids up to grade three. There was always a whitewater canoe group in the second week – even in the winter pupils chose to do it. On the fifteen mile river expedition from Builth Wells there were often capsizes on the bigger rapids. On reaching the bank it was quite normal for sodden and cold boys and girls to ask if they could have another go. The reader should know the pupils did not have wetsuits in those days!

My six years at the Centre instilled in me a great admiration for young people of this age range. I felt strongly that, whatever problems society might throw up, these youngsters would eventually make good citizens. I could also see clearly why the British had such a formidable reputation in times of war. When the youngsters had their backs to the wall, they normally responded extremely well and often with a sense of humour. So impressed did I become that I established, with the help of others, what eventually became the National Association for Outdoor Education, and wrote a book (The Adventure Alternative) in praise of this form of education.

Moving to the College of Education in Ambleside in the Lake District meant I was to train students to become adventure and outdoor teachers, for the Primary age range. I was wary of conventional adventure activities with such a young age group (up to eleven years). My introduction to a class of eight year–olds as I took them on to the hill underlined my concern. With whoops of joy within minutes they had vanished in all directions! They were manifesting their instinct for adventure with delight – escape from the classroom!

Once again, however, I grossly underestimated the abilities of young people. With the help of a local community programme the young people became very involved in the adventure activities for which the Lake District is famous. Some of them reached very high levels of skill. It also became a tradition for ten–and eleven–year old boys and girls in groups of up to ten, to train for and then complete five-day expeditions – both in the Lake District and down the River Wye (one hundred miles in kay-aks). These expeditions were self-reliant. Adults in charge of parties monitored the journey from a distance. Despite their tender age, to all intent the youngsters were on their own.

As I write this in 2007, I am acutely conscious of how, deep down, I am very angry and frustrated at what has not happened in adventure activities with young people in the UK. By the millenium it should have been normal for all young people in this country to have had Outdoor Education as a key part of their education – and in that programme the adventure should have been at the level of the needs and abilities of each pupil.

Instead of what should have happened, instead of adventure in the *natural* environment, adventure in the form of computer games has become immensely popular. In this world of virtual reality, adventure is neither real nor authentic. There is minimal *physical* involvement. The risks come from anxiety, an artificial or man-made stress, rather than from natural fear. In South Korea, for example, video games have become such a mania nationally that they are superceding even sport in terms of popularity. For the young especially, there are local rehabilitation centres, and suicides are not uncommon, such is the frenzy generated. (from a BBC World Service report in January 2008)

Young people today are often in the news for all the wrong reasons. Anti-social adventure, taken to extremes of murder and mayhem, is almost daily headline news – and often it is perpetrated by young people. If adventure is an instinct, then if society does not provide socially acceptable outlets, anti-social activities will often result. Not only that, but we need people in all aspects of society working on the edge of what is possible – and this of course includes the business sector. There are also other deeper reasons for young people to experience adventure in the natural, rather than the man-made environment. These reasons are to do with the human being essentially natural.

If the reader doubts there is an instinct for adventure then I would suggest they look at the circumstantial evidence that abounds. Pre-eminent are the theme parks or big thrill rides. These are a worldwide phenomenon which cash in on this instinct and are popular with the whole family. On a broader front there is a vast commercial market for armchair excitement through films and so on.

In the 1930s A.N. Whitehead, Professor of Philosophy at both Cambridge and Harvard universities wrote that he saw five characteristics of any civilised society. These were: *Beauty, Truth, Peace, Art and Adventure.* My experience underlines that adventure in the great outdoors can make a marked contribution to at least three of these characteristics: beauty, adventure and truth. Unlike so much of the man-made world, the natural world is totally honest – even if the more common word used would be 'real'. There is no dishonesty in Nature.

The following are the professor's words:

> *"A race preserves its vigour so long as it harbours a real contrast between what has been and what may be; and so long as it is nerved by the vigour to adventure beyond the safeties of the past. Without adventure civilisation is in full decay."*

3

Underlying Wisdom

In 1992 I took early retirement from my post of Head of Outdoor Education at the small college in Ambleside in the Lake District. Thoroughly disillusioned by the bureaucratic and financial pressures rampant in education at that time – more and more meetings and less and less time with students in the outdoors – I escaped with relief. As Annette, my wife, was still teaching, I was able to make trekking expeditions my normal life. In blocks of up to three months at a time I explored the Alps and especially the Pyrenees – mainly solo, with Annette joining me when she was free. The aim was always to explore new ground and to live as simply and frugally as possible, using a tiny tent. Back to wild Nature became a delightful existence and something of which I never tired. The only use of my office at home, apart from routine matters, was to study maps and plan the next journey.

By 1997 I had covered many thousands of miles. Beauty, wildness and adventure were my companions. My love of mountain flowers especially seemed to emphasise that I was not alone. In some elemental way, my natural surroundings were all my friends and I was truly at home.

In late 1997 I received an invitation to do a keynote lecture at a week-long National Outdoor Education Conference in Auckland, New Zealand. Delight at such an unexpected invitation and an opportunity to visit the country for the first time, was tempered by a sobering thought. The cost of going to the other side of the planet to give one lecture rather emphasised that it needed to be of high quality. I had, after all, retired from education five years earlier.

I sat in my office this time not to look at maps and plan my next expedition, but to find a topic and compose a lecture. To my great surprise, in what seemed no time at all, I wrote the following:

> **Everything in nature is alive in its own way, is on its own**
> **adventurous journey, and deserves its own well-being.**
> **Everything in nature, from the grain of sand to the cosmos,**
> **is no more and no less important than anything else.**

This statement was to form the basis of the keynote lecture. My expectation of how the lecture would be received was low. Having had several 'Kiwis' on my one year International Adventure Education course, I was well aware of their reputation for 'action, action, action'. They did not seem like people either to accept or be interested in the non-physical and unseen. After all, how could rocks be alive, even if it was 'in their own way'?

I comforted myself with the thought that my lecturing reputation would be less damaged by a lecture in far away New Zealand rather than if it had been in the UK.

My qualms were unfounded. The seven hundred or so delegates very warmly received the input. The organisers immediately arranged an impromptu lecture tour
throughout the length of the country. The National Outdoor Centre, the Outward
Bound School, Colleges and Universities were all to be visited. I returned home
knowing that I needed to put the ideas into book form (*Beyond Adventure*, 2001).

Commenting on this New Zealand experience at this early stage in the book will
be brief. First, and of considerable significance in terms of understanding myself,
the statement quoted did *not* come from my intellect or what might be termed my
thinking or rational aspect. It came swiftly from somewhere deep within – nearer
perhaps to my heart than my head. In the next chapter I will explore 'Who am I?'
and I will use the words 'insight' or 'intuition' stemming from my unconscious, to
describe the origin of such statements. The reader will have to bear with me here as
what I am writing about is beyond words. We are so used to using words with which
to communicate that it is no bad thing to stress that what is important – really important – in terms of being human is way beyond verbal or written communication.

What happened in that lecture hall was that somehow or other I had reached the
hearts of many of the audience. There were even, apparently, a group of ladies outside listening to the extension speaker, who were in tears by the end of the session.
Unsurprisingly, many 'Kiwis' have a great love of the outdoors generally and adventure in particular. 'Love' I would rate as the most important word in our vocabulary,
and something that is all but impossible to describe. We all *loved* wild Nature. The
journey through this book, I sincerely hope, will lead to some glimmerings of understanding, or confirmation, of the wonderful mystery as to how Love and Nature
and Adventure are all part of a natural and majestic unity.

To return to the matter of the origin of the statement. I sense the answer is simple.
Inevitably we are shaped by our surroundings. Look at the diverse characteristics of
different nationalities – the saturnine Finn and the excitable Spaniard, for example.
In my five years of solo trekking, my surroundings were wild Nature. It was my way
of life. Those who solo know that psychologically the experiences are a great deal
more intense than if with other people. Awareness tends to be considerably heightened. As I mentioned earlier, on these journeys not only did I not feel lonely, but I
felt I was surrounded by friends.

Somehow I *knew* that the statement 'Everything in Nature is alive in its own way...'
was true. It was *truth* in the deeper sense. The intellect, the rational thinking, did not
even come into it. Rumi's famous quotation seems so apt:[1]

  "Sell your cleverness and buy bewilderment" (Be-wilder-ment?)

4

Who Am I?

Ful wys is he that kan hymselen knowe

Chaucer, Canterbury Tales

I sense strongly that anyone who is certain that they know who they are is not only blind but is likely to possess both arrogance and have a closed mind. At best, unless we are an exceptional human being, we can only have glimpses of the truth.

If someone had asked me when I left school if I knew myself, I would have thought it a very stupid question. Of course I knew who I was. Asked the same question now, in my seventies, I would reply to the effect that I am *beginning* to understand who I am. As with knowledge generally, the more we know the more we should realise how little we know.

We tend to take ourselves for granted. Yet as each new discovery is made about the human being, the more we should accept that we are extraordinary. So many millions of parts that are in some wonderful way alive and unified. More than that, the construction of Nature has ensured that each of us, like the snowflake and leaf, is unique. Herman Hesse puts it graphically:

"Everyone is more than just himself; he also represents the unique, the very special, and always significant and remarkable point at which the world's phenomena intersect, only once in this way and never again. That is why every man's story is important, eternal, sacred; that is why every man, as long as he lives and fulfils the will of Nature, is wonderful and worthy of every consideration."

A sense of awe and wonder about ourselves would seem totally appropriate.

What I find even more fascinating about being human is that, to a considerable extent, we are in major ways the *same*. In our individualism we are unique but as a species we have the same characteristics. This common ground includes:

We are all essentially natural. We came from, and return to Nature. We are strongly influenced by natural instincts.

We all have the same basic needs.

We all desire happiness and a contentment factor from our lives.

We also have the same major aspects. These include the following four very obvious ones:

A Body: the physical aspect. Through the physical come so many of the major experiences of our lives. Its importance is huge. Not only is it capable (with training and good health) of a lifetime of manifold physical skills, but also it often has a major effect both on our attitudes to, and conduct of, life itself.

"If anything is sacred, the human body is sacred." — *Walt Whitman*

The Basic Senses: Sight, smell, touch, taste and hearing. As long as they are functioning we tend to take them for granted. They are of major importance in terms of helping us understand who we are.

The Emotions: These are our feelings. They are various in number, positive and negative; the basis of our moods. They can range from very shallow to extreme depth; from utter despair to feelings of great joy. Few of us would deny that, ultimately, how we feel seems more important than what we think.

"Life is feeling." — *Cecil Collins*

The Intellect: The rational aspect: the 'thinking' part so essential in modern daily living and the need to resolve problems. It is the home of ideas, theories and solutions. Because it is so often and so obviously important in our journey through life, we need to be particularly aware that it should *not* dominate our lives. It remains only *one* aspect of being human.

"Reason is like an officer when the King appears; the officer then loses his power and hides himself. Reason is the shadow cast by God; God is the sun." — *Jalal-Udin Rumi*

"The intellect is constantly betrayed by its own vanity." — *Anne M. Lindbergh*

"Western civilisation is distinguished by its worship of the intellect...the function of the intellect is not to satisfy itself but to contribute to the satisfaction of the individual's total needs." — *Alexis Carrel*

These basic human aspects – the intellectual or thinking; the physical and the emotional can each dominate at different times.

For example, on leaving University as a committed rock climber I was emotionally concerned about having a bad accident or worse. I was not paranoid exactly, but was very aware of two things. The first was that I was the only living ex-president of the Oxford University Mountaineering Club out of the four I had known. The other three had all died in the mountains, including my climbing partner and best friend.[1]

The second was that I knew I became frightened when leading climbs of Hard Very Severe standard, especially when protection was poor.[2] Not only was this an unpleasant feeling or emotion, but it also was often expressed physically in that my legs performed an 'out of control' sewing machine movement. This was not conducive to staying on the rock!

The problem needed to be solved, especially as I loved the movement of climbing, and wished to be among the best of climbers. Thinking came

[2] The top grades of British rock climbing at that time were Very Severe (VS); Hard Very Severe (HVS); Extremely Severe and Exceptionally Severe (XS).

into play and I decided I would use my school gymnasium for a winter of climbing training. As I was the PE teacher and it was a residential school I was in an ideal situation. I covered the wall with tiny wood blocks for climbing practice (this was probably the first climbing wall). I also carried a rucksack full of weights on my back for doing finger pull-ups on the up-turned beams.

The next spring when I returned to climbing my first climb in the Llanberis Valley, North Wales, was 'The Thing'. Not only graded exceptionally severe, it also had the reputation of being the hardest climb in the valley. Once climbing I became emotionally exhilarated as I found it comparatively easy. Physically I felt powerful. It was almost as if my fingers were made of steel.

There are other common aspects of being human apart from the four mentioned. To the aspects of Physical, Mental, Emotional and the Senses I want to add:

The Spiritual: This dimension is by far the most mysterious. Intriguingly, not only does the spirit not appear *physically* to exist but the wisdom literature through the ages clearly indicates the spirit is the *most important* part of being human.

The following quotations seem very relevant:

"The foundations of a person are not in matter but in spirit." — R.W. Emerson

"The thought of death leaves me perfectly calm for I am fully convinced that our spirit is absolutely indestructible: it is something that works on from eternity to eternity, it is like the Sun which only seems to sink judged by our earthly eyes and in reality never sinks at all but shines without ceasing." — Goethe

"Spirit is the God in all. It should be worshipped as the God." — The Upanishads

"The truest end of life is to know the life that never ends." — William Penn

"Life in the dimension of spirit is a mystery rooted in the joy of being." — John Main

The spirit is the base of our values, the source of our virtues and vices. Of necessity, it is shaped by our inheritance and upbringing, our education and our experiences. Along with our instincts and intellect it determines how we act and behave.

I use various words to describe this aspect, regarding them as largely synonymous. Apart from spirit, these include *Heart – Soul – Conscience.* Although invisible, there can be no denying the supreme importance of this part of being human.

As Jiminy Cricket advises Pinocchio:

"Always let your conscience be your guide."

There would seem to be a constant need for *reflection* upon the true values of our actions. Few of us have not experienced 'light-heartedness' or a 'heavy conscience'.

Another way to look at 'Who am I?' is to contrast the *conscious* self with the *unconscious* self. 'Conscious' self is the daily living part; that part of which we are almost constantly aware (apart from when asleep). In a sense it is the *interface* between our deeper, unconscious self and the world around us. A key word in this context is ego, which may be defined as that aspect that separates us from our surroundings. The ego can also make one separate (or attempt to make one separate) from one's unconscious or deeper self. The modern world, with its emphasis on materialism, hugely encourages 'separateness', and therefore, *self-centredness* (egocentricity). Probably most of us at some time or other will have experienced both the joys of being separate (e.g. a personal success) and the depression of loneliness caused by separateness.

After climbing 'The Thing' as a young man I don't think I was even aware of 'my ego'. I have no doubt, however, that it was inflated. It was difficult for it not to be, having led a climb with such a fierce reputation. Years later, the size of my ego, and my arrogance, were shattered by reading a single sentence:

"A man's ego is in direct proportion to the length of the bonnet of his car."

As the driver of an E-type Jaguar I had nowhere to hide!

If conscious self is the tip of the proverbial iceberg, then the rest of the iceberg is the *unconscious* self. Dreams and nightmares, of course, come from our unconscious, and may well be linked to the events of our daily life.

I still remember as a child waking up in a considerable panic, after a nightmare which ended in being beaten over the head. On opening my eyes I realised that not only had I rolled off the bed but had then rolled under it!

Whatever the specifics of these night experiences most people would agree that in the sleeping mode there can be a reality at least as real as in normal living when awake. Similarly, perhaps there would be much agreement concerning the depths into the unconscious that the most intense feelings or emotions can go. Extreme elation and joy on the one hand, and terror and panic on the other, are not easily forgotten.

So far I have stated obvious aspects of the unconscious. There is another obvious example in romantic love. Whilst conscious self is hugely involved, and not least one's emotions, there appears to be a 'larger than conscious self' involved. Somehow the entire human being is involved – both conscious and unconscious in a mysterious and wonderful way quite beyond rational explanation. I will try to cast some light on this mysterious word 'love' in a later chapter.

I want to move now to describe what was almost certainly the most profound and significant of all my experiences. Eventually it was to give me an insight into the importance of my unconscious that still amazes me.

In 1981 I did a kayak expedition with a friend to south east Alaska – a journey of about 750 miles from Prince Rupert northwards to Sitka. This magnificent environment – ocean, forest and mountains on a large scale; minimal habitation and minimal pollution was like a magnet. Put simply, I loved the environment and decided to return.

Two years later I set off north from Sitka for what turned out to be a 650 mile trip exploring Glacier Bay and the outer coast to the south. Inspired by John Muir, I was solo. I saw this trip simply as yet another of my adventures.

After the first few days of mainly poor weather I was especially conscious of two aspects. On land there were both black and grizzly bears, and because the forest came down to the high tide line, my tiny tent was always on the edge of the forest. No matter how tired I was after the day's efforts, sleep was always difficult. I carried no weapon. The forest was full of sound; and I knew a lone kayaker had been eaten in the Glacier Bay area the previous year.

The other aspect is difficult to put into words. I expected, of course, to feel relieved when on the ocean, as compared to the bear danger on the land. The feeling that developed when on the ocean was, however, way beyond mere relief. In 'Beyond Adventure' I described it as trying to imagine your kayak, which has no keel, has changed into having a keel that is so deep that it is bottomless. In other words, psychologically I was now stable. Beneath the surface all was stability. The depth of this feeling was immense, and much deeper somehow than the depths of romantic love which I have been lucky enough to have experienced.

This stability psychologically was to remain throughout the expedition when on the Pacific. The daily kayaking on the surface continued as normal with all the ups and downs physically and in terms of skills and attitude. The last full day was particularly interesting. Over about twelve hours, various adventures took place, including overcoming my fear of a large swell, giant beds of kelp and thick sea fog. By early evening, in pouring rain, I was in almost gale conditions. There were reefs everywhere, and I had to make a decision as to whether to push on or backtrack down a strait. It was also getting dark. Demands on my skill to prevent the kayak from capsizing were considerable.

From somewhere within, in the blink of an eye, came an insight. I knew with certainty then the truth of *'the most important thing in life is to die at the right time'*.

I had agreed with this statement when I read it many years previously. What it means in effect is 'we all have to die sometime. Ideally, therefore, depart this world when you are doing something you love doing.' (I loved both Alaska and sea kayaking)

Experiencing, rather than reading about that truth underlined for me the wisdom that *'there is no substitute for experience'*.

The reality of that 'oceanic experience', basic to the whole time I was on the water (apart from the first few days), took years for me to begin to understand. I eventually realised that there could only be one explanation:

That part of me that was the ocean had somehow been switched on.

I suspect that trying to explain is beyond words but I must try. The feeling within me when on the ocean had an immensity or depth completely beyond anything I had previously (or subsequently) experienced. Because of its depth it had to be from within my unconscious. I was aware of it as it had come into my conscious. After some years of reflection I came to accept that the only possible explanation had to be the ancient wisdom so well expressed in the Upanishads:

What is within us is without us.
What is without us is within us.

In other words wild Nature, or the entirety of what is natural is somehow, both wonderfully and inexplicably in rational terms residing within the unconscious of every human being. I had been incredibly fortunate in consciously experiencing this phenomenon in the form of the ocean. I had been engulfed by the ocean psychologically, or in more appropriate terms, experienced an 'oceanic feeling'.

Despite many subsequent expeditions, such an experience never re-occurred. I sense that is unimportant and feel privileged that it occurred at all. On return to the UK I was filled with a sense of awe and wonder and a distinct feeling of humility. I even felt uneasy at discussing what had happened.

My attitude to life was subsequently changed. I became more the pilgrim trying to understand than the adventurer who would return with tales of 'derring-do'. My glimmerings of understanding indicated that being 'self-centred' was 'feeding the rat' of the ego and the 'Hey! Look at me!' conscious self. Instead I began to delve into the mysterious and immense world of the unconscious, especially the writings of Carl Jung. Reading round the matter underlined that the base of the unconscious was a unity. In spiritual terms this emphasised that in essence, in my deepest unconscious, I *was* Nature. I was to discover in my reading that this was one of the most profound of wisdoms.

A possible problem for the reader is that my Alaskan experience is too extreme or remote from 'normal' living to feel relevant to their own experiences of life. Later in the book I will devote a chapter to extraordinary or transcendent experiences. They come unexpectedly, in a diversity of forms and can occur in all types of situations. I am certain that they are not at all uncommon and they have the same message of 'spiritually I am part of a unity'. What probably happens, especially in the rush of modern living, is that through lack of careful reflection, their elemental significance can be easily missed.

In this matter of the elemental importance of the unconscious, as opposed to the conscious self, I want now to refer to that aspect of the former known as *intuition*. In trying to solve a problem, for example, it may well be after considerable thought, that you decide upon a proposed action 'X'. Then from somewhere else suddenly comes another message: to take action 'Y'. I sense it comes from deep down, and certainly not from the intellect and careful thinking. It would appear to come from the unconscious and its messages, in my experience, tend to be correct. Kant, the great philosopher, described it as "the truth-finding wisdom" or "wisdom of the ages". I see intuition as a door into the unconscious and that in one sense, my major task in life is to bring my unconscious into my conscious state as much as possible. Only in this way will I really begin to know 'who I am'. It may simply be old age, but I find I increasingly regard my unconscious with great affection. At best it can help guide me through the rest of my life. Memories surface regarding this crucial role of the unconscious. Examples include the many times over a period of years when, driving back from work after a long day, I suddenly found myself in my driveway. I had been on automatic pilot for about eight miles of narrow road and innumerable bends, and could not remember any of the detail! Or the occasion in the Pyrenees when, nearing the bottom of a steep scree slope of large granite boulders, a block moved so fast that I did not have time to take evading action. 'Automatic pilot' took over, and my leg was moved out of the way of the danger at unbelievable speed. I was in awe and extremely relieved. The block would have severely crushed my foot, especially as I was using lightweight approach shoes. Even more recently, decisions not to return to New Zealand for the winter, and to move house back to the Lake District, came from my intuition. Somehow I knew they were 'right' decisions because of their origin.

I would agree with Gail Ferguson's description of this special human aspect:

> *"A sleeping giant of a capability in everyone, a wonderful phenomenon of Nature*
> *that we experience constantly and a readily available tool for building a*
> *better future for humanity."* [3]

Indeed it could well be the most vital element of all the instincts we have inherited.

> *"To be conscious of the unconscious means to be open, responding, to have nothing*
> *and to be."* — *Erich Fromm and Zen Buddhism*

---

[3] Ferguson, G. American writer and psychologist

5

Where Am I Going?

We appear to be free to decide our aims in life. Television displays many of them every night of the week; sex, shopping, fun and excitement, money, power and status; a convenient and enjoyable lifestyle. Sometimes these, or most of them, are all within a single advertisement. I have no wish to be a killjoy. Enjoyment remains an important and relevant aim in my life. All these aims, however, are what might be termed 'surface' or superficial, and they can easily trap the unwary into thinking these are the only aims.

As most people find out at some point in their existence, there is a serious or deeper side to life. I am sufficiently optimistic to sense that most people, especially the younger generation, would nod in agreement.

Since civilisation began people have discussed and written about the more discerning aims. These aims have included:

A search for Truth and Wisdom
A search for the Meaning of Life
A search for Freedom
A search for Beauty
A search for Peace

The Greek philosopher Aristotle had as his aim for living "to seek the virtues", as opposed to the vices. He equated the virtues with excellence.

Before the white man arrived on their land, many Native American Indian tribes sought happiness and well-being and found great freedom through:

> *"…an intense and absorbing love of nature; a respect for life; enriching faith in a Supreme Power; and of principles of truth, honesty, generosity, equity and brotherhood…"* [1]
> — *Luther Standing Bear*

I enthuse over their approach. For far too long a materialistic and greedy approach to living, so typical of Western society, has wreaked havoc on both planet and humanity. It is becoming increasingly clear that we need to return to a love of Nature and develop an affinity with the natural world. No longer can we justify treating Nature solely as a resource for human benefit.

Bernard Moitessier, famous round-the-world sailor, detested much about the modern world and described it as "the monster". He longed to find, when he returned from the sea and the simple life, a world of:

> *"…peace, respect for nature, feelings of brotherhood without borders, renewed awareness that we all belong to the same big family, their communion with things around them. All the beautiful and good the human soul can do, those true things we cannot live without."* [2]

In the Second World War (1939-1945), hundreds of thousands of young men from Britain gave their lives to fight Hitler and Nazism and we still annually celebrate them. If they were alive today and were asked what they were fighting for, I would strongly sense that they would say they were fighting for a decent and worthwhile way of life, for 'freedom' as well as all of the immediate enjoyments of life. I also suspect the majority of them would support the aim of leaving the world in a better condition for the next generation. If I am correct in my surmise then we should acknowledge their ultimate sacrifice. Not only that also but we should be determined to follow in their magnificent footsteps rather than succumb to the temptations to live mainly for immediate enjoyment with minimal concern for the future.

The serious aims of living can seem not only to be many, but often to appear both complex and easily confusing to anyone not used to studying them. There is another approach which is both broad and simple, and should have the benefit of being minimally contentious. "Where am I going?" can be answered by *fulfilment*. More accurately and honestly the answer should be *towards fulfilment*. In its deepest sense fulfilment is an ideal and therefore impossible to reach. If we are lucky, and work hard enough, however, we may experience glimpses of fulfilment – the land of our dreams.

Carl Jung uses the word *individuation*; the American, Abraham Maslow uses self-*actualisation* and, most recently, the Norwegian Arne Naess *self-realisation*.

There is another term for fulfilment. This is *maturity*, which I much prefer. We should never forget that we are essentially natural. This term, unlike the others, describes a process pertaining to *anything* in Nature. It is not restricted to humans, unlike the other terms. Like the acorn, then, I aspire to becoming the giant oak tree.

There I must stop the analogy and return to the human being and individual maturity. That maturity should include:

> *Physical potential*
> *Rational or thinking potential*
> *Emotional potential*
> *Spiritual potential*

To complicate matters further, as I have indicated in previous chapters, the individual should accept that he or she is not in *reality* totally separate. Each of us is linked to other human beings with responsibilities both ways and we also depend on the natural environment.

In chapter three 'Underlying Wisdom' the base statement was:

> *"Everything is alive in its own way…and deserves its own well-being…"*

This wisdom means, or comes down to, *minimal destruction* to everything around you, including yourself. Taking drugs for kicks, for example, is destroying oneself, at least in terms of long – term health and fitness. It may well also cause destruction to other people and your surroundings.

A summary statement of this section would be as follows:

The underlying or broad aim of living is *towards* individual fulfilment or maturity in every positive sense: physically, emotionally, mentally and spiritually.

The beauty of this situation, which at first may seem restrictive, is that you have the *freedom to work out your own journey through life* – in theory and practice. It is only *fair* that you allow that same freedom for everything else as far as this is reasonably possible.

Quotations

"Happiness…what is it? I say it is neither virtue nor pleasure…but simply growth. We are happy when we are growing. It is the primal law of all nature and the universe."
— *W.B. Yeats*

"I want, by understanding myself, to understand others. I want to be all that I am capable of becoming. This all sounds very strenuous and serious. But now that I have wrestled with it, it's no longer so. I feel happy – deep down. All is well."
— *Katherine Mansfield*

"…that man as we know him is not a completed being; that nature develops him only up to a certain point and then leaves him, either to develop further, by his own efforts and devices, or to live and die such as he was born, or to degenerate and lose capacity for development." — P. D. Ouspensky

6

If Only...

In this chapter I intend to reflect upon the period when, as a young man in my early twenties, my life was dominated by climbing. My criteria or evaluation will be based on the knowledge I have now gained over a lifetime in terms of who I am. In other words, I will try and put my youthful climbing life into a *mature* perspective.

If the *overall* or underlying aim of living is *individual fulfilment* in all positive senses, to mature like everything else in Nature, my youthful ambition to satisfy my drive to excel in something really challenging seems to be fine. Admittedly climbing was an activity that appeared senseless in that it could severely damage you. It also appeared to be useless in terms of being of any practical worth to society! On the other hand it stimulated the senses and brought me an intoxicating sense of freedom to which every adventurer relates.

In terms of the *aspects* of who I am, I was obviously very involved *physically, mentally* and *emotionally*. Every time I climbed I had to overcome fear. Whilst I seldom, and as little as possible, climbed with my 'heart in my mouth', fear was always an unwelcome companion, lurking on my shoulder. After all, I knew a slight error or momentary lack of concentration could spell disaster. Mentally, too, there were generally considerable demands albeit within a narrow focus. How to think under pressure was the name of the game. Not just using my intellect to control any fear, but also to work out *how* to climb a pitch. It was not unusual to feel you were playing a very taxing form of chess with death as your possible opponent – where the right moves were vital.

Physically when climbing at or near my limits, demands were twofold. Did I have the skill or technique to perform the moves, and in the right sequence? If so, did I have the relevant fitness – be it strength, endurance, or both? In addition to these major aspects of being human there was another facet the importance of which should never be underestimated. This was the *basic senses* of sight, sound, smell, taste and touch. Their use, or at least three of them, were both constant and fundamental to success.

On the surface, then, my youthful climbing would appear largely acceptable within the narrow interpretation of climbing as personal fulfilment. The alert reader will be aware that another aspect – the *spiritual* – has yet to be mentioned. The reader may also remember that I described this side as the most important part of being human. An obvious question now arises: was my spiritual side involved in my young climbing days? My answer, then, would have been "what has climbing got to do with the spiritual?" Now my reply would be "Yes, my spiritual side was involved but largely in my unconscious." In other words I was generally not *consciously* aware of what was going on in terms of my own spirituality.

What I mean by the 'spiritual' causes me some difficulty as I am acutely aware this word indicates an adventure into the unknowable. On the other hand it would seem of elemental importance to try to understand.

In the chapter 'Who am I?' I said that the *spirit* was:

> *The base of our values*
> *The source of our virtues and vices*

With reference to the first point, I valued climbing to such an extent that it dominated my life for about fifteen years. Nothing was as important. I loved climbing even if it did frighten me. To *love* something is the highest of values, providing that which is loved is not a vice and pertains to that which is positive about being human.

With reference to the second point, in terms of virtues and vices, I feel I must have known that some of the virtues were crucial to success. If I did know then, I did not either talk or think much about them. I will go into some detail at this point because the virtues we display and have as ideals are super important, not just for the individual but for the human race, and for the future of the planet.

Three virtues come immediately to mind: *Enthusiasm*, *Determination* and *Patience*. I would have rated myself highly on the first two and poorly on the third. Less obvious, possibly, was the virtue of *Self-Discipline*. I could not climb efficiently unless I had the self-discipline to control my fear.

I needed also to be very fit, so generally my lifestyle, whilst not spartan, was in accord with that concept. The virtue of *Humour* also was necessary at times, because of the seriousness of the activity. I still remember one of the lads doing a headstand at the top of a climb on gritstone with the vertical face adjacent to his hands. I also remember following Don Whillans up a 'Hard Very Severe' in the Lakes, in wet conditions. As I came over the top there was Don grinning at me. He had been coiling the rope round his knees as I came up. He was not belayed! (to belay is to rope yourself to the rock). My initial reaction of anger at his gross lack of safe practice was then subdued by the thought that he must have respected my climbing ability. As a mountaineer I knew that he was a consummate professional. I would have climbed with him anywhere.

There was the virtue of *Respect*, too – for the fitness and skill of outstanding climbers like Joe Brown, Martin Boysen and Don Whillans, with all of whom I was lucky enough to share a rope. They were teaching me, albeit unconsciously, about the virtue of *Honesty*. I *had* to admit to myself I could never have their skill and power, but I would never stop trying to reach their levels. There was the virtue of *Respect* too, for the mountain environment and especially the cliffs and some of the climbs. A line could be both beautiful and awe inspiring. I sense the seeds of 'a sense of awe and wonder' as well as matters of beauty were aroused or stimulated in my unconscious. They were to emerge into my conscious self much later in my life as I became more aware of their significance.

The importance of two other virtues was also beginning to become very apparent. One was *Courage*, or at least 'unbelievable determination'. My climbing partner, Bernard Jillot, personified this virtue. I particularly remember being his second on an attempt on a new route on the Avon gorge. He fell about ten metres when leading. Unhurt he proceeded to make further attempts on this vertical face. As it was limestone and raining, one half of me thought he was mad, the other half was full of admiration. Limestone is notoriously slippery in the wet! The second virtue is that of *Friendliness/Friendship*. Ours was of the strongest. That he should die so soon afterwards in the Himalayas in epic circumstances sent me into severe depression. Two remarkable experiences then occurred that somewhat rescued me, although I will forever miss his brilliant friendship.

The first was my college warden Eric Abbott who later became the Dean of Westminster. Never in my life have I met a more saintly or spiritual person. To my astonishment he insisted not only must I not give up climbing but I should henceforth climb even harder – for I was now climbing for Bernard as well. Much later in life I realised that what I felt in terms of awe in his presence, was caused by his deep *Humility* – another virtue and one of the most profound.

The second experience was that after I left Oxford I climbed regularly with Wilfrid Noyce. Again I was hugely impressed. He was a famous climber with two first class honours degrees from Cambridge; a writer and poet; and the survivor of a near-fatal long fall in the Lakes. Yet he was the quietest of gentle men – a magnificent example of *Humility*. In addition to this, his selfless action on the Dent d'Herens in my first

Alpine season displayed the virtues of *Courage* and *Integrity*.[1]

The following virtues then were involved in my young climbing life. Most were in my unconscious, and those in my conscious were qualities I seldom considered:

Enthusiasm, determination, patience, self-discipline, humour, respect, honesty, courage, friendship/friendliness, humility, integrity.

Of these virtues at least the first four were essential if I was to progress, i.e. develop my potential as a climber. They were used as key weapons in enabling me to express what I most deeply valued at that time: my love of climbing. Without them my skills and fitness would have been quite insufficient.

It would be unfair to myself if I did not mention the virtue of *Unselfishness*. I knew by taking the post of Warden of the Woodlands Outdoor Centre I would limit my own adventures – because of the lack of long holidays compared to teaching as well as the demands of the job. But I wished to be in a position to widen the experience of the young, to open their eyes to adventure and their own potential, along with providing an income and a home for a family.

What strikes me *now* about that time in my life was that I was extremely *self-centred* or *egocentric*. Perhaps I should not be too hard on my young male self as it was surely a natural instinct to want to prove myself. After all, throughout time there have been initiation rites for the young men of the tribe to prove they are adults by means of physical challenges.

The problem remains, however, that self-centredness or selfishness or egocentrism – whatever term is used – can quickly become a vice. Not only that, but like a cancer it can engulf you. Most virtues have an opposing vice, such as *Honesty* as opposed to *Dishonesty*. In the case of extreme egotism the vice is *Arrogance* as opposed to the virtue of *Humility*. As a young man in my twenties and thirties I was, I suspect, extremely arrogant. The only slightly mitigating factor was that I was largely unaware of this major weakness. There were two reasons for this. The first was that the society in which I lived encouraged the 'cult of the individual' and applauded 'success' to an excessive degree. The second was that Annette, my young wife, had an ethic of "never to criticise other human beings". I genuinely do not remember her calling me bigheaded! Einstein's remark is apt:

> *"The true value of a human being is determined primarily by the measure and sense in which he has attained to liberation from self."*

What he means here is 'freedom from the ego', freedom from the 'Hey! Look at me!' and 'I am important' type of syndrome. Never underestimate the threat that the ego poses, especially if you're experiencing success in your life. Simone Weil's words are both powerful and truthful:

> *"Ego is the prison of self."*

Imagine, for example, that as you go through life you become increasingly successful in what you do. You eventually become famous and a star with all the media hype. You may well either not have noticed, or more likely have ignored the fact that your ego is massive. What I am saying here is that one cannot begin to understand oneself until there is a genuine acceptance of the importance of the unconscious self and a realisation that the ego, the protector of the conscious self, can blind one to this reality. An extreme egoist is likely to have convinced himself that the unconscious is of no importance whatsoever in terms of living 'in the real world'. I am reminded of the wise person who said that what was important about any winner of a gold medal at the Olympics was how they behaved *after* winning. In particular, he was referring to the *modesty* the person hopefully displayed rather than his or her arrogance.

It would seem appropriate to re-state the basis of my New Zealand lecture given much later in my life: "Everything in Nature is as important as everything else, and deserves its own well being". Not only is the tiny flower or pebble no less or no more important than the human being, but no human being is more important than any other human being or part of the universe.

To summarise, in terms of what I now know of who I was. As a young climber I was extremely egoistic, living on the surface of life and largely unaware of the depths of my unconscious. I was completely unaware of the wisdom concerning my spiritual aspect, and even more unaware of the wisdom that the basis of everything was *unity*. My world was bound up in what I wanted: adventure in the outdoors and my immediate friends and my young family. Nature – the outdoors – was something I loved, but I took it for granted. It was an open air sports hall to be used for adventure – in my work and in my play.

I was a very ignorant and a very arrogant young male, who desperately needed the wisdom of a wise old man!

7

How Do I Get There?

If the reader is with me so far on my journey as to who I am and where I am going I will be pleased. Whilst I believe in the virtue of *simplicity* I sense I have already been a little complex.

It may be appropriate for the reader to take a deep breath before the next chapters. What now follows; for the rest of the book; apart from the final three chapters is my attempt to answer my own question. Having broadly answered *Who Am I?* and *Where Am I Going?* I now need to face the complexity of *How Do I Get There?*

In the introduction I mention that my initial attempt to write was solely for my own benefit. Very depressed by Annette's death I thought I might make more sense of what had happened so suddenly – find some clarity perhaps amidst my jumble of thought and feelings – if I put pen to paper. Several points seem worth making at this stage.

Of all the material I read about death one statement rang particularly loud:

"How you face the imminence of death depends on how you have lived."

The bell was loud because Annette had insisted in her final days, to all those very close to her, that she was in "a bubble of happiness". My intuition had from our earliest days together, intimated that she was somehow special – a naturally good person – if I can use that phrase. My reluctance to get married was entirely due to my love of climbing above anything else. Yet I knew that if we ever had children – which at that time I did not even want to think about – then they could not have a finer mum.

The next point is that I felt considerable remorse at how self-centred I had lived much of my life with her. I kept thinking: if only we could live our lives together again she might be more proud of me. Such an attitude, of course, is by no means unusual but it did make me determined to try and understand my strengths and weaknesses, and if I learnt anything worthwhile, to try and pass it on. I was conscious that Annette, as a spiritual presence at this difficult time, was a very powerful force indeed – if only I could begin to understand.

That first attempt at writing ended in a morass of virtues. I read more and persevered with what I had started, and eventually found glimmerings of understanding, which are revealed in the chapters on Love and Friendship.

What now follows is hopefully obvious from the end of the last chapter – where I describe myself as "a very ignorant and arrogant young male in need of the wisdom of an older man." The long section on virtues – a daunting list of 26 – and the following section on wisdom and specific wisdoms, is what I would like to take with me as ideals on my journey through life *if I was a young man again.*

This main part of the book has insightfully been described as "a book within a book". [1] I hope it is of particular value to young people – those in their last years at school, in further education, or beginning work. After all they are the citizens upon which the shape of the human world may well depend.

I hope also that other readers of all ages will not skip this long section ahead. To do so may well indicate a closed mind!

8

Values And Virtues

"Man is made by his belief. As he believes, so he is."

The Bhagavad Gita

This ancient observation I would have responded to as a young man by saying: "Yes, that is an obvious statement because I am a climber. I climb whenever possible because I believe in climbing". That precocious certainty of my youth, that arrogance of viewpoint, has thankfully been replaced by a more mature view. I would now say: "Yes, that is an excellent statement, because in my case I know I have been shaped by my deepest belief in the *value* of wild Nature, and my much more recent belief in the *value* of universal love." These two elemental forces have shaped 'who I am' and given me some understanding as to how I relate to everything around me.

Each of us needs to develop our personal beliefs which will both influence and create our *values*. They represent what is most important to us in life, and indicate our preferences and priorities. As they develop they create a deeper sense of who we are and focus increasing attention on what we consider important. They give meaning to our life and form the basis for our motivations. From the latter stem our actions. As our relationships develop so we build *shared* values. Historically this is how the world has produced a diversity of societies, each of which has a basis of shared values – often expressed in the form of a constitution.

The acceptance of specific ideas, expressed in terms of ideologies, politics or conceptual frameworks determine beliefs and moralities. Ultimately it is ideas that drive people to peace or war, that shape the systems under which they live, and which determine how the world's resources are shared among them. Ideas *matter*, and so therefore does the question of reasoning, by which ideas often live or die.

In a large society like the UK we are familiar with the frustration of having to live with decisions taken by a government that we feel to be impossibly remote. Fortunately the wisdom in this matter points most strongly to the crucial importance of developing a *personal* set of beliefs and values. I would want to call this a *personal values framework*. Lewis Mumford puts it succinctly:

> *"The production and conservation of values is one of the main concerns of human existence: all that a man does and is, depends on his taking part in this process."*

William Barclay is helpful in how we go about this challenge:

> *"The only way to get our values right is to see, not the beginning but the end of the way, to see things not only in the light of time but in the light of eternity."* [1]

The biologist Julian Huxley says something similar:

> *"Above all the individual should aim at fulness and wholeness of development. Every human being is confronted with the task of growing up, of building a personality out of the raw materials of his infant self. A rich and full personality, in moral and spiritual harmony with itself and with its destiny...in its attainment the individual possibilities*

of the evolutionary process are brought to supreme fruition."

Both of these quotations are similar to the idea of *positive fulfilment*. By looking to the end of our life and asking ourselves what we would like to have achieved by that time, we have at least sorted out our dreams or ideals.

The scientist Albert Einstein has something to say in this respect:

> *"The ideals which have lighted me on my way, and time after time have given me new courage to face life cheerfully, have been kindness, beauty and truth...the trite subjects of human efforts – possessions, outward success, luxury, have always seemed to be contemptible."*

I find his three ideals fascinating. Life is an *individual* journey but sharing is extremely important. Providing the sharing is *constructive* this literally makes the world go round. The first of his ideals – *Kindness* – I have as one of the key virtues. *Kindness* is not just an ideal but an action. Presumably Einstein displayed kindness whenever possible. Ideally he would display this virtue in every situation—not just to all humans, but to everything that is 'alive in its own way'.

The second ideal of *Beauty* has my full support to the extent that a later chapter is devoted to the belief that life should, or could, be approached as a search for *Beauty*.

His last ideal, *Truth*, again has my full agreement – I regard it as both a major aim and one of the key wisdoms as we journey through life.

Kierkegaard, the Danish philosopher wrote the following:

> *"In a significant sense you are your values.*
> *Decisions and actions are motivated by values."*

Although simple, this statement is extremely important because:

Almost all of our actions are based on our beliefs and values.

The actions we take define us as individuals. They largely define our *character*. In turn our character is essentially made up of our individual traits or qualities which are our virtues and vices.

The Outward Bound movement, started in the early years of the Second World War, was dedicated to character training and improving the fitness of the young men of the country. The training courses – originally of a month's duration – were held in mountain or coastal centres. At the end of each course, 'reports' on each individual noted all the relevant virtues (and vices to a lesser extent) and how they developed and were displayed over the month. Such courses, and they are a worldwide phenomenon today, tend to be held in the highest regard by all those involved.

In my educational involvement using wild Nature I have long been convinced that the character (the amalgam of virtues and vices) of a person is by far the most important aspect of being human. I regard the virtues as more important ultimately than any achievements. How someone lives their daily life, and the virtues they consistently display, shows their calibre as a human being.

I am also convinced that all the virtues and vices, like the wisdoms, lie dormant in our unconscious until they are brought into use. Like our muscles, they will then only progress if they are further used – ideally in a progressive and consistent manner throughout life. If they are not used they will either remain dormant in our unconscious, or possibly, like some of our senses, atrophy or even die.

Quotations

In preparation for submission of the manuscript to publishers I considerably reduced the number of quotations at the end of chapters. The exception to this reduction is this chapter. In a materialistic society based essentially upon dishonesty and other vices, I regard the positive voice of history – the importance of the virtues – as the cornerstone of what is best about being human.

"There is something more important in man than is apparent in his ordinary consciousness, something which frames ideals and thoughts, a finer spiritual presence, which makes him dissatisfied with mere earthly pursuits. The one doctrine that has the longest intellectual ancestry is the belief that the ordinary condition of man is not his ultimate being, that he has in him a deeper self; call it breath or ghost, soul or spirit. In each dwells a light which no power can extinguish, an immortal spirit, benign and tolerant, the silent witness in his heart. The greatest thinkers of the world unite in asking us to know the self."
— *Radhakrishnan*

"All sober inquirers after truth, ancient and modern, pagan and Christian, have declared that the happiness of man, as well as his dignity, consists in virtue."
— *John Adams*

"The existence of virtue depends entirely upon its use." — *Cicero*

"Virtue is a way of being, but an acquired and lasting way of being." — *Aristotle*

"There is a capacity of virtue in us and there is a capacity of vice to make your blood creep." — R.W. Emerson

"We must revolutionize this system of life, that is based on outside things, money, property, and establish a system of life which is based on inside things." — D.H. Lawrence

"It is good to be without vices, but it is not good to be without temptations." — Walter Bagehot

"Virtues and vices are like life and death, or mind and matter: things which cannot exist without being qualified by their opposite." — Samuel Butler

"The crown and glory of life is character. It is the noblest possession of a man...character is human nature in its best form. It is moral order embodied in the individual." — S. Smiles

"The safest road to Hell is the gradual one – the gentle slope, soft underfoot, without sudden turnings, without milestones, without signposts." — C.S. Lewis

"When you see a worthy person endeavour to emulate him. When you see an unworthy person then examine your inner self." — Confucius

"Our whole life is startlingly moral. There is never an instant's truce between virtue and vice." — H. D. Thoreau

"The central task of education is virtue." — W.J. Bennett

Introduction To Specific Virtues And Vices

It should be obvious from the last group of quotations, that the virtues are, or should be, of very considerable importance both to the individual and to society.

In compiling the following personal list of virtues I found only one modern book on the subject that was valuable, and that was translated from the French! [2]

This apparent dearth of books on such an important subject – for the virtues displayed by an individual largely define the quality of an individual – is both astonishing and revealing about the modern world.

E.F. Schumacher clearly saw the problem in the 1970s: [3]

> "In ethics, as in so many other fields, we have recklessly and wilfully abandoned our great classical – Christian heritage. We have even degraded the very words without which ethical discourse cannot carry on, words like virtue, love, temperance. As a result, we are totally ignorant, totally uneducated in the subject that, of all conceivable subjects, is the most important. We have no ideas to think with and therefore are only too ready to believe that ethics is a field where thinking does no good. Who knows anything today of the Seven Deadly Sins or of the Four Cardinal Virtues? Who could even name them? And if these venerable, old ideas are thought not to be worth bothering about, what new ideas have taken their place?"

In any society dominated in practice by money; power; status and 'success at all costs', the *vices* tend to become prominent rather than the virtues. The latter become 'an inconvenient truth'. Such societies tend to be characterised by the vices, and not least by the seven deadly sins. *Greed, envy, lust, gluttony, pride, sloth* and *anger* are no strangers in our midst. In practice many of them support the market economy.

Any individual has an undeniable responsibility – to himself, to others and to the planet – to sort out a personal list of their own virtues. They are ideals and they should be regarded as something of both truth and beauty towards which to strive. They are meaningless as simply words. Action is always required.

In the next section the specific virtues are given in a bipolar manner, that is with an opposing vice. When reading about a virtue/vice imagine a situation where that virtue/vice occurs and how you would react in that situation. For example, you walk down a street. Someone in front of you drops a banknote. You have to make a decision and take a course of action. At one extreme you pick up the note and disappear as rapidly as possible. At the other extreme you pick up the note, run to the person who dropped it and return it. These two extremes can be represented thus:

It is important when *reflecting* on a situation that has arisen and an action taken, to realise that it is crucial to be as honest as possible in what can be very complex situations. Did I take the right action? It depends on the individual, based on facts, as far as possible, and is *always situation specific* (like every accident!).

Ideally if someone drops some money in the street, then naturally and spontaneously you *always* return the money immediately, regardless of the circumstances. That is *honesty* at its best. If you had *no thought* of doing anything else in that situation that is also the virtue of *purity.*

Of course we do not live in an ideal world. Here are some of the factors that could affect the action you take when someone drops money in the street in front of you:

- *How far you have developed a Personal Value Framework within which you wish to live.*
- *The psychological mood you are in.*
- *Your financial state – the larger the sum dropped (e.g. a £50 note rather than a £5) and/or the more impecunious you may be, the greater the temptation.*
- *Whether you are alone or not and whether that would make any difference.*
- *The situation e.g. how easy/safe would it be to escape with the loot?*
- *Your feelings about the person who dropped the money (e.g. it could be an old lady or business man).*

Simplicity is a key virtue on my list for many reasons; one of the main ones is the opposite vice of *complexity*. Many situations and ideas seem to become more complex the further they are explored. This path could lead to mental illness! Treat reflection on actions and seeking the 'Truth' as *fun* wherever possible. Exploration in this area with good friends can be fascinating. In a lovely way your conscience ideally should always inform you whether you made the correct decision. *Temptations* are always around (and need to be!) and to be human is to be fallible. That is why *forgiveness* is a key virtue!

The matter of virtues deserves a complete book. I suspect it would be a weighty tome as the subject is both complex and elusive. In a sense each virtue is part of the spirit of the individual and each one should be regarded as sacred, or as an ideal. Here there is scope only to make important points about the virtues and vices.

There are no dividing lines in nature. Often the *virtues* merge into each other. They also often *overlap* and should be regarded as *inter-dependent*.

There are virtues and vices unmentioned. When one is found see if it relates to any on the list given.

Viewed in isolation and taken to an extreme a virtue may become a vice (e.g. determination can become stubbornness which in some situations would correctly be described as a vice).

The Motivation behind an action is crucial. It is possible for example, to apparently display the virtue of *Courage* when the reason for action is essentially because one wants maximum publicity for self-centred rather than self-less reasons.

Although I have indicated that virtues and vices are bi-polar they can sometimes be seen as a summit between two vices. Examples given by André Compte-Sponville are *courage* between *servility* and *selfishness*; and *gentleness* between *anger* and *apathy*.

Like everything else in Nature virtues are dynamic. It may be simplest to view them like muscles. With frequent and progressive training they will become stronger. Without consistent and constant use they will atrophy.

An unmentioned virtue, that of *politeness* as opposed to *rudeness*, is of major importance. Put simply the latter leads eventually to aggression and war, the former towards peace. At a more immediate level people need to be able to *discuss* things – the positive – without becoming involved in *argument* – the negative. *Politeness*, despite its importance is a *precursor* rather than a key virtue and I have included it in *respect*. Another unmentioned virtue is *connection*, or to use Professor MacIntyre's word, *connectedness*.[4] Again this is of major importance – we need to accept our relatedness (non-separateness) to everything else. I have included it in the key virtue of *awareness* which I see as broader and deeper than one that tends to be confined to human beings only.

Comments on the personal list of virtues

In many ways these virtues, as opposed to their corresponding vices, are at the heart of the book. The combination of virtues and vices largely define any individual in terms of their beliefs through their actions. In my own case this list of virtues has developed extensively as I have become more mature, more aware of my deeper self; and more aware of my responsibilities in all aspects. The death of Annette accelerated that process and this book has been the result.

I suspect that each virtue has occasions when it is the most prominent one in a specific situation. I have made little attempt to compare these virtues as this is beyond the scope of this book. It will be obvious, however, that some of them are of very major importance throughout life. The virtue of *Honesty*, I see as the *foundation* virtue – the one on which my life needs to be built. If I were to live my life again I would spend it in education, devising experiences, not least in the outdoors, where these virtues would become both alive and meaningful to the young people experiencing them. I sense that at some time in the future this will be accepted as conventional education, providing the human race still exists!

Grouping of the virtues

There are almost endless permutations. All I have done here is to present the specific virtues in what might be a helpful way.

All virtues are to be based on *Honesty* as the foundation virtue. The next three – *Awareness, Respect, Compassion* I see linked as follows. As the lifelong process of *awareness* grows, then it should naturally lead to more *respect*. When, for example, I learnt about the annual migration of the arctic tern across the planet – about 20,000 miles annually – my respect for them grew. From respect I would hope love – *compassion* – would eventually emerge, as happened seamlessly in my feeling for terns. As this whole process develops – from awareness to respect to love – then I would hope the individual develops an increasing attitude of *minimal destruction to everything in Nature* (unless it poses a threat to one's existence).

The next five virtues – *Determination*; *Patience*; *Self-discipline*; *Self-reliance* and *Concentration* – unlike most of the other virtues, can also be used for egocentric and even evil purposes.

The next group of virtues are very much concerned with the individual's relationships: These are *Altruism*; *Empathy*; *Friendliness*; *Kindness*; *Gentleness*; *Gratitude*; *Tolerance*; *Forgiveness* and *Justice*.

The next seven virtues include some of the great universal virtues, especially *Humility*; *Purity*; *Courage*; *Vitality*; *Creativity*; *Responsibility* and *Simplicity*.

The final virtue is that of *Humour*. The matter of vices and virtues in the way each of us lives is so serious that this virtue is essential!

Honesty

HONESTY	DISHONESTY
Conscientiousness	Lying
Truthfulness	Deceit
Integrity	Hypocrisy
Exactness	Immodesty
Morality	Cheating
Sincerity	Insincerity
Genuineness	

This virtue is closely linked to Purity, Humility, Awareness, Fairness, Respect, Responsibility, Vitality.

Honesty should be seen as *the foundation virtue*. In other words, it is the base for all of the other virtues. To be honest should never be underestimated in terms of its importance as we grow and try to understand who we are and how we relate to all of our surroundings. As Abbott Jamison notes:

"The real task of being true to oneself is a slow and profound work; it is not a fixed way but involves search and change."

To be truly conscientious – to act with purity of heart – is to display the highest form of honesty. To live in this manner, as for example like my heroes – the polar explorer Dr Edward Wilson, and Albert Schweitzer of Africa fame – or the young heroine Simone Weil – is to demonstrate the highest levels of being human.

From the East, from the ancient writings of the Upanishads and Brahman come the strongest echoes of the importance of this virtue. It is one's duty to work towards absolute truthfulness. Not only is 'truth' the great educational influence, but men of wisdom down through the ages suggest *any* life should be a search for truth. The link between honesty and truthfulness, if the words are not synonymous, must be of the strongest.

The key virtue of *awareness* is most important in this context. We need to be especially aware when we are being less than honest. Both good friends and an active conscience are essential in this respect. There is a need for *reflection* on all of our actions and indeed even our thoughts as we journey through life. Almost all of our actions are based on what we value, and honesty is the essential base.

It may be helpful to view this virtue in three ways:

Honesty with oneself

To reflect *honestly* upon one's thoughts, feelings and actions. To be very aware that one can nearly always find reasons or excuses for all those occasions which do not reflect the best of oneself.

Here is a memory of this type of honesty:

It is the early 1960s and my partner and I are attempting the second ascent of a recent new climb of the highest standard. We are well up the west face of 'Cloggy', the majestic crag that dominates a high flank of Snowdon. I am probably at my peak as a young rock climber, and the previous day we have completed the second ascent of another recent new route. Despite this I do not feel confident when I look up at the blank corner above me. The corner is steep, appears bereft of holds and the only protection I can see looks very poor. Below the corner, the crag drops vertically to the ground. This pitch is the crux and it looks it! Bridging is apparently the key to the problem. Voices on the track below cause me to look down. I recognise a famous climber, later to become a household name. To my intense annoyance words float up to the effect that I have no chance. My anger fuels me and almost without hesitation I layback up the vertical corner (a layback is a bold and strenuous climbing technique). With hindsight I now know that was by far the most exposed and tenuous layback of my whole climbing career.

I expect the next pitch to be easier. It is not, as it is damp. By now, however, I am very determined and eventually I climb it. The feelings of success after a hard climb are this time somewhat muted if I am honest with myself. My first reaction is one of relief as I reach the top of the climb. On the one hand I have proved to myself that I am capable of climbing something that I thought beyond me. In addition I realise I must have shown a high level of skill and strength – otherwise I would have fallen off. On the other hand I have allowed myself to react to overt competition – the comment from below was particularly galling as I had climbed with the person who had made it and intuitively sensed that I had more natural skill as a climber. I am not proud of my impetuous reaction. As a careful climber I decide I still prefer the latter approach. As the years go by and certain climbers become increasingly famous, when I seem to have more talent, I content myself (or try to) with thoughts that my comparative lack of determination might mean I live longer. Despite these thoughts I hate the thought that I am a coward or 'lack bottle'. Only much later in life do I find that is untrue when it comes to the crunch in a mountain situation. There is also another factor here which I dislike intensely. The open competitiveness somehow seems more appropriate to the games field. Much later in life I am to learn the importance of my misgivings and the need for the most honest appraisal of my motivation for climbing, and indeed for everything else I do in my life.

Honesty with other people

The second way to view *honesty* is in terms of relationships with other human beings. This means constantly to appraise your attitude and actions concerning others. To be honest with others is to show them respect and to link the virtue of *kindness* with honesty where relevant. The following situation is again in the mountains:

> August 1959, my first alpine season. I am climbing with two very experienced mountaineers, Wilf Noyce of Everest fame and Jack Sadler, an American. My snow and ice experience is extremely limited to one short visit to Ben Nevis the previous winter. This alpine trip is regarded as essential training especially for me. The following year we are going together to the Himalayas to try and climb the unexplored peak of Trivor (7732 metres).
>
> We go up to the Schonbiel hut. Our objective is the Welzenbach route on the north face of the Dent D'Herens, a large peak adjacent to the Matterhorn. I note with some trepidation that it is graded 'VI' – the most difficult snow and ice grade. The concern increases when Wilf declares that we breakfast at midnight. He has decided to ignore the advice of the hut guardian (himself an experienced climber). This is that the route in question had not been done that season because the main face is completely out of condition.
>
> Dawn arrives as we reach the foot of the north face. A snowbridge over the bergschrund (deep crevasse) and we scramble up easily for 300 metres. Here we traverse right unroped along an easy although exposed narrow ledge system above the steep lower face. I make the classic beginner's mistake and catch one crampon spike on the other foot. In a trice I have tripped up and I hurtle down the face – it is steep and ends in a yawning chasm. Motivation is of the highest order as I learn to ice axe brake! I finally stop about 50 metres from the bergschrund. As I climb up and rejoin my companions I am fully awake.
>
> At the end of the traverse we have a choice to reach the foot of the main face proper. It is either a slightly overhanging wall of snow and ice of about 10 metres, or a very long traverse left and then back right at a higher level. I persuade my friends to let me have a go at the former. They are dubious, but, using skills learnt in artificial climbing on rock, I put our axes to good use. Somewhat strenuously I overcome the problem. With much grunting and a very tight rope my colleagues join me.
>
> The face on which we stand rears upwards impressively. Below the face there is an abyss, with the hut a dot a long way below. My heart sinks. Even with my very limited experience I can see the hut guardian was correct.

The face is completely out of condition. Covered in tiny scree and a veneer of ice it is not possible to place protection – or so it appears. Then I heard Wilf speak. His words are etched in my brain: "I suggest we stay roped up". What in effect he was saying was simple: "I have taken the responsibility of bringing Colin, a novice, here against the local professional advice. I have made an error of judgement and I accept the responsibility". The reality is stark. The face is highly dangerous. One slip could mean disaster. By being roped, if that event occurs, means that all three of us will fall into the abyss and oblivion.

I often wonder about the element of luck in completing the climb. Certainly our concentration was total. The reason the experience is written up here was that Wilf was acting in the best sense of being human. To describe a person as having 'integrity' is to pay them the highest of accolades. His action displayed the highest form of honesty and was in the best traditions of mountaineering.

Integration is synonymous with *unity*. If we were going to depart then we would go 'as one'. Unity is also the most profound message that comes from Nature.

Honesty with the surrounding world

The third way to view *Honesty* is in terms of our relationship with the surrounding world: to try to accept the implications of the fact that one belongs to the unity of Nature. Also to accept, ideally that one is no more and no less significant than everything else in Nature. It was only in old age, especially after years of solo expeditions that I truly accepted this radical premise without question. I *felt* it to be true. It had been a long journey from extreme egoism. The personal experience I will relate took place in the summer of 1983.

I am several weeks into a solo sea kayak 650-mile expedition, off the Alaskan coast from Sitka to Glacier Bay. The experience, as I expect after a two-man kayak trip in 1981, is exciting and impressive. This particular day has seen my first meeting with sea lions, and I am not keen to repeat it. This is followed by a traverse round a headland made difficult by a strong wind and confused sea. Once round, conditions become progressively easier and I am now about to erect my tiny tent on the first and only official campsite of the expedition. Glacier Bay is the largest of the American National Parks and boasts both a hotel and a campsite, the only habitation in a large pristine wilderness.

I search for and finally find a low covering patch of vegetation amidst the bare ground under the canopy of trees. Whilst erecting the tent, a National Park Ranger appears and in a gentle yet firm manner, suggests I should erect my tent on the **bare** ground. I feel stupid. I love the Alaska wilderness yet have been so self-centred, so unaware, as to ignore the **fragility** of that tiny area of vegetation. Upon reflection there is more than enough challenge for that vegetation to grow, without me camping on top of it. It was a lesson I never forgot.

To summarise:

Bearing in mind that honesty is the major route towards truth and wisdom, and that dishonesty is a major characteristic of modern societies I have described *Honesty* as:

The Foundation Virtue

To act honestly is to act truthfully or conscientiously. Both truth and conscience are central to the human spirit. If Emerson was correct in his statement "Truth is the summit of being", then honesty would be a major route in the search for it.

Quotations

"Lies are not only evil in themselves, but infect the soul of those who utter them." — *Plato*

"Love loves honesty." — *Tennyson*

"The most difficult thing in life is to live and not to lie
– and not to believe in one's lies." — *Dostoevsky*

Awareness

AWARENESS	IGNORANCE
Attentiveness	Inattentiveness
Perceptivenes	Unawareness
Open-mindedness	Close-mindedness
Consciousness	Blindness
	Prejudice

This virtue is closely linked to Concentration, Empathy, Vitality, Patience, Respect, Compulsion, Humility, Simplicity.

If *Honesty* is the foundation virtue, on which we must always build and refer back to, then *Awareness* is, or should be, a major companion as we journey through life. Without continuous attention to *Awareness*, growth will always be restricted or even worse become misshapen. Each of us possesses the means necessary to explore our deepest nature. No one else can do this for us. The responsibility and opportunity for becoming aware of all that we truly are and then sharing it with others is ultimately our own.

If these comments seem formidable then it is because I believe that everything in Nature is a unity. As a young man I would have dismissed that statement as 'ridiculous'. The key, I sense, is *at minimum* to have an open mind and to accept the possibility of the wisdom or truth of the ancient statement from The Upanishads:

> "What is within us is without us.
> What is without us is within us."

Initially this means accepting the unity of *self.* Any individual is made up of conscious self and unconscious self. In an attempt to accept this unity it may be helpful to return to the analogy of the ocean. Conscious self is *the surface*, and the depths beneath are unconscious self.

Awareness like *Honesty* may also be seen initially in the three aspects:

Awareness of Self
Awareness of Others
Awareness of the Environment

Herewith a relevant personal experience involving two of these aspects:

A Monday in the summer of 1977. The weather forecast is for high pressure and settled weather. I have a couple of spare days and so I know it is time to take on a particular kayak journey. The Isle of Man lies off the west coast of Cumbria. It can be seen on a clear day from the mainland. Mostly though, it lies hidden, as it is 40 miles offshore.

I spend most of the day checking and packing my sea kayak. I deliberately do this slowly and methodically. There must be no mistakes on a solo trip, especially as I have also chosen a night crossing.

By early evening I am at Selker, a tiny village on the Cumbrian coast. The view west is magnificent. Beyond the extensive beach is the great red orb of the setting sun. Villagers help me carry the kayak to the distant edge of the sea (it is low water). With cries of "Good Luck" in my ears I am on my way. It is 7.45pm. Paddling into the red sunset is beyond words. I feel engulfed by the immensity and beauty of the scene and my place within it.

I begin to concentrate on keeping a specific bearing. Tidal streams run across the kayak and demand awareness. Nearer the Isle of Man there are tidal races. If I am pushed off course I do not wish to miss the island and meet them instead. Visibility is only a few miles at best. I also try and keep very relaxed. In rough conditions I need to be a firm part of the kayak, at least below the waist. That means the maximum movement of my toes is only an inch or so if I need to stretch them. Cramp, potentially, is a major enemy on a solo trip. Rafting up with other kayaks and thereby being able to ease out of the cockpit in order to stretch and remove the cramp, is not an option. I try to take psychological comfort from all my lone training on Lake Windermere in the winter, where I have become used to being 12 hours in the boat without getting out.

The sunset, around 10.30pm is breathtaking. By 11.30pm it is very dark and I feel very lonely. No lights anywhere. Just a dark vault of sky and the gleam of an occasional wave over the deck. I am undeniably tense and need to keep a tight hold on my imagination. Suddenly I am aware of a small bird fluttering around the boat and my interest is immediately aroused. Years of sea kayak trips, especially around the islands of West Scotland, have given me a love of sea birds. Often they appear to be the only form of life around me, and their beauty and skill is always attractive.

For several minutes the bird stays around. It is as if it is as interested in me as I am in it. I am excited by its presence. Never before have I seen a storm petrel. It is the tiniest of sea birds, around six inches long and weighing hardly an ounce. I knew it was normally only seen well offshore. Apart from its diminutive size, its major characteristic of fluttering is more like a butterfly than a bird.

With its departure I continue to head west into the darkness. To my surprise, and relief, I realise my mood has changed. I am no longer tense. Intuitively I sense that the meeting had in some way been very special if not extraordinary.

A short time later I can just make out lights close together way off to the west. Checking the chart by pencil light I am over the moon. The lights are Maughold Head on the east coast of the Isle of Man. I am on course and, at last, have a definite guide.

By dawn the wind has become a north easterly force 4, and I am beginning to feel tired from the cold shower effect. My mood, however, is positive. I can eventually see the land, and finally I surf into Ramsey harbour. It is 4.15am and the trip has only taken eight and a half hours.

Looking at this experience it is obvious that it is generally related to awareness of self. Any solo experience, especially if dangerous and over a length of time emphasises and accentuates the loneliness of the situation. Everything is simply more intense psychologically. The specific situation of meeting the storm petrel was much more profound than I realised at the time. It was a highly positive experience which dramatically improved my 'feel good' factor. In contrast, my awareness of the sea, which I love, had a fearful effect because of its immensity and potential to change for the worse, especially after sunset and before meeting the bird. The profundity of the bird situation I eventually realised was that in that meeting my separateness had somehow been suspended. It was almost as if two long lost friends had been briefly reunited.

Another type of awareness had taken place before I left my house.

As I packed the kayak I tried to be aware of all the things that could go wrong on the trip. This *foresight* was essential in that I might well need a particular piece of equipment quickly in an emergency. It would need to be in exactly the best place to access it as easily as possible. As usual much of safety in such adventures means being prepared in *detail*.

Awareness Of Others

It is difficult not to overemphasise the importance of this aspect of *Awareness*. From *Awareness* hopefully should develop the virtue of *Respect* and if this continues the positive growth should lead to Love. By the latter I mean Universal Love – the most challenging of all ideals.

Sensitivity and attentiveness like empathy, are key elements of this *Awareness*. The same is true in developing the ability to listen. The more you feel you have to contribute, the more essential it is to be able to listen.

We live in a time of the cult of the individual. Emphasis is on the freedom of the individual, restrained only by the framework of the law. Whilst this is often highly convenient for the individual it is unacceptable as an attitude to life. We also need to have *awareness* of our connection to past human beings.

As Professor Alasdair MacIntyre reminds us, we also need to be aware that we are born with a past – a human link extending from immediate family back through the mists of time when our ancestors were hunter-gatherers and lived in caves.

Aldous Huxley was probably correct in 1959 to note that 'connection' and what Professor MacIntyre called 'connectedness' is the most important lesson history can teach us. That connection, however is not merely to our human ancestors but to everything else in Nature.

From Fritjof Capra the scientist:

> *"As I looked over the ocean my awareness of the unity of all things became very real and compelling…a wave can be viewed as an individual entity, and yet it is obvious that the wave is the ocean and ocean is the wave: there is no ultimate separation."*

And the Native American tribes, through the words of Chief Seattle:

> *"All things are connected. This we know. The earth does not belong to man; man belongs to the earth. This we know. All things are connected like the blood which unites one family."*

To live believing and acting as though one is separate is not only to live a lie but to hasten the decline of civilisation.

And from nearly seven centuries ago, Meister Eckhart speaks:

> *"All things are contained in the One, by virtue of the part that is one. For all multiplicity is one…"*

These words from the Upanishads also seem highly appropriate:

> *"As is the human body*
> *So is the cosmic body.*
> *As is the human mind*
> *So is the cosmic mind.*
> *As is the Microcosm*
> *So is the Macrocosm.*
> *As is the Atom*
> *So is the Universe."*

These are strong words, yet deliberate. Genuine unawareness of connectedness first needs to be acknowledged and then acted upon in terms of one's ideas and actions.

This recent personal experience seems worth recounting as an example of gross *unawareness.*

> An International Mountain Film Festival. At the end of a lecture by a famous mountaineer I have an informal word with the speaker and ask him if he had read *Beyond Adventure*. His reply was to the effect that "I don't have time for that sort of stuff" and I was dismissed. Now I may make a wrong judgement here but the picture this produced in my mind was to the effect that "I am far too busy living (on the surface of my life) to look beneath my surface. In any event I enjoy being on the surface because I am both a very good climber and very important in the bureaucratic world of mountaineers."
>
> What really saddens me is that the person concerned was not a young climber trying to make his mark. He was well educated and occupied a prominent position in that specific world of adventure.
>
> I am even more saddened when I look wider. I sense that the *"Hey look at me, who I am and what I have done"* is doing very well in the modern world.
>
> And "hey, who needs all this awareness stuff? "

It is only with awareness that one can learn about the deeper aspects of self. For most people this is likely to be a lifelong process. In old age I feel I am *beginning* to be aware of how I relate to everything natural in my environment. For many years I have been aware, for example, of the possibility that as I pass a tree, the tree is looking at me in some intangible way. That awareness, I sense, is very much only a beginning. The same is true in terms of my awareness of most other human beings with whom I make contact.

Quotations

"So what I do feel is that man's task is to become more and more aware, and more and more obedient to his own intimations of greater awareness." — L. van der Post

"It is a very rare matter when any of us at any time sees things as they are at the moment. This happens at times…that we become aware of what is going on about us and of the infinite great worlds of force, of feeling and of idea in which we live, and in the midst of which we have always been living. These worlds are really in progress all the time; and the difference between one man and another, or the difference in the same man at different times, is the difference in his awareness of what is happening."
— John Jay Chapman

"We look across the water towards the West and upward into the soaring arch of the sunset; Stillness – our lives are one with that of this huge far-off world, as it makes its entry into the night." — Dag Hammarskjöld

Respect

RESPECT	DISRESPECT
Appreciation	Rudeness
Value	Contempt
Politeness	Impoliteness
Courtesy	Discourtesy
Consideration	Inconsiderateness
	Selfishness

This virtue is closely linked to Awareness, Humility, Unselfishness, Compassion, Tolerance.

The 1990's. I am about halfway through a solo east west traverse of the Spanish Pyrenees and now face the crux of the whole expedition. I am high on the shoulder of Monte Perdido (3355 metres). Because it is still early in the year snow has hidden the route over the top of the Anisclo Canyon. After climbing exposed snow slopes, I cross the ridge at about 3000 metres. I then descend 200 metres to a prominent limestone shelf. Fifty metres below lies a much larger and wider shelf which I know will contain the proper trail. Between the two shelves lie vertical cliffs. Following the top shelf northwards for about a kilometre I can find no possible descent. Increasingly concerned I return to my start and then head south along the shelf. Eventually I find a tiny cairn at the top of a dark overhanging gully. "No thank you". It appears far too dangerous. I then examine the arête on the south edge of the gully. It is vertical but the rock is dry. Heart in mouth I climb down. Difficulties of about severe standard test me considerably as I am wearing trekking shoes and am carrying a large rucksack. Camping that evening on the broad shelf below, despite almost no food and being very cold, is brilliant. In the mountains I have always regarded myself as a coward. No longer. I have committed myself in a most exposed place. It is so early in the year that I have seen no one. I could have been on the moon. I know I have at last found my self-respect in the mountain environment.

In a broader sense *Self–respect* essentially means behaving with dignity, in a manner of which your conscience would approve. This includes, of course, your relationships with other human beings. *Politeness* and *Civility*, if genuine, are the very basis of civilised living. In addition it is always worth remembering that how another sees you may well depend on how you see him. If you respect him, he will likely respect you.

The philosopher A.C. Grayling underlines the importance of this virtue:

> *"…civility is our best hope for finding and maintaining that subtle and constantly renegotiated equilibrium on which the existence of society depends."*

The modern age suffers from both a loss of politeness and a deficit of good manners. There is every reason for the young to be educated in terms of behaviour and not least in their attitude to everything and everyone around them.

So far my comments have been confined to human beings. With my view, however, of "everything in Nature is alive in its own way and deserves its own well-being" I need crucially to show *respect* towards all aspects of Nature. Logically I sense that by use of *awareness*, *respect* should follow. Perhaps even more hopefully, from *respect* should come Love in its universal sense.

My view concerning everything that is not an obvious part of Nature – i.e. things made by man as opposed to not made by man has been somewhat ambivalent with regard to *respect*. I suspect I need to include the man made world but would add a rider: providing the thing is not destructive in itself or is not used destructively.

I came to love, for example, both my sea kayak and paddle. In demanding conditions they kept me alive providing I executed the appropriate skills. More than that they had my complete respect. I often wondered how such inanimate objects could be felt by me to be an extension of myself. Getting into the kayak always felt like I was putting on old slippers and yet, like the delicate wooden paddle, the boat could perform brilliantly in brutal conditions.

At a more mundane level I now try to respect everything I own or use. When I wash up I try to be aware that the items have inherent energy, that their materials came from the earth and that its makers have produced objects that are beautiful in their simplicity.

Quotations

"If a man be gracious and courteous to strangers, it shows he is a citizen of the world, and that his heart is no island, cut off from other lands, but a continent that joins to them."
— *Francis Bacon*

"Respect yourself if you would have others respect you." — *Baltasar Gracian*

"Is there no respect of place, persons, nor time in you?" — *Shakespeare*

Compassion

COMPASSION	INDIFFERENCE
Concern	Apathy
Pity	Insensitivity
Charity	Egoism
Sympathy	Unconcern
Mercy	Detachment
Tenderness	

This virtue is closely linked to Awareness, Humility, Empathy, Fairness, Kindness, Unselfishness, Respect, Responsibility, Patience, Humanity.

This great virtue of both Christians and Buddhists relates not merely to humans but to all living things.

When it comes to compassion for other humans recent personal experience is seared into my brain. As usual, we begin really to understand when we are truly and deeply involved in the suffering itself. Working on a busy mountain rescue team often involved the feeling of compassion. Inevitably, however, there was a necessary detachment in order to act efficiently, in what were sometimes dangerous situations. Having a wife dying unexpectedly from cancer on the other hand was at a much more painful level. I marvelled at the *Compassion* of those who worked in the hospice. I was utterly out of my depth, and immeasurably moved, by my dying wife consoling *me*, insisting that I must find someone else. If she had not insisted that she was in "a bubble of happiness", I am not at all sure I would have eventually made something of a recovery. The senior nurse at the hospice was also very moved by Annette's positive attitude and compassion. She was unused to having terminally ill patients who took time to be compassionate with their fellow sufferers.

In terms of compassion for other life forms, I have a particularly vivid memory from my first expedition to Alaska.

Barry and I have completed our journey and we have returned to Sitka, with a few days to spare before our flights home. A small island is decided upon for rest for a couple of days, and I go fishing alone over a reef a mile or so offshore. The weather changes suddenly and the calm sea begins to become rough. My problem is that I have caught a red snapper of several pounds. Eventually I pull in the line and, with difficulty, place the frantic fish under the strong deck elastics in front of my cockpit, before quickly grabbing my paddles to stabilize the kayak before I capsise. As I paddle back to the shelter of the island I watch this magnificent fish die in front of me. Conditions have been too dangerous to take my hands off the paddle to release the fish.

I have never fished again. I sense that even if my life depended upon fishing for food my decision would remain.

I would like to see *compassion* extended to relate to *everything* natural, as I believe everything is alive *in its own way*, and seeks and deserves its own wellbeing. My intuitive belief is that everything in Nature is no more or less important than anything else. I do not regard, for example, my view as extreme, that the stone kicked clumsily off the footpath, should not be returned immediately to its original situation; or that I should try to avoid the cobweb in front of me. By behaving in a positive least destructive manner with as much *awareness* as possible I sense that I help my own growth and well-being.

Indifference, the opposite of compassion, can only exacerbate feelings of pain and suffering, whilst emphasizing cruelty and egoism. The doorway into compassion may be the imagination, which indicates a strong link with the virtue of *empathy*. There is also a strong link with *unselfishness*. Whilst compassion is often seen in a universal sense, I feel it may be only one aspect of universal love, because it is concerned essentially with sympathy with suffering in some form or other.

To be genuine, compassion must be based on respect for the other, and on the realisation that others have the right to be happy and overcome suffering just as much as you.

Quotations

It is still my firm conviction that human nature is essentially compassionate, gentle. That is the predominant feature of human nature. Anger, violence and aggression may certainly arise but I think it's at a secondary or more superficial level; in a sense they arise when we are frustrated in our efforts to achieve love and affection.
— *Dalai Lama*

Compassion is the motive force behind morality. — *Schopenhauer*

Compassion was the chief and, perhaps, the only law of all human existence.
— *F. Dostoevsky*

A story from Native American Indian culture:

They used to inform a tree it was going to be cut down to make a canoe. All trees around then fainted with shock and were thus anaesthetised. A different tree was then cut down. As he didn't know anything about it, he had no experience of the fear of something happening to him. The original tree who was told, woke up with relief that he was still alive.

(As told to the author by a friend)

Determination

DETERMINATION	IRRESOLUTION
Will-power	Weak-will
Hard work	Passivity
Commitment	Submissiveness
	Feebleness
	Half-heartedness
	Inconstancy

This virtue is closely linked to, Vitality, Patience, Responsibility.

In comparison with almost all the other virtues, *Determination* has by far the greatest number of synonyms. This tends to emphasise its importance in life's journey. These synonyms include: persistence, resolution, industry, willpower, perseverance, purposefulness, tenacity, endeavour, resolve and resilience.

When compiling a list of relevant personal experiences, to illustrate this virtue, I was initially confounded. Of all the virtues, this one had been a major characteristic of my life. There were simply too many experiences to choose from. Then I had an idea. Why not use the experience of trying to write this book. After all I am now in the third year of its gestation, have at least another year to go, and my heart lies more outdoors than indoors. Both previous books have felt like irksome indoor expeditions, not least when the sun shone!

I then realised there was a flaw in this idea. I *love* this exploration of trying to understand what my life is about, and then trying to communicate what I seem to have learnt. Because of this love I accept implicitly that there will be times when I will need all my determination to make progress. This is not infrequent because of the complexity of the subject and the knowledge that what is really important in life is *beyond* words!

I doubt I am alone in finding determination more difficult when in situations which I do not love. The ideal however, seems clear: *to be determined to do one's best at every moment.* This living 'in the now' is one of the great wisdoms and, unsurprisingly, a formidable challenge.

Very closely linked with determination are two other key virtues. That of *Patience* is very obvious. That of *Vitality* perhaps is less so. I include in the definition of the latter "Taking a positive approach to the problems of life". By that I mean acting in good faith and according to one's conscience! This is why *motivation* is always so important. One needs to be sure that one's reason for being determined is for positive rather than negative reasons. If it is the latter then determination becomes a vice such as stubbornness, inflexibility and even ruthlessness. Similarly extreme selfishness and foolhardiness can be displayed. The point at which determination can become foolhardiness is a fascinating one, not least for those who adventure. Preventing one, the virtue, becoming the opposing vice, necessitates the use of the basic senses. The importance of common sense cannot be overstated.[5] Many would agree that there is another sense involved here – that of intuition – an innate and deep-down sense of whether to go forward or to retreat. History shows mystery here. There are no simple answers, as there are no straight lines or compartments in Nature.

If determination now appears more complex than at first sight, it should not detract from its magnificence. The history of the human race shines with outstanding stories of endeavour, not least from exploration and adventure. It is important however to avoid looking at a virtue in isolation, especially one such as determination. *Courage*, for example can be defined as an extreme and ultimate form of determination in certain circumstances.

Quotations

"The glory is not in never failing, but in rising every time you fall." — *Chinese Proverb*

"The drop of rain maketh a hole in the stone, not by violence, but by oft falling."
— *Bishop Latimer*

"Before you begin a thing remind yourself that difficulties and delays quite impossible to foresee are ahead…you can only see one thing clearly and that is your goal. Form a mental vision of that and cling to it through thick and thin."
— *Kathleen Norris*

Patience

PATIENCE	IMPATIENCE
Restraint	Hastiness
Stoicism	Restlessness
Self-control	Impetuousness
Calmness	

This virtue is closely linked to, Self-discipline, Determination, Concentration, Reflection, Self-reliance, Vitality, Awareness, Tolerance.

Summer 1969. My four-week vacation from running the Oxford outdoor centre is based at my new home in Saundersfoot, Pembrokeshire. Now an enthusiast for open boat coastal sailing I have a second catamaran. The *Shearwater* is far sturdier than the original beautiful *Unicorn*.[6] It also has a jib as well as a mainsail and the latter can be reefed. Nevertheless it remains a tiny open craft for what I have planned. Around seventy-five miles west of Fishguard, across the exposed southern approaches to the Irish Sea lies Rosslare in Ireland. The likelihood that such a trip would be a first in such a boat added to the excitement of the plan. There are two problems. The first is finding a crew. I am very fortunate. Roger Stephens lives and works in Saundersfoot and is an experienced dinghy sailor. The other problem is more difficult, in fact much more difficult. We have to have the 'right weather'. We could not justify having to be rescued unless we have at least set off in settled weather, which meant a high-pressure system, or at least a 'weak ridge of high pressure'.

Patience is severely stretched and it is nearly two years before we decide to go in June 1971. It turns out to be a very memorable 11½ hour journey, including being becalmed, and then almost looping the boat end over end out of sight of land. It is a relief to sight eventually the famous Tuskar Rock and know Ireland is close. Next day we plan to sail back to Wales. The shutters onto our hotel bedroom window wake us up early. They are slamming as an easterly gale hits them. We return by the main ferry. The captain invites us on the bridge. He has seen us crossing the previous day and said how small we had been. I knew what he meant!

Nearly a quarter of a century later I now know that *Patience* is literally one of the most important of all the virtues. It is an ideal towards which I will continue to strive and which I will try further to understand.

Living in the modern world does not help, indeed it hinders making progress with this virtue. As Norman Douglas notes:

> *"Impatience…is the white man's characteristic, and his curse."*

Indeed the modern world seems to spin faster as the years go by. Unsurprisingly many people (especially in cities) become stressed by the unnatural pressures and seek their sanity in more natural settings.

A letter to *The Times* in 2005 from Father Bryan Storey:

> *"Sir, when I was young (a good few decades ago) it was usual to wait for two or three minutes before a doorbell was answered. Now if I haven't answered my front door in 30 seconds, almost invariably the bell is rung again or I find that the person at the door has disappeared. Isn't it a pity that we have grown so impatient?"*

Many years ago I had placed *Patience* as an important aspect of *Determination*. Whilst that may be true it does an injustice to patience. I should have taken more heed of Emerson's wisdom that:

> *"The most important thing that Nature can teach us is patience."*

And this Turkish proverb indicates its rewards:

> *"Patience is the key of paradise."*

I now see that Patience is a *central* virtue in terms of self-fulfilment, in the deepest of senses. It is a matter, a formidable matter, of trying to live 'in the moment', and to be as peaceful and relaxed as possible in that process.

A Sikh guru perceptively notes:

> *"Let patience be your purpose in life; implant this with your own being. In this way, you will grow into a great river; you will not break off into a tiny stream."* — *Guru Arjan*

The reader, no doubt will be familiar with the saying, *'needing the patience of a saint'*, a not uncommon feeling in modern life. There is a deeper implication: try to have the patience of a saint. John Dryden knew this well:

> *"Possess your soul with patience."*

As did John Ruskin:

> *"People are always talking of perseverance, and courage, and fortitude, but patience is the just and worthiest part of fortitude – and the rarest too."*

Quotations

"Patience is needed with everyone, but first of all with ourselves."
— *St.Francis de Sales*

"I am managing, more and more to make use of that long patience you taught me by your tenacious example: that patience which, disproportionate to everyday life that bid us haste, puts us in touch with all that surpasses us."
— *Rainer Maria Rilke*

And a final, brilliant comment:

"Patience is not passive, on the contrary, it is active; it is concentrated strength."
— *Edward R. Bulwer-Lytton*

Self-discipline

SELF-DISCIPLINE	INDISCIPLINE
Managing emotions Guided by conscience in resisting desires and temptations	Uncontrolled, impetuous and irresponsible behaviour

This virtue is closely linked to Honesty, Purity, Responsibility, Awareness, Determination, Simplicity.

There is an idea that all major feelings stem from the emotions of either fear or love. I believe that fear can be the major block in making any sort of progress in life.

I support this idea and have become convinced that, using natural outdoor settings especially, young people should learn to control their fears, to use self-discipline, and then move forward in terms of actions. In this natural adventure way they learn by experience that they can take up this challenge, overcoming fear with success, and of course, gain markedly in terms of self-confidence and self-respect. It has always impressed me that no matter how much psychological support a fearful person has, ultimately, only that person can control their own emotions. I have lost count of the number of times I have seen a young person in an adventure situation, such as half way up a climb, having problems with fear. The rope linking them to the instructor on top of the climb seems very thin; the ground below looks a long way down and is covered with rough boulders. To make it worse the climbing moves in front of them now look more difficult and the cliff seems to be very steep. Friends below shout their encouragement. The instructor above emphasises the moves are not as difficult as they look. No matter what the support, the beginner has no escape from trying to overcome his fear.

In the broader world of resisting desires and temptations, and being guided by my conscience I suspect I do not score highly. It has, for example, taken until 2006, to give up fast cars – and even then it was a major psychological battle!

Desires can be strong and temptations lurk around every corner. I am not alone I suspect in experiencing an ongoing problem in this respect. An indication of a wise person is perhaps not only one who learns to control his desires, but also one who is content with the minimum of possessions.

In a broad context, the value of this virtue can be seen when one looks at the considerable amount of anti-social behaviour in our societies. *Self-discipline*, if practised on a much larger scale than at present, could markedly help to reduce this fundamental problem. *Discipline* that is imposed from outside the person, such as by the police, is generally the least satisfying in terms of personal growth. There is something pathetic about people who seem to delight in being anti-social, when they nearly always have a personal choice as to how they behave. There is no substitute for exerting control over oneself.

Indiscipline, the opposing vice, would seem a trait to discourage. Uncontrolled, impetuous and irresponsible behaviour is largely self-damaging, as well as often damaging to others.

Quotations

*"Freedom is not procured by a full enjoyment of what is desired,
but by controlling the desire."* — *Epictetus*

"From intellection comes desire. From desire, will. From will, our deeds. And from deeds our destiny. Self-control, therefore, is so essential for the spiritual life and a practical life well led that it is even favourably compared to martial conquest."
— *C. Johnson*

"When he is lord of himself, he will deserve his self chosen title of homosapiens."
— *W.R. Inge*

Self-Reliance

SELF-RELIANCE	DEPENDENCY
Independence	Unnecessary compliance and acquiescence ˟
Self-sufficiency in thought and action	Seeking assistance more than is helpful or necessary

This virtue is closely linked to Honesty, Purity, Self-discipline, Responsibility, Determination, Vitality.

Castle Rock of Triermain, a steep and impressive crag, lies at the head of St. John's in the Vale in the Lake District. It is 1960 and I have spent a few days leading two schoolboys up routes graded Extremely Severe. They have previously only climbed with me on the small gritstone edges in Derbyshire and I am impressed with both their skill and coolness on these bigger crags. At the end of the afternoon I point them at a crack line up the centre of the southern face of the crag. The forty metre line, though steep and open, is obvious. I explain the route is called Via Media, is graded 'Very Severe', and they are to be very careful as they lead through. (they have been taught to belay and place protection). I depart to the campsite half a mile away. They are fourteen years old, from a secondary modern school in Derby, where I have a temporary job. They are in shoes.

Around twenty-five years later, I am at Glasbury-on-Wye in South Wales. This time it is a group of ten boys and girls from the Lakes. They have spent a term learning to canoe-camp, and have about three years of kayaking experience up to grade III whitewater standard. They carefully pack their tiny kayaks and then, with waves and smiles, set off down the River Wye, which is in summer spate. My college student and I return to the minibus and set off to the next bridge downstream to check them. The group are on a 100-mile, four day trip to Chepstow, without adults. They are ten-and eleven-year olds.

It will be obvious from these two memories, as well as from my own expeditions, that I am a strong believer in the importance of self-reliance.

Emerson in his famous essay 'Self Reliance' from 1897 makes the powerful point that Nature suffers nothing to survive unless it learns to be self-reliant. Self-reliance is also the basis of Darwin's *Theory of Natural Selection*. A recent television programme (2006) on the migration of tracked young ospreys from north of New York to South America was deeply impressive. The birds had only recently learned to fly, parents

˟ to self satisfied without taking opposition is. to account.

were absent from their journey and they travelled solo facing many dangers. The contrast with life in the modern world can be considerable. In a consumer society there are powerful interests at work to make people, and not least the young, *conform*, in the interests of making money. Individuals can be robotically reduced to being consumers.

There is a natural logic in progression through life from total dependence as a baby to eventual independence or self-reliance.[7] Independence of thought and action, regardless of popularity, are important characteristics of a mature person. This virtue, like determination, however, needs to be linked to other virtues. *Honesty*, for example is essential. In the first instance there is a need to acknowledge that it is impossible to be completely self-reliant. We are all dependent on the planet for basic needs of water, food, air, light, warmth and shelter. In the second instance there needs to be honesty in terms of *awareness* of ones capabilities. Is one ready to be self-reliant? In the two examples given, the awareness of the adults as to the capabilities of the youngsters was of crucial importance. Nature does not suffer fools gladly.

In addition, unless we can live as hermits, we need relationships with other people. In other words dependency, the opposite of self-reliance, in important ways, is not a vice, but a virtue. Interdependence is a basic attribute of Nature.

One of the most pleasing aspects of the second type of expedition mentioned was that each member had at times, and especially on the water, to be fully self-reliant, and at other times they also had to depend on each other and work as a team.

It is possible to become too self-reliant. Very often self-centredness or egoism is the root cause. I became particularly aware of this on one expedition where my fellow expeditioner showed his bachelor background. In contrast to living alone, being married meant I accepted as normal the principle of sharing equally. It took a while for me to realise that I was the one who carried all the dirty, awkward equipment!

Quotations

"Whosoever would be a man, must be a nonconformist...nothing is at last sacred but the integrity of your own mind...I am ashamed how easily we capitulate to badges and names, to large societies and dead institutions." — R.W. *Emerson*

"The reason Wakantank does not make two birds, or animals or human beings exactly alike is because each is placed here to be an independent individuality and to rely on itself." — *Teton Sioux Indian*

William Blake captures the essence of self-sufficiency:

"No bird soars too high if he soars with his own wings."

Concentration

CONCENTRATION	DISTRACTION
Attentiveness	Inattentiveness
Application	Mental and emotional
Centering	disturbance or interruption
Being wholly present	
Focus	

This virtue is closely linked to Awareness, Determination, Patience, Self-Discipline, Sympathy, Vitality.

Summer 1976. Six of us are attempting the first circumnavigation of the Outer Hebrides by kayak. After lunch at Castlebay we head west down the narrow Sound of Vatersay. Despite sunny weather we are on edge. As the swell from the west comes up the Sound it explodes on the numerous reefs. After about three miles we are out of the Sound, past the reefs and into deep water. A new danger now becomes apparent. The swell on the nearby beaches is huge. Landing would only be attempted as a last resort. Return down the Sound is also not an option unless we wish to play Russian roulette because the location of the reefs cannot be seen when looking **down** *wave. This means the explosions that will occur spasmodically could be* **under** *us. I study the map on my deck with what seems a laser like focus of my brain. I do not think I have ever read a map with such* **intensity**. *I knew if I did not find a solution to where we could possibly land – we would be faced with a night offshore. In an area as exposed as this it was not to be contemplated. Eventually I found one possibility – a tiny beach ten miles away round the north side of a headland. We eventually landed safely – to our relief and that of the coastguards.*

Such focusing of attention is common sense, of course, and what might be termed situation specific. Those humans involved with danger – from the surgeon to the racing car driver – commit themselves to years of hard practice to develop the necessary levels of concentration to be as safe as possible. In one sense these are examples of the *skill* of concentration rather than the virtue of concentration. My belief is that concentration as a key virtue is very much broader. It can be basic to our entire approach to the journey through life itself.

Complete concentration is an ideal. In other words, it is almost impossible to achieve. By 'complete' I mean the *entire* self is focused on the situation. At these advanced levels this is what I would term *relaxed concentration*. Tenseness of any kind has been removed, as it is not possible to perform at your highest level if there is tenseness. When one realises how incredibly complex is the make up of a human being, and how the mind is seldom still, it is not difficult to appreciate the enormity of this challenge. This becomes even more so if the personal approach to living is to try and live fully in each moment of existence! [8]

Careful reflection upon a few personal experiences of a transcendental or extra-ordinary nature have convinced me that there is a higher level of existence where the separateness of self is suspended and unity prevails. For example:

*The last five minutes of a ten-mile sea kayak training paddle on Lake Windermere. Unexpectedly and the only time it ever happens I suddenly **flow**. No effort is involved which is rationally inexplicable. Myself, my kayak, my paddle and the water become a unity.[9]*

Richard Jeffreys, in his celebrated *'The Secret of my Heart'*, enjoys a not dissimilar experience:

"It is eternity now. I am in the midst of it. It is about me in the sunshine. I am in it, as the butterfly floats in the light-laden air...now is eternity..."

This profound type of concentration is like a diamond, a brilliant focussing of our energy, intelligence, and sensitivity, and ideally, our very being. As growth occurs deepening levels of concentration can become contemplation and the eventual appreciation of unity as the basis of all existence.

Quotations

"To concentrate – to bring to, or towards a common centre..."
— *Shorter Oxford English dictionary*

It is the profound implications of this simple statement that I find meaningful and at which I have hinted.

"Zen is not some kind of excitement, but concentration on our usual everyday routine."
— *Shunryu Suzuki*

"Every instant of our lives is essentially irreplaceable: you must know this in order to concentrate on life." — *André Gide*

Altruism

ALTRUISM	SELFISHNESS
Unselfishness	Egoism
Charity	Self-centredness
Public-spirited	
Co-operation	

This virtue is closely linked to Compassion, Empathy, Honesty, Humility, Tolerance, Respect Responsibility, Generosity.

Unselfishness is the more commonly used word, though I prefer the more traditional term of *Altruism*. Whichever term is used, however, is unimportant. What matters is to recognise that this virtue is of *massive* importance. We live in a modern world where the cult of the individual and consequently self-centredness is deliberately encouraged. This is inevitable in a capitalist world where in practice the bottom line is making money. The phrase 'I want' or 'I must have' is basic to modern living. This is even more emphasised in a society where freedom without responsibility is the norm.

Whatever the situation, the unselfish action and the unselfish lifestyle deliberately puts others before oneself in terms of importance. Commitment to this virtue has long been recognised as a major pathway to both inner contentment and to love in its deepest sense. One of my heroes comes to mind.

In 1965 a human legend died aged ninety. This was Albert Schweitzer, philosopher, theologian, musician, doctor, Nobel Prize winner and admired the world over. As a young man, a student in Strasbourg, he wrote:

"It struck me as incomprehensible that I should be allowed to lead such a happy life whilst I saw so many people around me wrestling with care and suffering."

He allowed himself ten years for his pursuit of the intellect and then devoted the rest of his life to the service of humanity. This began with training to become a medical doctor and then setting up a hospital in deepest Africa. His unselfishness was eventually to inspire millions across the globe. Not only has he been one of my heroes but I cannot believe that any civilised person is not familiar with his life story.

At a personal level I feel uneasy because I now sense that for most of my life I was far too self-centred to really appreciate the depths of importance of this virtue. When I think about it, being married to Annette for over forty years emphasises this feeling. By nature she was unselfish, and I now don't accept that was because she was a woman and a mother and I was a man who had to achieve. It is true that from the time that I ran the Woodlands Centre I increasingly accepted that I was heavily involved in a movement dedicated to providing adventure for all young people. My life was largely consumed by all that this involved, and as a result my family involvement suffered. My *unselfishness* was largely restricted to this specific adventure area. Commitment to unselfishness as a way of life is at a different level altogether. I suspect that the truth of the matter is that most of us are a mixture of selfish and unselfish acts. With growth and maturity one hopes the latter becomes much more prevalent. In our modern world, for example, voluntary work of all kinds is always required. It is pleasing to see just how many people of all ages are involved in society in this way. Without such commitment society would all but grind to a halt.

Quotations

"If a man thinks or acts with a selfless thought, joy follows him, as a shadow that never leaves him." — *Buddha*

"Human history is the sad result of each one looking out for himself." — *Julio Cortazar*

Empathy

EMPATHY	SELF-CENTREDNESS
The ability to project oneself with sensitivity into the object of contemplation (human or otherwise) and as far as possible without self-centredness. Intuitive Awareness	Insensitivity Conceit Egoism

This virtue is closely linked to Awareness, Respect, Compassion, Reflection, Friendship, Humility, Altruism, Vitality.

A working life largely spent in outdoor adventure situations with young people of all ages has made me realise that I was constantly using the virtue of empathy. This was in the sense that I was very aware of the emotional turmoil going on within each individual as they attempted to overcome their fear of the situation: the "what if I fall in or off if I carry on?" and "why don't I retreat?". I knew their feelings because of my own experiences in such situations. More importantly most of them intuitively knew that I knew how they felt and also that I expected them to go onward and not retreat (in other words they were expected to use another virtue, that of *vitality* by being positive).

Empathy is a word that can be easily misunderstood. It is a quality that requires one to move as far as possible outside the importance of oneself, and then to try to *understand the world, situation or person*, from *that other standpoint*. Its use is not as is often commonly thought, restricted to human beings. It is relevant to our relationships with *anything*, and ideally, *everything*. Here is another personal experience:

> I am having a lunch break on a solo west-east traverse of the Spanish Pyrenees. The morning has seemed endless. Hours uphill along a deserted forest track in sweltering heat and the glare of the sun. Lunch is minimal. I care not for I am resting on a giant flat boulder. As I rest I realise I have a companion. No more than a foot away is a lizard and he periodically looks at me. He appears completely unafraid and I have no reason to move suddenly. Somehow I sense there is communication and I marvel that he enjoys this tremendous heat. Maybe he knows that I too love the sun, but I long for some shade and an icy pool to immerse myself in. As I move on he remains in my thoughts, and still does!

I feel this virtue to be of profound importance in terms of how I relate to my surroundings whether these be man-made or natural and regardless of whether they are animate or inanimate. My reasoning is as follows:

Most of us are conditioned to believe that we are separate from both other human beings and the environment and the fact that we are part of both tends to be lost. Empathy can break down these feelings of separation. Not only that, but these feelings should ultimately lead to strong feelings of the underlying unity and connectedness of everything.

The more we can identify with what is around us, and especially with reference to the natural world, the more we can grow. To see the world from a viewpoint other than one's own can make a profound difference to understanding oneself. This remains true whatever the object of contemplation might be. Empathy can also lead to a natural tendency to encourage other virtues rather than the self-centred vices.

Quotations

"A man to be greatly good, must imagine intensely and comprehensively; he must put himself in the place of another and of many others, their pains and pleasures must become his own." — Shelley

"When we cease making materialistic claims over objects and persons...and allow them to be what they are in their own right, then we can touch the inviolable strangeness which is their sacredness...the object comes into focus and is respected and relished in its otherness." — Sam Keen

"You never really understand a person until you consider things from his point of view... until you climb into his skin and walk around in it." — Harper Lee

Friendliness

FRIENDLINESS	UNFRIENDLINESS
Warmness	Unsociability
Amicability	Aloofness
Congeniality	Uncongeniality
Approachability	Distance
	Coldness

This virtue is closely linked to Cheerfulness, Humour, Kindness, Tolerance, Vitality.

If you want the atmosphere around you to be friendly, you must create the basis for that... whenever I meet someone new, I feel no need for introductions. The person is obviously another human being...there is not so much difference between us all. — *Dalai Lama*

This quotation makes me smile. Having met various Buddhists I am always impressed by their peaceful and open manner. I know that this is not my character. Not that I in any way try to be unfriendly. It is simply that since I was a young man I have found social situations difficult, often preferring my own company. I have wondered if this tenseness and awkwardness is altogether a bad thing. I have spent my life searching for answers to my existence. Would I have bothered if I had been happier and more sociable? I somehow doubt it. My situation, my awkwardness in company, was emphasised by a lifetime with Annette. She was naturally happy, outgoing, and friendly in manner. Since she departed I have had to try to be friendlier and more relaxed. The alternative of loneliness is not to be contemplated. It has been and still is an interesting experience. Friends who have known me for a long time say they have seen positive changes in this respect. I remain unsure!

It may sound odd but I sense in the first instance one needs to be friends with oneself. By that I mean to be comfortable with oneself, accepting that tenseness is invariably counter-productive in all senses. Accepting also that being positive, if not cheerful, rather than negative, is always a productive way forward.

Ideally we should start the day with a smile. This simple word may well have profound implications. We all know that our lives are made and marred by our relationships with other human beings, as well as with ourselves. No amount of wealth, health, fame or power can compensate us for our loss if these relationships go wrong. This perforce should include the 'inner' smile, the acceptance of the fact that there is beauty and worthwhileness within us, even on our darkest days. It may be that the smile is on the direct path to love in its universal sense, a subject I will try and look at in a later chapter.

Being friendly and *receiving* friendliness are two sides of the same coin. In the two-way process of course, friendship can emerge. That relationship can be for both mutual utility and mutual pleasure.

There is also a higher level of friendship for mutual good, which Aristotle termed the 'supreme human relationship'. I take this to mean friendship that accepts that the most important aspect of living is to share ideas on how to live in such a way as to leave the world a better place. This is obviously the most complex and difficult of tasks even in theory, never mind the practice. Again I smile as from all the responses to earlier editions of this book I somehow *know* I have friends in various parts of the world, some of whom I have never even met.

Friendship can also arrive spontaneously. Stuck in Madrid very late on a Saturday night with my wife, little money and bewildered by the crowds, unfamiliarity and noise, and barely able to speak Spanish, a night on the tiles seemed inevitable. Out of the blue came help. A Spaniard picked us up and after much searching he found us a cheap and cheerful lodging. In good English he explained the same happened to him in London and we were to pass on the gesture.

Such friendliness may not be that unusual. Round the world French sailor Bernard Moitessier, just six hundred miles into another round trip is stuck with a waterlogged boat and is penniless:

"A guy came to see me. I did not know him. He brought a crew of professional caulkers. He paid for everything and he was not rich. Then he said 'Pass this on to a stranger as I did for you. Because I got it from a stranger too'..." [10]

And the words of Saint Exupery after a plane crash in the desert; days without food and water, and trying to walk to habitation:

"You Bedouin who saved my life...you are humanity...I in my turn shall recognise you in the faces of all mankind...it did not seem to me that you were rescuing me; rather did it seem that you were forgiving me and I felt that I had no enemy left in the world."

It could well be that if there is to be a future for the human race then 'the brotherhood of man' will have to be much more of a reality than it is at present. There needs to be maximum focus on those positive aspects which unite and link all human beings.

Neither should we forget friendship with the non-human world. Millions of humans have the strongest of friendships with dogs and cats, for example. That also makes me smile. On several expeditions Annette and I have been befriended by dogs. They have literally joined our expedition sometimes for many hours[11] – as if to say "I am bored with my static existence and wish to join you on your adventure!" One memory in particular stands out.

> Spring in Cyprus. A week into a traverse of the main mountains and Annette and I have to follow a road as there is no track. A beautiful yet cold day with recent snowfall. Out of nowhere comes a huge white Alsatian. I am very wary. I need not be. He has come not only to be our friend but also to protect us from all dangers!
>
> For the next few hours our life is surreal. Every vehicle – and it is the main road along the mountain spine – is seen as the enemy by the dog. Quite fearless it attacks even buses and lorries. Someone calls the police, who try to entice it into their van. No chance! We three continue. A coffee stop is difficult. The man is clearly frightened; the wife terrified. What an experience. We thankfully leave our (exhausted) friend swimming in a large pond!

Less dramatically and yet wonderful, on all my recent expeditions, and especially the solo ones, I sense the friendship of my wild surroundings – from the trees and flowers to the rocks and stars.

> *"We are all travellers in the wilderness of this world, and the best we can find in our travels is an honest friend."* — *R.L. Stevenson*

Quotations

"A friend may well be reckoned the masterpiece of Nature…with him we are easily great. How he flings open the door of existence. What questions we ask of him. What an understanding we have. How few words are needed…a real friend doubles my possibilities and adds his strength to mine." — *R.W. Emerson*

"The shortest distance between two people is a smile." — *Attributed to Victor Borge*

> *"Don't walk in front of me*
> *I may not follow.*
> *Don't walk behind me*
> *I may not lead.*
> *Just walk beside me*
> *And be my friend."*
> — *Anon.*

Kindness

<table>
<tr><td>KINDNESS</td><td>UNKINDNESS</td></tr>
<tr><td></td><td></td></tr>
<tr><td>Goodness</td><td>Cruelity</td></tr>
<tr><td>Humanity</td><td>Callousness</td></tr>
<tr><td>Warmth</td><td>Insensitivity</td></tr>
<tr><td>Affection</td><td>Inhumanity</td></tr>
<tr><td>Generosity</td><td></td></tr>
</table>

This virtue is closely linked to, Awareness, Compassion, Friendship, Gentleness, Empathy.

In old age I would hope that I am well aware of my virtues and vices. I knew I was going to find it difficult to personalise this virtue, or so I first thought. I knew I was not by nature what is conventionally seen and understood as kind. I would hasten to add that I don't think of myself as an unkind person by nature either. All this seemed very obvious to me when married to Annette who was the epitome of kindness as I understood it.

Then a dear friend noted most helpfully that an early meaning of this word, which has perhaps become a bit obscured, was 'likeness to your own nature' and 'if you acted kindly you acted like a human being, one of your kind'.

Into my mind then came the phrase 'to be cruel is to be kind'. Almost like 'hey presto' I understood where I stood with this virtue. Firstly though I would change that phrase to 'to be hard is to be kind' and add the rider 'providing it is in the best interests of the person on the receiving end'. I could then think of many occasions when I needed to tell someone the truth about what I saw in them, but always tried to do this in a kindly manner.

I have long been a believer in the Outward Bound concept of 'impelled into experi-ence' [12], although again I would add a rider of 'having maximum awareness of the individual concerned'. Here is an extreme example:

A standard fourteen-day course at the Oxford Outdoor Centre in Wales. The activity is abseiling down a ten-metre steep rock slab with a safety rope. Nine out of the ten fourteen-year olds complete the task. I send them off to the next activity half a mile away. I now have a tubby girl who has refused to have a go. I eventually have her equipped at the top. She still refuses to descend. I physically place myself on top of her and the two of us go down the rope. There is screaming and then silence at the bottom. She eventually agrees to have another go – like the first time, though I will remain at the top this time. She has obviously realised that she can cope psychologically with the problem. She does it twice more. I then suggest she could do it *without* a safety rope (which no one else in the group had done). She does it and we rejoin the group. I take no pleasure from being so extreme. On the other hand her *self-confidence* and the *respect* from the rest of the group towards her are both enhanced.

It is probably unnecessary to remark that I have always been a hard taskmaster, not least to myself. To balance that is a long developed and deep concern to see progress in terms of people generally and young people in particular, realising their enormous potential in all positive senses of being human.

To move to the more conventional understanding of kindness, there can be no doubt of its importance. In many ways it is difficult to separate it from love. In a way it is a key aspect of *compassion*, along with the quality of *gentleness*. It can be seen as an essential striving towards *universal* love and the essence of being human.[13]

Quotations

"Kindness in words creates confidence
Kindness in thinking creates profoundness
Kindness in giving creates love"
— Lao Tzu

"So many gods, so many creeds,
So many paths that wind and wind
While just the art of being kind
Is all the sad world needs."
— Ella Wilcox

"What wisdom can you find that is greater than kindness." — J. J. Rousseau

Gentleness

GENTLENESS	HARSHNESS
Tenderness	Pitiless
Considerateness	Grimness
Humanity	Austerity
Mercy	Severity

**This virtue is closely linked to Friendliness, Kindness,
Unselfishness, Empathy, Compassion, Awareness.**

My immediate images of *gentleness* were watching my youngest daughter with her first born. The second was as a beginner transferring some seedlings from pot to garden. I have seldom felt so inadequate and yet so aware.

It is no coincidence that gentleness is probably the nearest virtue to Love, as I have no doubt the latter word is the most important word in any language! This virtue of tenderness is often known as the feminine virtue. In this modern world of equal opportunities, however, it is salutary to realise that there is probably an increasing number of women who often behave more like men than women and viceversa. We are all inevitably shaped by our surroundings and the modern world tends towards aggressiveness rather than gentleness.

For the Greeks, gentleness was the opposite of war and barbarism. As harshness, anger and aggression lead down the road to strife and to war, so gentleness is the major highway to peace. Gandhi comes to mind as a supreme example. His stance against the British Empire reminds us of the power of this virtue. In the same way, I also see gentleness as a major pathway to peace. In contrast, anger, which was seen as the third worst of the seven deadly sins, is on the increase. Road rage, yob anger, and the anger of terrorism are all modern phenomena. The concept of the 'gentleman' also seems to be disappearing.

> *"A gentleman is a man whose principle ideas are not connected with his personal needs and his personal successes." — W.B. Yeats*

I would have thought it axiomatic that a gentleman always apologises where appropriate. Such an event, for example in the House of Commons and in business, is a rare event today.

It is probably difficult to appreciate the immense depth of this quality. Shambhala provides an insight: [14]

"When you are fully gentle, without arrogance and without aggression, you see the brilliance of the universe. You develop a true perception of the universe."

My own insight links this key virtue to the natural rhythms of Nature, which may not be dissimilar to the words from the Shambhala. There may well also be a link with the idea of flexibility in contrast to being inflexible or fixed whether it be in terms of ideas or actions. This in turn links to everything in Nature being dynamic and in a state of interdependence rather than static.

Quotations

This was the noblest Roman of them all;
All the conspirators save only he
Did that they did in envy of great Caesar;
He only in a general honest thought
And common good to all, made one of them.
His life was gentle, and the elements
So mixed in him that Nature might stand up
And say to all the world, 'This was a man!'
— Shakespeare

But let us return to gentleness. What is, or seems to be, feminine about it is its courage without violence, its strength without harshness; its love without anger."
— Compte-Sponville

"The quality of a gentleman is so very fine a thing that it seems to me one should not be at all hasty in concluding that one possesses it." —Gerald Manley Hopkins

Gratitude

<table>
<tr><td>GRATITUDE</td><td>INGRATITUDE</td></tr>
<tr><td>Appreciation</td><td>Self-centredness</td></tr>
<tr><td>Acknowledgement</td><td>Egoism</td></tr>
<tr><td>Thankfulness</td><td>Selfishness</td></tr>
<tr><td>Grace to receive</td><td>Unawareness</td></tr>
<tr><td>Recognition</td><td></td></tr>
</table>

This virtue is closely linked to Awareness, Humility, Empathy, Kindness, Friendliness, Unselfishness.

Winter in the early 1970s. I have a new enthusiasm. Instead of climbing it is now white water kayaking and I am into exploring rivers. It has been raining for a week and rivers are very high. The target is the river Vrynwy in mid Wales. It is not in the guidebook but the map shows, from the closeness of the contours, that it should be swift flowing. As Steve, the Manchester Grammar School captain and I approach the river, a minibus and a trailer full of kayaks pass us going **away** from the river. (We later discover this contains the experienced members of Birmingham Canoe Club who, after inspection, decided it would be suicidal to attempt the river!)

Somewhat tense because of the roar from the river around the bend below the start, along with the speed of the brown swollen mass of water before us, we get into our kayaks. We stop on the bend; get out and climb up to look down on the next section. The river roar is because the flooded river enters a gorge. Almost reluctantly we decide there is no logical reason not to continue as there are no rocks and no big drops! (In our ignorance we did not know that when looking vertically down on waves from 30 metres above there is no way of assessing their size, which was immense!)

We return to our kayaks and continue down river. The rollercoaster ride of my life ends abruptly as I am wiped out by a side stream hitting the main river. I somehow manage to eskimo roll. Steve is capsized by the same wave, fails to roll and ejects from his kayak. With massive effort I manage to rescue him and tow him to the bank. We find his kayak about half a mile below wedged near the top of a (flooded) tree. We then complete the trip to a bridge at the end of a gorge, where Annette is very relieved to meet us. Two years of experience was far too minimal for what we had done. It was probably (or felt like) Grade VI of which the international system says 'cannot be attempted without risk to life'.

Our thankfulness, our *gratitude* in surviving, to whoever, or whatever, was heartfelt. Luck certainly played a part. I was especially concerned about Steve. He was fearless but still a schoolboy. I *had* to bring him back.

Inevitably with a lifetime of adventure, there were near misses. My view in theory was simple – reduce the element of luck to a minimum. In practice of course it was never that simple.

In the modern world the virtue of gratitude has to be of major importance. The cult of the individual, along with the emphasis on speed, often seem to leave little time for appreciation and thankfulness. As I have got older I have a distinct impression that time is going faster, or at least that people have to hurry: "Sorry, have to dash!" and so on. To show genuine appreciation requires a certain graciousness or politeness. In a time of much rude or crass behaviour, characterised by so many TV programmes, and not least the soaps, the acceptance of this virtue becomes ever more desirable.

In times not that long ago, it was de rigueur that the family were together for the evening meal, and grace preceded the event. This thanks for the food itself and the provider of it, is now a rarity. How sad when, as we eat, there are people, including children, who are dying of starvation.[15] Even worse is the greed encouraged by the 'buy one get one free' mentality. Obesity is already obvious within western societies and destined to become a major cause of death in the next few years

Displaying gratitude not only costs nothing, but also can make a very positive contribution in terms of a 'feel-good factor' for both giver and receiver. I wonder how many of us remembered to say 'thank you' to our teachers when we left school. It is almost a tradition *not* to say anything – selfishly to take what they offered, and often with criticism.

At its deepest levels gratitude is strongly linked with love, with *humility* and a recognition that life is 'a state of grace' and a window on eternity.

For Thomas Merton, the monk, the whole motivation of the solitary life was gratitude.

The opposing vice of ingratitude stems from self-centredness (egoism) and consequent selfishness. Such a vice shows either a dislike of acknowledging debts to others or a considerable lack of awareness; it may also show a marked lack of desire to share and to give.

Quotations

"Gratitude is the heart's memory." — French proverb

"How could one not be grateful to the sun for existing? To life, to flowers, to birds and the whole universe?" — Compte-Sponville

"The chief idea of my life…the doctrine I should always have liked to teach. That is the idea of taking things with gratitude and not taking things for granted."
— G.K. Chesterton

Tolerance

TOLERANCE	INTOLERANCE
Open mindedness	Narrow mindedness
Charity	Bias
Magnanimity x	Dogma
Munificence	Prejudice

magnificent liberality in giving; bountifulness

This virtue is closely linked to Forgiveness, Awareness, Patience, Empathy, Compassion.

I suspect I would rate poorly in my degree of *Tolerance* with regard to human affairs. Perhaps to some small degree I have mellowed in old age, but my negative feelings about increasing materialism as the basis for living and at the expense of destruction of the natural world have strengthened as the years have gone by. There is always choice in human matters. For example any action we have taken can be assessed in terms of its value, by whether it was self-centred, human-centred, or eco-centred. In other words was the motivation essentially for self-interest reasons; for the interest of humans (whether a specific group or, at the other extreme, the whole human race); or for the benefit of the planet? Put very simply, if we are to leave the planet in a better condition for the next generation then we have to be eco-centred to the best of our ability. I realise, of course, that even with the best of intentions, our actions are likely to be a mixture of all three attitudes; that these attitudes are dynamic; and that there is a logical, if not natural, progression from self-centredness through to eco-centredness. My intolerance is based on a lifetime of work in wild Nature within a state education system, whereby progress as I saw it was unacceptably frustrated by self-interest, egoism, and closed and fearful minds. A tiny example will have to suffice, in defence of my *Intolerance*!

Work at the Oxford Outdoor Centre had convinced me of the magnificent educational potential of adventure for all young people. I wrote a book, lectured extensively, and instigated what became the National Association for Outdoor Education. As its initial chairman (bad for my ego!) I was able to get acceptance for the first aim of the Association which was to the effect:

> *"To provide outdoor and adventure experiences relevant to the needs and abilities of each individual young person."*

When, as chairman, I retired early being seen as too radical (I was laughed at for suggesting that there was a group of virtues that we should all encourage!), I was sickened to see that the number one aim of the Association quickly became:

"To protect and safeguard the needs of the members of the Association."

I would accept the wisdom of these words by Alexander Chase (1966):

"The peak of tolerance is most readily achieved by those who are not burdened with convictions."

It is obvious that *Tolerance* is of particular importance because this trait should form the base of our values. Throughout history millions have died and are still dying in the name of a specific religion because it has 'the truth'. There are many groups around the world today who believe *they* have identified evil. The Taliban's perspective of Americans and vice versa is but one example. Such groups can dedicate their lives to opposing that evil. They demonstrate *intolerance* at its worst unless its values are based on a broad framework of minimal destruction to everything around them. 'Live and let live' would seem to be a common-sense policy and yet closed minds and prejudice are very much a feature of our modern age.

There is an urgent need to heed the words of Gandhi:

"Even as a tree has a single trunk, but many branches and leaves so there is one true religion (the one religion is beyond all speech) but it becomes many religions as it passes through the human medium…hence the necessity for tolerance."

Quotations

"The highest result of education is tolerance." — Helen Keller

"True goodness is not without that germ of greatness that can bear with patience the mistakes of the ignorant." — C.C. Colton

Forgiveness

FORGIVENESS	CONDEMNATION
To pardon	Disapproval
To show mercy or clemency	Censure
To be gracious	

**This virtue is closely linked to Tolerance, Compassion, Humility,
Honesty, Awareness, Kindness.**

Running an International Adventure one year course means inevitably
there will be dangerous situations. In the wilderness Nature does not suffer
fools gladly. The following experience remains especially vivid. Almost at
the end of a particular course and my group of ten sea kayakers are returning from the Shiants, uninhabited islands off the west coast of Scotland, to
the east coast of the Outer Hebrides. The crossing is ten miles; the area is
notorious as a place not to be in in bad weather; and a gale is forecast that
day. As we come out of the lee of the islands into the Minch, we meet the
full force of a northerly force five. Many of the group are comparative beginners although they have all learnt to eskimo roll. It will not take much
to have several of them *simultaneously* upturned. If this happens their eskimo
rolling cannot be guaranteed. I am the only member of staff and there are
ten mature students. I sense considerable potential danger.

To my consternation, the one very able mature student – able in the sense
of being competent in dangerous conditions and helping with rescues – suddenly accelerates away in front of the group. All too quickly he is out of
earshot because of the wind. To say I am furious would be to put it mildly.
How could he not know that his help might become essential? To this day
he remains unforgiven. I know we are lucky not to lose someone that day.
No more than an hour after landing a full gale is running. It is, however, too
easy to blame others. I have the total responsibility for the group and made a
mistake. I had presumed, as he had worked at an Outdoor Centre, that I did
not need to spell out the danger as it seemed so obvious.

Another memory of unforgiveness surfaces. In March 1989 the captain of the giant
oil tanker the Exxon Valdez split his vessel asunder on the pristine Alaskan coastline.
The weather was fair and he had been drinking. I loved that coastline not least for
its beauty, lack of pollution and lack of habitation. To imagine it covered in oil was
all but unbearable.

It makes sense, however, to live in a world where forgiveness is commonplace, providing that it is within acceptable limits. It makes sense also to accept the need to forgive oneself, no matter how reluctantly.

In the latter case it is at least a step in a positive direction. This may be particularly important with regard to trying to live by such a large number of virtues. There is a danger of undue self reproach and thoughts of "Oh I'm useless" or "I should be better".

To err is human. Unlike compassion, which stems from the heart and is more spontaneous, forgiveness has strong links to the intellect. Mental effort can be considerable.

Our society, at least in terms of its media, seems almost to delight in finding fault and apportioning blame. We live in a 'blame culture'. As lawyers well know, money is to be made by indictment and litigation. There is generally an urgent need to stop blaming, as it is both negative and can be a great waste of energy. Life is too short to justify anything other than a positive approach to life and concerted attempts to reduce, rather than encourage, friction. This is true not just in local, national and international senses, but *within* oneself.

Quotations

"Mutual forgiveness of each vice, Such are the Gates of Paradise." — *William Blake*

"To err is human. To forgive is divine." — *Alexander Pope*

"Generally there is far too little forgiveness in this world, but just occasionally, there is too much. There are those who get the wrong signals from forgiveness and learn nothing."
— *D.H. Lawrence*

Justice

JUSTICE	INJUSTICE
Fairness	Unfairness
Integrity	Prejudice
Rightness	Inequality
Equity	Discrimination
Truthfulness	Bias
Virtuous	
Impartiality	

This virtue is closely linked to Honesty, Responsibility, Reflection, Courage, Empathy.

It's not surprising that *Justice* has long been recognised as a cardinal value and, in a *social* sense, as the most important of all the virtues. Aristotle describes it as "the complete virtue" and "an absolute good" and further "the just then, is the lawful and the fair; the unjust the unlawful and the unfair".

In one sense *fairness* encompasses other crucial virtues such as Honesty, Responsibility, Compassion and Humility. Fairness, or Justice, also implies the use of *consistency*, which if used for positive purposes is a virtue in itself.

Throughout history there have been 'just' wars. In a civilised society peace would, or should, be a major objective. War would tend to be a last resort for obvious reasons. The importance of weighing all the evidence honestly and openly before making the decision whether to go to war cannot be overstated.

Current events in the Middle East emphasise the importance of making 'just' decisions. History is littered with wars based not on justice, but revenge. The former is characterised as 'well-meaning endeavour'. The latter is a primitive and emotional reaction. Ideas of revenge may be understandable but should be recognised as unacceptable. The strength of such heroes as Nelson Mandela, his magnanimity in not taking revenge, is always impressive.

A personal experience of an unusual nature may illustrate the virtue:

> A beach in Pembrokeshire in the late 1960s. I have a group of a dozen 14-year-old boys and girls on a General Adventure day. The tide is out and the name of the game is coasteering. The group are to traverse (move sideways) across the base of the steep cliffs above the sand. The rules are simple.

Do not go higher than 3 metres up the cliff. If you fall onto the sand, then rejoin the group at the back end and have another go. This is a fun and safe activity, demanding some climbing and balancing skills, providing the rules are accepted. There is often one in a group who dislikes rules, even if the latter are common sense. This time it is a large red-haired lad who has a reputation of being a bully. In the face of a difficulty he tries to avoid it by going above 3 metres. He gets to about 5 metres above the beach and gets stuck – too frightened to move in any direction. (The group are unroped). There is tension in the air. I am relaxed because I have foreseen such an event. Eventually the inevitable happens and he falls off. I field him but he is bruised and his ego severely dented. Inwardly I smile. Rough justice has been served. Nature can be brilliant in providing ideal learning situations.

Disraeli famously remarked:

"Justice is truth in action."

He was referring, of course, to equality among individuals, and the necessity for everyone to conform to the laws of the land.

Various organisations extend this justice to include animals and birds. It may be very radical but I feel this key virtue should be further extended to 'everything natural' because "Everything in Nature is alive in its own way and deserves its own well-being" as I proposed in my lecture in New Zealand in 1998.

Herewith a couple of experiences that have helped me develop this viewpoint:

On a walk across Northern England I was entertained to a pot of tea by a retired stonemason. I asked him if he thought the stone he had worked on over his lifetime was alive. He seemed unfazed by such an odd question and replied in the affirmative!

After my years in surf and on the ocean in tiny boats I came to accept implicitly the great tradition amongst such users that the sea was not only fully alive but was the greatest woman of them all!

The implementation of justice in this widest of senses would ensure a world of minimal destruction and minimal pollution. The contrast could not be greater than with justice in the modern age. Not only is it heavily biased in favour of the human race, but also it is prejudiced very heavily in favour of those who are most able to pay.

Quotations

"All virtue is summed up in dealing justly." — Aristotle

"The probability that we may fail in the struggle ought not to deter us from the support of a cause we believe to be just." — Abraham Lincoln

"Love should be inseparable from justice." — Iris Murdoch

Creativity

CREATIVITY	DESTRUCTIVENESS
Imagination	Harmfulness
Perception	Perniciousness
Invention	
Inspiration	
Originality	

This virtue is closely linked to Awareness, Concentration, Determination, Patience, Simplicity, Vitality.

As a young man so much of life seemed simple, at least in theory. The word Creativity, for example, would bring Annette immediately to mind. Much of her recreation was in the delights of the arts and crafts. Music and art in college were 'the creative arts'. This was a different world from my world of adventure. Not only that but I viewed adventure as a much more serious way of life.

When I began writing and thinking about the virtues I included creativity in substantial part because of its opposing vice. The idea that one had a choice between being either *creative* or *destructive* made its inclusion essential. I was well aware how easy it was to be destructive – the glee for example in rolling giant rocks down steep and remote mountainsides!

I then began thinking of creativity in a more positive manner. The word has the same roots as 'creation' – from 'creare' (latin) meaning 'to bring forth, to produce'. I came to realise that in my own way, I was creative.

As my love of sea kayaking developed, for example, I began to see that this modern recreation activity had little tradition of multi-day trips abroad. In mountaineering, on the other hand, expeditions had a long tradition and were popular. Why should the sea be different from the mountains in this respect? The sport was certainly as dangerous and challenging. Once I had the idea of sea kayak expeditions, I then had to create a journey. Mountains as objectives were comparatively easy. I knew, further, that as the first *modern* expedition it would have to capture the public's imagination if it was ever to become a tradition.

Eventually the idea comes of an expedition to Nordkapp or North Cape – the most northerly point of mainland Europe. I plan an expedition from Bodo, a town on the Arctic Circle – a journey up the Norwegian coastline of five hundred miles. I also manage to obtain a Churchill scholarship to lead the six man trip, emphasising that it will further Anglo-Norwegian relation-

ships. This cultural idea works brilliantly.[16] *We are front-page news in all the main newspapers in Norway – the six mad English in their tiny kayaks meeting the worst summer since 1874! Sea kayak expeditions have subsequently become commonplace worldwide.*

What this episode demonstrates is that almost every human activity has creative possibilities. Each human being has, I believe, the potential to be creative: to look at the world with new ideas and embrace the opportunities that come to light. There is an obvious need to encourage this virtue at every opportunity, and to discourage its opposite of *Destructiveness*, whether in thought or deed. Each of us might benefit considerably if we reflected upon our actions in terms of whether they were creative or destructive.

It could be that Adventure and Creativity are synonymous. The latter is about moving on and progressing, building on what has gone before and making new connections. Adventure is no different in that sense. It seems fitting that I now see having an adventurous approach as essential to growth across the spectrum of anyone's life. The word evolution probably is also synonymous.

Beneath the obvious characteristics of creativity I sense inexpressible depths concerned with 'creation' itself. In this area I feel very 'out of depth'. Suffice to say that recently experiencing the joys of a new grandson I was struck by the implicit non-separateness and unity. Amidst the physical intensity and the radiant love between mother and child, I later realised that there was something else as profound. In its own way, the birth of each new day would seem equally immense yet so easily taken for granted.

Michael Mayne expresses well my sentiments:

> "So much of what I want to share with you in succeeding letters could be summed up by saying: to ask 'What is art?', 'What is poetry?', 'What is music?' is one way of asking 'What is a human being?' For I believe the mystery of what I am and what you are has to do before all else with our capacity to create, and be possessed by, such things. It is a sharing in the creative act that is no less than God-like, and that, too, is a source of wonder."

Krishnamurti powerfully and brilliantly joins in:

> "So we are enquiring into what makes a bird. What is creation behind all this? Are you waiting for me to describe it, go into it? You want me to go into it? Why (From the audience: To understand what creation is). Why do you ask that? Because I asked? No description can ever describe the origin. The origin is nameless; the origin is absolutely quiet, it's not whirring about making noise. Creation is something that is most holy, that's the most sacred thing in life, and if you have made a mess of your life, change it. Change it today, not tomorrow. If you are uncertain, find out why and be certain. If

your thinking is not straight, think straight, logically. Unless all that is prepared, all that is settled, you can't enter into this world, into the world of creation."

Quotations

"Man unites himself with the world in the process of creation." — Eric Fromm

"Every individual who is not creative has a narrow, exclusive taste and succeeds in depriving creative being of its energy and life." — Goethe

"In order to create there must be a dynamic force, and what force is more potent than love." — Stravinsky

Responsibility

RESPONSIBILITY	IRRESPONSIBILITY
Duty	Unreliablility
Obligation	Untrustworthness
Onus	Thoughtfulessness
Accountability	Egotism
Trust	

This virtue is closely linked to Honesty, Justice, Awareness,
Empathy, Vitality, Reliability.

January 1979. A Sunday morning and at 8am I am enjoying being in bed. It has been raining for most of the week and is now snowing. The doorbell rings. Annoyed I go downstairs and it is as I feared. On the step a diminutive ten year old boy declares that "the group are ready to go canoeing". Unsuccessfully trying to smile I inform him that I will be with them 'in about thirty minutes'. Hurriedly I alert my eldest daughter (also ten) that we will be off shortly. She is also a member of the advanced junior kayak group.

Lake Windermere, at its southern end, is linked to the sea by the river Leven. Monthly in winter the owners of this salmon river give access permission to kayakers. Normally it provides rapids to grade III before finishing above a large and dangerous weir. A trip down is generally 'good fun'. This gloomy Sunday I am very tense. Whilst the youngsters are ready to tackle some big water, the river is about six feet above winter level. It is in full spate, moving very fast and, to my imagination at least, menacing. I am acutely conscious that even if the group is highly skilled it is extremely young for such paddling. I also know that in Nature there are no certainties about outcomes. It is an "on the edge" situation and the group is my responsibility.

I'm so worried I decide that the four boys only, and not the four girls, will do the upper section which includes shooting a flooded weir. I wait in the eddy for each boy to complete that section in turn. It looks spectacular but each performs well and there are no capsizes. At the eddy below the weir the girls get on the water and we all continue down river. In what seems no time at all we have ridden the brown monster and arrived at the exit point. As this is just above the big weir, the thunderous roar of the fall seems to emphasise how very careful we need to be. After seeing them all safely ashore, my relief is considerable.

This type of situation, where my responsibilities could not be more serious if things go wrong, I have always found stressful. Yet I have no doubt that was what I should have been doing.

The Latin root of the word 'responsibility' reveals something of its true meaning:

'the capacity to respond, to react'. There needs to be added 'in the best way according to one's conscience'. In other words we should always be accountable for our actions. It was Victor Frankl who suggested that instead of just having the statue of Liberty in New York on the east coast, there should be another statue, of Responsibility, on the west coast of the USA.[17] There can be no freedom without responsibility. It is a spurious freedom that despises responsibility and chooses to live without it.

As John Donne famously noted "No man is an island". Apart from hermits the rest of us need other human beings. This implies responsibilities in all our relationships at whatever level. In the world of business for example, at a time when passing the buck is commonplace, the good workers, managers and bosses are the ones who take responsibility and get things sorted positively. It is also pertinent to remember that we are members of the human race. This is especially important if we are fortunate to belong to the affluent West and life is materialistically comfortable, in comparison to life in some other parts of the world.

Nor should our responsibilities be restricted to human beings. If I am correct in that "everything is alive in Nature in its own way and deserves its own well-being", then it points very strongly to living with a policy of *minimal destruction* to everything around us. In extreme form this is Jainism, a religion that has been described as the most compassionate of all ways of life and certainly represents an ideal.

In a way, especially in the light of the threats of global warming, we should all become 'responsible warriors', or warriors for responsibility.[18] By so doing we are more likely to find an inner stillness and a peace of mind.

Quotations

"To be a man is, precisely, to be responsible." — Antoine de Saint-Exupery

"There is no freedom without responsibility. We need to be very aware not to regard this virtue as a 'detachable burden' which is so easily shifted to the shoulder of God, fate, future, luck or one's neighbours." — Ambrose Bierce

"Only individuals have a sense of responsibility." — Nietzsche

Humility

HUMILITY	ARROGANCE
An unpretentious modesty which accepts that no one individual is more important than another, regardless of one's abilities, power and status. Accepting that one is part of nature, and that, in terms of wisdom, the ego is unimportant. Accepting that the more one knows, the more there is to know.	Self-importance Egoism Pride Contempt

This virtue is closely linked to Patience, Purity, Reflection, Honesty, Empathy, Awareness.

Sam, a fellow instructor at the Woodlands outdoor centre, and I leave Saundersfoot in Pembrokeshire at 4 am on a grey summers morning in 1968. As we head due south I ponder on what we have taken on – an overnight expedition around the Bristol channel taking in Lundy island, the Devon coast, and South Wales. Our craft is very beautiful but no more than a "flimsy tea-tray" plus sail. A catamaran with hulls of 5.5 m length and a maximum width of 30cm, built of 3mm plywood, a trampoline deck bolted to the hulls and a 14 sq. metre (150 sq. foot) single sail with no reef points. Total weight is a very light 50kg.

The sky and sea stay a dull grey as dawn comes. I can see the bolts joining the crossbeams to the hulls moving as we skim the surface in a gentle sea. What if the sea gets up? I sense we should not be here in this boat! By 10 am land has disappeared. The gloom of the day matches my mood. There is no shelter on the trampoline. In those moments I realise my insignificance – I am no more important in the great scheme of things than a matchstick. (We were to do 100 miles on that day, at one point becalmed for several hours again out of sight of land, eventually landing near Porthcawl in the late evening).

Throughout my life the great outdoors has served me with severe reminders of the importance of humility. Any seafarer, for example, needs this most crucial of virtues.

An ideal introduction to this virtue, for young people at least, might be to ask them to remove footwear and then do a barefoot journey on grass or a beach. The root of humility is from humus meaning soil or earth. To be humble is to be down to earth. Mother earth had total respect from many primitive American Indian tribes. To be realistic, honest and truthful is the path to humility and to be human means to be made from the humus. Perhaps it is no coincidence that there is a parallel with the journey in bare feet that takes in mixed terrain. Awareness becomes of high priority. With freedom of bare feet comes responsibility.

Humility in the most profound sense seems difficult to define. Meeting people who possess it is like seeing a cobalt sky after weeks of grey weather. In their presence, any thoughts of self-importance are likely to evaporate. The obituaries of the late Cardinal Basil Hulme, for example, all agreed that humility was the essence of the man. Perhaps to possess a depth of this virtue is to be on the pathway to saintliness. One major way to develop it would be to try to avoid arrogance, its opposing vice. In practice that presents considerable challenges. Unless we have been singularly fortunate, from our earliest days we are likely to have been taught, consciously or otherwise, that the human race is superior to anything else in Nature. Even *if* our intellectual powers are greater than those of other life forms I feel certain that we should try to avoid any feelings of superiority and keep man in perspective within the vastness of the universe. It may well be, for example, that a sheep is better at being a sheep than we are at being human!

The unhappiness and anxiety among so many in the human race, along with the increasing devastation of the natural world clearly indicates that our feelings of superiority are unjustified, unacceptable, and ultimately, self-defeating.

In the modern world there is every opportunity for the individual to be arrogant rather than humble. Arrogance separates us even more from the world and encourages egoism. The undue importance given to success promotes an aggressive outlook on life. I find it unsurprising that such societies produce leaders, in almost all walks of life, who tend towards arrogance. Humility is not putting oneself down but seeing the good in the whole world and within oneself. In the modern world this trait must be one of the least recognised and yet most precious.

Quotations

"In itself, humility is nothing else but a true knowledge and awareness of oneself as one really is." — Anon

"The greatest enemy of truth is prejudice and her constant companion is humility."
— S. T. Coleridge

"To be humble is not to make comparisons. Secure in its reality, the self is neither better nor worse, bigger nor smaller than anything else in the universe. It is — is nothing, yet at the same time one with everything." — Dag Hammarskjöld

Purity

PURITY	IMPURITY
Innocence	Defilement
Perfection	Pollution
Clearness	Materialism
Goodness	Egoism

**This virtue is closely linked to Honesty, Simplicity, Humility,
Vitality, Self-discipline, Concentration, Awareness.**

Corsica. The summer of 1991. Annette and I have just completed the famous
G.R. 20 trek along the mountain spine of the island. To celebrate, and in
view of the intense heat, we decide to spend our last day by a river high in
the hills. There is perfection in purity as well as simplicity. If we aren't sun-
bathing, we are swimming. Our food a loaf of bread and fruit, our drink is
straight out of the river so pure is the water. Now I also remember reading
how something like over three quarters of the rivers in the world are so polluted that they pose a dangerous health risk to humans. Even when recently
spending time in thinly populated New Zealand I am both surprised and
disappointed to find that their lowland rivers are heavily polluted.

Consumerism has become, in practice for so many, the modern God. No religion has
ever swept the planet like gross materialism. Like a disease, it has found its way into
every corner of the human world. Man's greed – one of the worst of the seven deadly
sins – is evident everywhere. The pollution of wild Nature is the work of man. As
someone who has spent much of his life travelling simply and self-reliantly in wild
places, I know an excess of stuff is not a path to true well-being. It is no coincidence
that mental illness has now become a major killer worldwide, and suicides are in the
region of 900,000 annually.[19] The more you have the more likely you are to want.

The radical problem of materialism demands a radical solution. I propose rejection of
materialism as a way of life and, in its place, suggest we find ways of life that accept
the 'goodness' of being human. This is why I have included Purity as synonymous
with Spirituality. To have purity as an ideal is to reject materialism as a vice, where it
belongs. Purity is the acceptance of 'Being' in all its positive senses, and the rejecting
of 'having and wanting'.

D.H. Lawrence is very succinct in this matter:

"If we think about it, we find our life consists in this achieving of a pure relationship

between ourselves and the living universe about us. This is how I 'save my soul' by accomplishing a pure relationship between me and another person, me and other people, me and a nation … me and the animals, me and the trees and the flowers, me and this earth, me and the skies and sun and stars … that makes
our eternity for each one of us."

When Laurence refers to "a pure relationship between me and another person" I find I reflect on all my relationships. It would be less than honest not to admit undisclosed motives and intentions in some of them where the other person has largely been a means to my own ends. Thank goodness that in my old age I can enjoy friendships of the highest order that are unsullied by either person.

Arthur Koestler, the writer, experienced in the degradation of both communism and Nazism, saw strongly the value of purity:

"Hatred of evil is as necessary as love if the world is not to come to a standstill."

And more recently, Schumacher, the author of the classic '*Small is Beautiful*':

"The Buddhist strongly endorses the concept of right living: sees the essence of civilisation not in a multiplication of wants but in the purification of human character."

Purity, then, is a lofty ideal. A friend described it thus:

"An awareness of, and a positive, proactive rejection of what is impure – for example lust, foul language and immodesty."

In my reading on this virtue I was very taken with Simone Weil, who died a young heroine towards the end of the last World War. Two examples from her letters follow:

"The idea of purity, with all that this word can imply for a Christian, took possession of me at the age of sixteen, after a period of several months during which I had been going through the emotional unrest natural to adolescence. The idea came to me when I was contemplating a mountain landscape…"

"To possess is to soil; to assume power over is to soil."

Quotations

"If I were to choose one sentence to sum up my philosophy, I should say 'allow no evil in your thoughts'." — *Confucius*

"If you speak and act with a pure mind, happiness will follow you as a s hadow clings to form." — Buddha

"Growth is a process of purification." — Anon

As I check through what I have written and quoted concerning Purity I am forcibly struck by how close it seems to be to universal love.[20]

Simplicity

SIMPLICITY	COMPLEXITY
Uncomplicated	Duplicity
Unpretentious	Pretension
Elemental	Complication
Straightforward	Elaborateness
Natural	Tortuous

This virtue is closely linked to Purity, Awareness, Creativity, Self-discipline, Humility, Honesty.

Three simple words: *less is more*. Over a lifetime I have come to appreciate the wisdom of these words. Memories of expeditions abound, and one in particular.

> The aim is to tackle the G.R.20 in Corsica (mentioned briefly under Purity). Because the mountain spine of the island not only has a reputation as the best mountain trek in Europe but also involves scrambling, I decide we would go very lightweight. I am concerned that Annette, my partner, might be stretched by scrambling with a multi-day sac. In the event I take it to an extreme. This involves considerable hard work, weighing everything in grammes, keeping everything minimal conducive to having an efficient safety framework. My notes show our rucksacks weighed 26 lbs, which includes food for 6 days, and water for a day. Once we accept that we are very basic in every sense, travel becomes a joy. There are times when I feel so free I have to check I still have my rucksack on! The reward for the long hours of preparation and the simplicity of our travel and outdoor living is a real appreciation of the word freedom.

When I retired in 1992 my life became trekking expeditions for about the next 10 years. When at home, with rare exceptions, spare time was spent looking at maps to prepare for the next expedition. Annette, when not working would join me, although mostly I travelled alone. The essence of that travel was *simplicity* – in almost every sense, be it equipment, routine, or aims and objectives. I became part of the great rhythms of Nature including awakening pre-dawn, and bed by dusk. Crucially, although I usually prefer more exciting activities, I realised I loved what I was doing. I realised also that I was being *natural*. We are built to walk and run.

The contrast to living in the modern world could not have been more extreme. The word *complexity* screams at me and I long to retreat back to the sanity of wild places. I am sure I cannot be alone in finding that as each year goes by almost every aspect of modern living becomes more complex – so much so that I have the strongest of suspicions that it is all to do with making money – as much as possible and as quickly as possible. Shopping, for example, I find often very irritating. There is simply both too much choice, and the information you require either stated, if at all, in tiny letters or in diverse ways. I sense the implications can be immensely damaging for the future of the planet.

Schumacher makes a good case, for example, of linking simplicity to non-violence. A modest consumption of finite local resources by local people can closely relate to non-violence in comparison to people whose existence depends on worldwide trade systems.

It seems very obvious that to have a life of simplicity and yet live in a modern world is a very considerable challenge. To have any success will demand other key virtues such as *Honesty, Determination, Patience* and not least, considerable *Self-discipline*.

In its finest sense *simplicity* has deep implications, is profound and along the path to saintliness. Dag Hammarskjöld hints at this:

> *"The life of simplicity is simple but it opens to us a book in which we never get beyond the first syllable."*

Quotations

"Would that you could meet the sun and the wind with more of your skin and less of your clothing? For the breath of life is in the sunlight and the hand of life is in the wind."
— *Kahlil Gibran*

"The ability to simplify means to eliminate the unnecessary so that the necessary may speak." — *Hans Hofmann*

"When my guide wanted to compliment me, he called me simple: when he wished to chide me, he called me clever."— *Stephen Levine*

Vitality

VITALITY	APATHY
A positive approach to life with the	Laziness
characteristics of Energy and Enthusiasm	Indifference
Hope	Pessimism
Optimism	Unresponsiveness
Unremitting Effort	Bored Outlook

This virtue is closely linked to Awareness, Determination, Patience, Responsibility, Goodness, Cheerfulness.

1959 Summer. I arrive by train from Chamonix at Zermatt to meet Wilfrid Noyce, the Everest climber. His age and alpine experience make me feel very young. I am fresh out of Oxford and it is the start of my second week of my first alpine season. My first view of the Matterhorn from Zermatt convinces me that it is the most beautiful mountain I will ever see. It looks impossibly high and remote. About a week later, after two grade VI snow and ice routes, Wilf and I bivouac near the rubbish dump by the Hornli hut at the base of the popular route up the Matterhorn. Not long after midnight we traverse to the foot of the Furggen ridge. Wilf has agreed that I can return to my world of rock, as distinct from the unfamiliar world of snow and ice. In addition I am allowed to lead the climb. The route has never had a British ascent. To add spice, the Direct Finish is around Hard Very Severe and supposed to be exposed. Few young climbers in those days could have had such an opportunity, in such company, in their first season.

It becomes one of the most memorable of days – all 20 hours or so of it. The ridge is loose, non-technical yet a little dangerous. The Direct Finish is wonderfully exposed, strenuous and well protected by in place pitons. The summit amazes me, devoid of human beings but the habitat of several alpine choughs, which I never expected to see so high in the sky.[21] Black clouds and a strengthening wind say not to linger. Within half an hour a full blizzard rages. Wilf, now in the lead, is simply brilliant. He knows the Hornli ridge. If we pass one climbing party we pass hundreds. The blizzard continues down to the Hornli hut. A brief respite then down to Zermatt. Somewhat shattered – it is around 11pm – Wilf smiles and says "a quick shower and I will buy you the best meal in town".

The reason for using this experience here is probably obvious. Making the best use of a day doing something you love, something for which you are *enthusiastic*, always leads to good feelings about self. The energy and unremitting effort are accepted as unavoidable. The high level of fitness demanded by such a day was built on months of 'living climbing' back in England. Most importantly there was, from both of us, a high degree of optimism and cheerfulness.

The vitality shown in that experience, however, had a narrow focus of climbing. Ideally our whole journey through life, with all its ups and downs, should display this virtue of vitality. An impossible challenge perhaps, but no less important for that.

Kurt Hahn, the founder of Outward Bound emphasised in his lectures and writing that *apathy*, the opposing vice, was the worst vice. In an affluent society with a comfortable lifestyle it is much too easy to 'not bother'. It is I suspect, a challenge for almost all of us, as we journey through life. How can we always be *optimistic*? How can we be positive, give of our best, in the unending battles with the myriad of temptations that are so typical of modern living? The answer of course is that we cannot. But at least we can try as best we can. And like anything else the more we try the more we will positively grow. A positive and cheerful attitude is always full of possibility and aspiration. As one reads the biographies of giants like Mahatma Gandhi, Rachel Carson or Albert Schweitzer for example, one can see how important *Vitality* really is in a world of complexity and vices. It is unsurprising that Bertrand Russell, the famous philosopher, placed *Vitality* as the most important of all the virtues.

Quotations

"You work that you may keep pace with the earth and the soul of the earth. For to be idle is to become a stranger to the seasons and to step out of life's procession that marches in majesty and proud submission towards the infinite." — *Kahlil Gibran*

"Human vitality is so exuberant that in the sorriest desert it still finds a pretext for glowing and trembling." — *Ortega Y Gassett*

"…we should practice as though we had 99 more lifetimes… but not waste a moment." — *Stephen Levine*

Courage

COURAGE	COWARDICE
A virtue of the spirit which can be exposed both physically and morally. It can be used to describe heroic commitment to a lifelong cause or single acts.	Taking the easiest option Faint-hearted Lacking spirit

Summer 1995. I am on expedition across the French Gorges and then up the G.R. 5 in the Maritime Alps towards Chamonix. I wait impatiently in Modane for Annette to join me. She is coming out by train from the UK. Companionship is strongly desired. I have been solo for 67 days. My aim is 1000 miles and 1000 different wild flowers. A hundred more miles and 6 new flowers remain to achieve my goals.

By day 74 in the Queyras a broad leaved helleborine signals my thousandth wild flower. Moving further south we reach the small town of St Etienne de Tinée in the Mercantour Park and I pass 1000 miles. The last week has seen an unduly oppressive heat wave. Despite the popularity of the G.R.5 there are very few walkers and none with full camping gear. Having restocked and rested we continue south again. Day 81, unfortunately, is to become etched in my memory. It had begun with a 2 hour climb up through forest to the ski village of Auron. Even early in the morning I sweat profusely from the exertion. During the next climb up to Col du Blainon (2071m), I note an odd feeling in my stomach, but dismiss it as hunger pangs. By the time I near the Col, however, my abdominal area feels severely graunched, and I all but collapse. At first no body position seems to relieve the discomfort and it takes an hour, plus a couple of painkillers, before I feel ready to descend to the village of Roya. The descent presents me with no problems and, after a coffee at the village, we proceed up the final climb of the day, to an intended high mountain camp and rest day. As I labour uphill in the intense heat, my abdominal discomfort returns with a vengeance to such an extent that I have to stop. Annette goes ahead, finds a campsite and then returns for my rucsack. Even without it, I can only move a hundred metres or so before I sink to my knees. It seems to take forever and a huge effort of will before I collapse into the tent. I can still find no relief from the pain and it becomes obvious that I need medical attention. Annette returns to Roya. Within three hours, in darkness, she is back at the tent complete with rescue team and doctor. I am given oxygen, carried off the mountain, and taken by ambulance to hospital in Nice. A battery of tests revealed nothing. By 11am the following day the pain had gone. Severe dehydration seemed the most likely explanation. At home I discovered I had lost nearly two stone!.

I have included this personal experience here with some reluctance. Not because it shows personal weakness – to have been a member of a mountain rescue team and to have to be rescued yourself is regarded as a gross indignity – but because I sense that Annette would frown at the very idea that she behaved courageously. She would likely have said she did what she had to do. In my search for truth, however, I have no doubt that she was courageous in this instance, and further, that it was but one example of how she lived her life. This quotation from Shambhala is particularly apt:

"Courage is to…live in the world without any deception and with tremendous kindness and caring for others."

When I glance at the list of virtues already mentioned and bearing in mind the latter quotation, the following were strongly in evidence in this situation: *Awareness*; *Compassion*; *Respect* (for my trying to carry on); *Altruism* (unselfishness); *Empathy*; *Friendliness*; *Kindness*; *Gentleness* and *Responsibility*.

When I bring in another highly relevant quotation from C.S. Lewis concerning courage:

"Courage is not simply one of the virtues but the form of every virtue at the testing point."

then many of the other key virtues on my list demand attention as they were so strongly relevant to this expedition situation. These include: *Determination*; *Patience*; *Self-discipline*; *Self reliance*; *Concentration*; *Simplicity* and not least *Vitality*.

The reader should know that simply accomplishing the day's journey with full sacs was epic, even if I had been fit. The heat, we later discovered, was so extreme, that local workers were collapsing and being taken to hospital, and many locals kept indoors. Annette was simply brilliant. I could not have been with a better companion – in every sense. As I write this, I remember when I took the post of Warden for Woodlands, the City of Oxford Outdoor Centre, Annette was appointed housekeeper. After a month or so she was sent to the local hospital for a check – an unusual occurrence. Eventually she was diagnosed as suffering from fatigue. We found out that she had worked 94 hours that week!

In ordinary life the use of courage is far more common than may be supposed. The human condition almost by definition demands coming to terms somehow with grief; illness; pain; disappointment. Terror and poverty are also evils many have to face. We need to be mindful, too of the many whose work demands acting courageously to help people. The Rescue Services especially are to be admired.

Throughout history and in all forms of endeavour, there have been people who have exemplified this virtue. Similarly there have been many single acts of courage where people have risked everything, in a moment, in order to try and save others. Maybe the more appropriate word in this context is 'heroism'. It is heartening to find that, in a world where so much is moral wasteland, courage of this type is still both revered and highly publicised. The media tends to use 'courage' to describe extreme personal performances. This seems an inappropriate use of the word unless, for example, it pertains to recovery from traumatic or debilitating injury.

It may be helpful to see 'courage versus cowardice' as one of the recurrent themes in life, throughout which there are, or should be, unending opportunities to tackle this challenge. That process is likely to be both hard and sometimes frightening. But that is as it should be. Courage, like heroism, brings its own psychological rewards.

Quotations

"The way of cowardice is to embed ourselves in a cocoon in which we perpetuate our habitual patterns." — Shambhala

"The courage we desire and prize is not the courage to die decently, but to live manfully."
— Thomas Carlyle

"How favoured by the gods is he, whose character is tested in situations where courage has meaning for him – perhaps even a tangible reward. How little does he know about potential weakness, how easily he may be trapped and blinded by self admiration."
— Dag Hammarskjöld

Humour

HUMOUR	HUMOURLESSNESS
Funniness	Solemnity
Amusement	Gravitas
Entertaining	Bigotry

This virtue is closely linked to Cheerfulness, Vitality, Empathy, Creativity, Friendliness

As a new P.E teacher it is my first swimming lesson at Manchester Grammar School. The first form class line up dutifully against the wall. They face the pool and I face them – dressed casually but smartly. I begin to pontificate and for some reason take a step backwards. It is deep! As I surface, I notice ghosts of smiles everywhere. They then have a very hard lesson!

A campsite in the Lakes – a cold night in early spring, two of us in the tiny tent on a slightly sideways sloping campsite. I awake early to a 'sticky noise'. I cannot believe the sight. We had gone to bed with a candle raised up on books and a full tin of syrup. At some point one of us had knocked the tin over. The tin had all but completely emptied. My climbing partner had had a restless night. His entire sleeping space and sleeping bag were covered in syrup. I, being on the upside of the tent, am completely clear of this disaster. I am the one with the sweet tooth. Life can be so unfair! Whoever is 'up there' must have a really wicked sense of humour.

1991 Corsica. After the end of the expedition over the mountains on the famous G.R.20 we descend to the north coast. Our last night is spent on a typical campsite by the sea. What seems like thousands of large frame tents surround us. Our tiny tent has just sufficient space. As the evening progresses, snug in our bags in preparation for an early walk to the airport the next morning, I gradually become aware that we are becoming a centrepiece of attraction for the Saturday evening walkabout by the multitudes of campers. The French goes something like this: "Deux personnes dans cette petite tente? Non! Ce n'est pas possible!" It is hard not to smile. The tent, a single skin goretex model, is so tiny that all gear is outside, and we have to shoehorn into the tent itself. The comparison with the canvas palaces around us could not be more extreme.

A comic sense of ourselves probably helps greatly as we journey through life. A review of my last book, *Beyond Adventure* made me smile. It was to the effect that it raised more questions than it provided answers. I remembered the story of 'the one up there' giving the disciple the choice: "In one hand I have the Truth. In the other I have the Search for Truth. You must choose." The answer seems so obvious and is also humorous in that wicked sense again. I expect with each step forward I make in terms of understanding to be more confused. I enjoy this state of affairs even though it nearly drives me up the wall at times!

Alan Watts would seem to agree when he refers to

"*The ultimate humour of spiritual exploration.*" [22]

In a less esoteric sense it is important to differentiate between jokey behaviour and crude laughter – that quickly leads to malicious behaviour and bullying – and self-deprecating humour that helps life move forward gently. One of the problems I find, is that in keeping up with the news of world events, much of what happens appears to be surreal. The trouble I find is that much is a sick joke of the worst kind because we are supposed to live in a 'civilised world' – a phrase that epitomises what I am saying. One does not need to watch the 'soaps' on TV when constant news is available! The problem is compounded for me by the so-called 'humorous sketches' on television. Many of them appal and seem to be more evidence of a sharp decline in civilisation.

It is a fault to take oneself completely seriously. Humour can change sadness into joy and free the ego from itself. Good humour is an expression of generosity that contains sympathy but is no substitute for actions. At its best humour can shake up our beliefs, values and illusions. It can also demonstrate a level of wisdom, understanding and humility.

Quotations

"*Unmitigated seriousness betokens a lack of virtue because it totally despises play which is as necessary for human life as is rest.*" — *St. Thomas Aquinas*

"*True humour springs not more from the head than from the heart; it is not contempt, its essence is love ; it issues not in laughter but in still smiles, which lie far deeper.*"
— *Thomas Carlyle*

"*Humour is an affirmation of dignity, a declaration of man's superiority to all that befalls him.*" — *Romain Gary*

Overleaf: View of summit of Trivor from camp IV, Karakoram, 1960.

Clockwise from above: MGS Expedition, Arctic Norway, 1965; Girdle of Cenotaph Corner, Dinas Cromlech, N. Wales, Early 1960's; Unicorn Catamaran, Training on Langorse Lake, January 1968; Beginners (14yrs), Woodlands, Langattock, S. Wales, 1968.

Clockwise from top left: Dinghying (14yrs), Woodlands, River Wye in winter spate, 1968; Abseil (14yrs), Woodlands, S. Wales, 1968; Polybagging (14yrs), Woodlands, Black Mountains, S. Wales, 1969; River Crossing (14yrs), Woodlands, River Wye (Glasbury), 1970; Coasteering (14yrs), Newgale Beach, Pembrokeshire, 1969; Gorge Walking, Woodlands, River Hepste, S. Wales, 1969.

Clockwise from top left: Gorge Walking (Advanced), Woodlands, River Ystwyth, Mid Wales, 1971; Coasteering (14yrs), Woodlands, Tenby Beach, Pembrokeshire, 1971; Competition on Jungle Gym, Woodlands, Glasbury, S. Wales, 1971; Equipment (one person), Start of Nordkapp Expedition at Bödo, 1975; Jungle Gym (14yrs), Woodlands, Glasbury, S. Wales, 1971.

Clockwise from top left: Vember and Senja, Bivouac, Orkney Islands, 1977; Rafting (10&11yrs), Lake Windermere, Lake District, 1977; Family Expedition, West Scotland, Annette/Tiree, Senja, Vember, a friend, 1978; West Coast, Orkney Islands, 1979.

Clockwise from top left: Annette Expedition, Bressay, Shetland, 1979; Ishbel Grant 12yrs), River Leven, Lake District; 1980; Sea Kayaking (11&12yrs), over sea to Skye, 1980.

Clockwise from top left: Peter Astles (11yrs), 5-Day Expedition (no adults), River Wye, 1981; Alpine Rose, Pyrenees, 1996; Burnt Orchid, Pyrenees 1996; Typical terrain, Spanish Pyrenees, 1999; Alaska Solo Expedition (Day 8); 1981; Rafting (10&11yrs).

key down from the Col to our last high camp near Lac de Pousarrae... in the high valley which is the source of R.

From Annette's Pyrenees Diaries

View up to Col de la Pez
from our tent on the riverside

follow. We left the sheep behind and
to negociate the morraine of boulders worn
shallow ?ravines by the spring thaws. It be
strain — looking ahead for small cairns and
same time keeping a balance on the rocks
the gloom of the day it was hot work. w
down to vests as the track steepened
though we were now parallel to the s
The cairns became more frequent + yello
marks began to appear. A route thread
way up a steep spur which seemed end
A definite NEED to stop for lunch! Che
cakes, sweet cake and water — refreshed
difference! By now we were in true
territory — formidable. Steep cliffs, clou
snow fields — waterfalls. The route beca
but suddenly we were on a good par
alpenrose — + the flowers began to ap
nearly all the favourite alpines. We ?
on a series of zig-zags which gained
quickly until we were suddenly sto
the edge of a big snowfield. The slig
of a track across it could be made o
tested it — HARD + glassy! Time for ice ?
did the hard work of kicking steps, driv
handle as deep as he could into the
I followed close behind — not dwelling on
down! A brief glimpse of steep snow — its
in cloud — was enough. I felt safe in Col
— jamming my axe handle into the holes he
The palm of his hand was bruised with
our axes are light weight and it required
force to make them penetrate the hard
We stepped onto a large patch of su
and entire ?leaved primroses, on the oth
pleased to have got across. Zig-zags
alpenrose continued — evenly steeper
before and then ran out into an ?ex
rocky path — severely eroded in pla
demanded 100% concentration and 100%

9

Wisdom

If the purpose of our complex journey through life is to seek positive fulfilment – physically, emotionally, intellectually and spiritually – then we need all the help we can get. A major source of assistance is wisdom. But what is wisdom?

It is a question that has long intrigued philosophers. Aristotle, for example described wisdom as *"Knowledge of the most precious things"*. He also said *"Wisdom is the answer to the eternal problems of life and death; god and man; time and eternity."*

The monk, Thomas Merton, perceived it as:

"Truth in its inmost reality."

The Roman, Marcus Aurelius described it as:

"Knowledge of all things divine and human."

Those three quotations, for me, are reflected in the three central questions of this book: Who am I? Where am I going? And how do I get there? Certainly I can be helped, perhaps greatly, if I can begin to understand something of the meaning of wisdom.

I intend to look at a specific incident at the end of the solo Alaska expedition already mentioned in the chapter 'Who am I?' By the final full day I was battling with conditions that threatened to overwhelm me. I then wrote:

"…from somewhere within, in the blink of an eye, came an insight. I knew with certainty then the truth of 'the most important thing in life is to die at the right time'."

That last statement (*the most important thing…*) I had read many years previously and had accepted it as true, or as 'a truth' or 'wisdom'. Aurelius speaks of wisdom as *"Knowledge of things divine and human"* but what does he mean by *"knowledge"*? It is a crucial question if we are to begin to understand wisdom. My interpretation, apropos my specific situation, is that my *intelligence* or thinking accepted the wisdom concerning when to die and in that sense I had 'knowledge'. But that knowledge was *theory*. I did not really *know*. In the practical, or real, situation I simply *knew* from that flash of insight. I knew from the depths of my being that this was *truth* or *wisdom*. I was in a situation where virtually the whole of me – physically, mentally, emotionally and spiritually – was very involved. Even more fascinating was that the intuition – the moment of understanding – came not from my conscious intelligence, but from my unconscious. And at least as interesting is that, as a result of that expedition in particular, I became convinced that the whole of wild Nature resided within me, as well as around me.

Carl Jung refers to:

"The wisdom of the unconscious."

Confucius says something similar:

"The heart of the wise, like a mirror, should reflect all objects without being sullied by any."

Saint Francis of Assisi would appear to agree:

"Brother, in thine own heart seek wisdom. There shalt thou find it."

Emerson in 1857 says the same thing:

"Wisdom has its roots in goodness."

I sense most strongly from these and similar writings, as well as my own experiences, that wisdom is deep within us, but, if I can put it somewhat oddly, tends to be asleep. Like the virtues and vices it is not only innate also but always ready, and I suspect is very keen, to be woken up.

Although the wisdom about the right time to die came, therefore, from within, it was not fully meaningful until I had a relevant practical experience. Or, in the words of the proverb:

"Experience is the mother of wisdom."

Henry James has an excellent description of experience: [1]

"Experience is never limited, and it is never complete; it is an immense sensibility, a kind of spider-web of the finest silk threads suspended in the chamber of consciousness, and catching every airborne particle in its tissue."

My experience is that it is the building blocks of my life. In practice this meant, for example, that with each adventure activity that I took up I attempted to *live it*. I simply wanted to perform to the very best of my ability and fitness, and ideally make it as easy as walking down the road. It took years however to realise that action, action, action alone, no matter how accomplished, was neither the path to contentment nor wisdom. There needed to be, in the words of Meister Eckhart:

"The life of wisdom must be a life of contemplation combined with action."

This is very similar to Aristotle's man of *phronesis*, which can be translated as 'man of practical wisdom'.

Along with the importance of experience in searching for wisdom I would state unequivocally that interaction with wild Nature has the greatest potential for the individual becoming wise and beginning to understand.

Bertrand Russell, the philosopher, did not have wild Nature in mind, I suspect when he wrote:

"To conquer fear is the beginning of wisdom."

But certainly fear, as well as love, are key features for most people when they adventure outdoors in self-reliant ways.

Nevertheless, although there was some truth in the old Eskimo saying that "Wisdom is only attained by suffering and solitude in the great outdoors", it is not, however, the only environment in which to develop wisdom. Human situations in the man-made world have produced and continuously produce great wisdoms – not least as a result of suffering.

As Aeschylus noted so long ago, that sorrow and suffering were:

"The profoundest teachers of wisdom."

In trying to summarise my sentiments concerning wisdom I would look to the work of Thomas Berry. In *The Dream Of The Earth* he notes the need for reverence for the elemental "mystery of existence". He regards it as a base from which wisdom may be found from any human activity.

Michael Mayne, one time Dean of Westminster Abbey, hints at something similar when writing towards the end of his life. He notes that increasing awareness or increasing maturity leads to a decreasing need "to cling to intellectual baggage".

A reason for writing this book was that I sensed I had glimmerings of *understanding* of what my life was about. I could equally have written glimmerings of *wisdom*. What wisdom or understanding I may have, has come from reflecting, especially on solo expeditions. In addition, and most importantly, there has been the reflecting on the way Annette led her exemplary life, along with the extraordinary experiences that have come my way.

As I seek to discover further wisdom, I try to see myself both as a conscious and unconscious entity *within* whom lies the whole of Nature. Whilst I journey – and as far as possible this will be in wild Nature – I will heed the advice of Confucius from his Analects:

There were four things from which the Master was entirely free:

No foregone conclusions
No arbitrary pre-determinations
No obstinacy
No egoism.

I interpret those four as: an open mind; no certainties or fixed views and conscious self, in its egoistic separate sense, to be dismissed as far as possible because I and Nature are a unity.

The erudite Professor Whitehead assists my understanding:

"But Wisdom is persistent pursuit of the deeper understanding, ever confronting the intellectual system with the importance of its omissions. These three elements, Instinct, Intelligence, Wisdom, cannot be torn apart. They integrate, react and merge into hybrid factors. It is the case of the whole emerging from its parts, and the parts emerging within the whole. In judging social institutions, their rise, their culmination, and their decay, we have to estimate the types of instinct, of intelligence, and of wisdom which have co-operated with natural forces to develop the story. The folly of intelligent people, clear-headed and narrow-visioned, has precipitated many catastrophes."

Quotations

"Common sense mellowed and experienced is wisdom, and wisdom in its ripeness is beauty." — A. R. Orage

"Here is the test of wisdom
Wisdom is not finally tested in schools
Wisdom cannot be passed from one having it to another not having it
Wisdom is of the soul, is not susceptible to proof, is its own proof."
— 'Song of the Open Road' by Walt Whitman

"Wisdom denotes the pursuing of the best ends by the best needs."
— *Francis Hutcheson*

10

Specific Wisdoms

I have indicated that wisdoms lie deep within our unconscious. They wait to be awakened into full alertness and to enter into our consciousness. I hope that I can be helpful as an 'old hand' to the younger person or less experienced person. What I propose to do, is to put forward *specific* wisdoms that, if I was young again, I would like to be very aware of as I journey onwards. From this premise, that if I am at least aware of them and their importance in *theory*, they are more likely to be fully awkened when I have a relevant practical experience.

The specific wisdoms to follow are concerned with:

Action — Reflection

A Sense of Awe and Wonder

The Search for Truth

The Individual as Singular – Universal

Heroes and Heroines

Action – Reflection

I regard the following as the foundation wisdom:

Quality action or experience and quality reflection on that action or experience are of fundamental and equal importance.

Quality action means operating as much as possible at, or near, our capabilities. We tend to give our best when most challenged or stimulated. The same is true of experiences, such as meeting people and having conversations. In all the things we do, we should try to involve as much of ourselves as possible – to be wholehearted.[1] The higher the demands of the action or experience, the greater the opportunity for learning, evolving and eventually fulfilling our potential.

On the other hand if our actions and experiences are too uninvolving and demand little from us, then our progress through life will slow considerably, and may even regress. When life becomes too easy or too affluent then stagnation in terms of our true capabilities can quickly become the norm. Phrases like 'laid back' and 'why bother?' become the order of the day.

Quality reflection is more difficult to describe than quality action. Using the 'self as ocean' comparison again, it means thinking beneath the waves rather than just on the surface. Suppose I have just finished leading a hard and dangerous climb. There is often a strong urge to talk about it or to reflect upon it. If it is in the climber's pub the talk is likely to be loud and lively; how hard it was; how a particular move was the crux; what a beautiful line up the cliff, and so on. As the beer flows the climbing descriptions become livelier and the difficulties often become easier in the telling than in the reality! This can be all good fun but very often it is surface chitchat.

A bomb, or better still, a depth charge could be thrown into the conversation which would likely cause havoc. I have in mind something like *'Don't you realise that you are all likely to be adrenalin junkies because you are so dependent on your climbing fix every week-end and don't you think this is pathetic?!'* [2] I would be lucky to get out of the pub in one piece! But it is a serious question and *'why do people climb?'* has led to many articles and books on the subject. My example is provocative, but may be helpful. Quality reflection is asking oneself the deeper questions concerning the action or experience.

Only recently I was talking to a young and accomplished mountaineer. He had just returned from an exciting trip to Ben Nevis in winter and was questioning what he had done in view of the fact that he had very recently had a son, and his wife was expecting another child. These are serious reflections on what are the *values* of what one is doing with one's life. There are a multitude of other pertinent reflections.

Here is a sample. Did the experience:

Make me more or less aware of my self-centredness?
Contribute to a search for Truth or Beauty?
Have relevance to my virtues and vices?

Summary

Modern living often means almost constant activity and action, with reflection confined to the toilet break or soak in the bath. Even the bath is often dismissed as the shower is quicker. Action, action, action, no matter of what quality, on its own is a dead end road. It may not be not the road to Hell, but certainly it is not the road to finding deep contentment as a way of life. It is essential to make time to reflect seriously upon one's actions in the deeper senses of what being human really means. Decisions need to be taken on what values your life is to be based and then how to live your life *in practice*. An inner contentment will then come from a continous interplay between action and reflection to the extent that it can become a natural way of life. To skate on the surface of existence – no matter how apparently successful this might seem to be – is to live both a lie (in the sense of not being true to the depths of self) and is a personal contribution to further decline in civilisation.

Quotations

I sense profound truth here:

> *"The highest form of lifestyle is that which combines contemplation and action."*
> — *Meister Eckhart*

> *"Contemplation is the highest expression of man's intellectual and spiritual life. It is spiritual wonder. It is spontaneous awe at the wonder of life, of being. It is gratitude for life, for awareness and for being. It is a vivid realisation of the fact that life and being in us proceed from an invisible, transcendent and infinitely abundant source."*
> — *Thomas Merton*

I find this quotation visionary:

> *"... I think there is a place both inside and outside religion for a sort of contemplation of the Good, not just by dedicated experts but by ordinary people: an attention which is not just the planning of particular good actions but an attempt to look right away from self towards a distant transcendent perfection, a source of uncontaminated energy, a source of new and quite undreamt-of virtue."* — *Iris Murdoch*

A Sense of Awe and Wonder

We live in a hard-edged man-made world with its overemphasis on meeting targets and delivering results. The genuinely important aspects of being human are way beyond results, success, convenience and having a good time. It is also a world with ever increasing reliance on high technology. In this rushed artificial world there are real dangers in losing some of our natural senses, and not least our sense of awe and wonder. It is as if by no longer living in harmony with Nature but instead treating it as a resource, such senses, at very least, may become blunted or distorted. Without frequent use they will atrophy and may even disappear into a world of darkness and cynicism.

Here is a personal experience, a particularly vivid memory, of a sense of awe and wonder. This is what I wrote in my first book, *The Adventure Alternative*:

After the successful Nordkapp kayak expedition in 1976, I have decided to have an easy summer and to attempt the first kayak circumnavigation of the Outer Hebrides. The Norwegian experience, along with various journeys on the British west coast lead me to believe that this journey is to be an enjoyable and not a particularly difficult challenge, providing that we have reasonable weather and sea conditions.

> After taking the ferry from Skye to Loch Tarbet on Harris, our group of five paddles south down the sheltered east coast of the Outer Hebrides, to camp on the isolated and immensely attractive island of Mingulay. The follow-ing day we are to paddle west through the Sound of Berneray and round Barra Head, the southerly tip of the Outer Hebrides. As we expect this to be somewhat exposed, we double-check tidal patterns and weather forecasts. The weather is excellent, the tides favourable, and the swell on the west side is what the locals term 'small'.

> Once through the Sound of Berneray we enter another world. In our kayaks the swell seems huge, with companions disappearing for what appear to be long periods of time. It is my introduction to the vast difference between sea swell and ocean swell. We do not linger and are soon round on the east side in the lee of the island. We land and walk up to the lighthouse on top of the cliffs. The lighthouse keeper is surprised to see us, and emphasised how lucky we are to have such a good day. He explains that the lighthouse is generally either in cloud or covered in spray. He then goes on to explain that there is a lichen that only grows on the top of the cliffs because it is frequently doused with salt water, and that fish have been found on top of the cliffs. What is 'mind-blowing' is that the west facing cliffs on which the lighthouse is built are 620 feet above sea level! It is hard to believe. Yet, as we have just kayaked around these cliffs, we have no doubt that it is true. It just happens to be a place where the Atlantic, with a fetch of 3,000 miles,

meets land and the continental shelf. There are other places too that on the west coast, as well as the most northerly point – the Butt of Lewis – which emphasise both the majestic power of the Atlantic, as well as the need for kayaking with great caution and humility.

As scientific research moves on we increasingly understand how other life forms migrate, on land, sea and in the air. Many of their annual journeys are in themselves a cause for a sense of awe and wonder. First year ospreys, for example, were recently tracked from north of New York to South America. They were not only solo but had only recently learned to fly. There was also Miranda, the godwit who flew 7,000 miles from the north to New Zealand non-stop! The cathedral bells at Christchurch were rung to celebrate her arrival. There are countless other examples to excite the imagination.

Before moving on, a few words on what are called the basic senses. Far too often they are taken for granted because they are so familiar. Yet our use of them is often at a low level and there is considerable scope for their development. This can be seen in the way that blind people develop compensatory skills in the use of the other basic senses.

D.H. Lawrence wrote:

> *"The sense of wonder*
> *That is the sixth sense*
> *And it is the natural religious sense."*

Whether it is the sixth sense or not is immaterial. What is important is the phrase 'natural religious sense' or what I would term spiritual sense. I feel this sense of wonder often does atrophy – it is almost inevitable at a time when secularism and anti-religious sentiments are in vogue.

I am unsure of the relationship between a sense of awe and wonder and a sense of beauty but at minimum there must be strong links. They may even be, if not synonymous, then parts of some other profound sense. John Lane makes out a case that our forebears who lived in, and were much more in tune with the countryside, had a sense of beauty.[3] I think this is very likely for their surroundings were dominated by natural beauty. The reverse could easily be the case in modern living – surroundings often more dominated by ugliness, sameness or drabness rather than by the beauty and almost endless wild diversity in Nature. It is a wisdom that we are shaped by our surroundings.

Privileged to have spent most of my life in wild Nature I feel I have a well-developed sense of awe and wonder, as well as a sense of beauty and mystery. A kaleidoscope of memories surfaces: the immensity and eternity of the night sky; the almost unbelievable beauty of the Northern Lights as seen from a solo bivouac on a mountain in Arctic Norway; the feelings of awe at watching fifteen metre waves surging into St. Bride's Bay and covering me in salt spray as I sat on a ridge thirty metres above them; watching a seven metre flood on the river Wye and imagining I was that log, careering crazily through the waves; the world of tiny flowers – such beauty and growing in such high and exposed places. The list is almost endless – and it should be as one becomes increasingly aware of one's natural surroundings. As Matthew Fox wrote recently, the universe has been evolving for around fourteen billion years. It seems completely sensible to view this natural world with a sense of the sacred.

When it comes to a sense of awe and wonder about *self* it is, at first sight anyway, easy to agree with St. Augustine:

> *"People travel to wonder at the height of mountains, at the huge waves of the sea, at…*
> *the rivers, the vast compass of the oceans and at the circular motion of the stars; and they*
> *pass by themselves without wondering."*

Modern knowledge of the human being should leave no doubt that we need a sense of awe and wonder about self. Watching the behaviour and growth visually of the foetus in the womb is one example. There are countless others.

At this moment, for example, you have in your physical body, about seven billion billion billion atoms (7×10^{27} or 7 followed by 27 zeros!). One deep breath and you inhale 10^{22} atoms from the universe and exhale roughly the same amount. These exhaled atoms have their origins in every cell of your body. Those breaths are exchanging atoms all of the time with other living things.[4] Was this why Peter Matthieson , author of *The Snow Leopard* wrote:

> *"In this very breath that we take now lies the secret that all great*
> *teachers try to tell us…"*

Or, again, our body contains something akin to a quintillion (10^{18}) microscopic cells, most of which aren't human! About eighty percent of the body's living matter is bacteria and other micro-flora and fauna, much like the way trees alone are not the forest. The forest includes many other plants, fungi, invertebrates, birds, animals and bacteria. The ecological web of inter-dependence is evident within every human being.

Also, as I understand it, each of those cells makes a decision whether to live or die in the interests of the whole body; and this is going on all of the time! I was made aware of the latter when, just prior to making the descent to Los Angeles (from London), the man next to me decided to start a conversation. In a loud voice he exclaimed, "Do you realise that everybody on this plane is dying?!" What he said was true although I did not warm to his iconoclastic approach to a conversation, especially in view of the circumstances!

Whilst I do not know the authenticity of the figures mentioned above, and I am not a scientist, I think they point the way for a need to wonder about self. The way for me, however, has not been through science but through powerful extra-ordinary experiences. They leave no doubt in my mind.

Whilst they leave no doubt, however, they do leave a great worry. It is this: I know from experience of the immense potential for all the *positive* things about being human from my work with young people in the outdoors. Reading has considerably enhanced this viewpoint. There have been immensely impressive human beings in all walks of life throughout time. I sense also that *each* human being has positive potential almost beyond their wildest dreams. Against all the good news about human beings there is undeniably the bad news. Almost all of us have immense potential for evil and destruction – to ourselves and to everything around us. The concentration camps are the tip of an iceberg of evil that can be read about daily in most parts of the world. It is up to each of us. We always have choice between what we decide is good or evil, positive or negative.

Summary

It is essential to develop:

A sense of awe and wonder as we journey through life.

This should be with reference to all positive aspects of being human.

Quotations

"The smallest mosquito is more wonderful than anything man has produced…so man must never lose his sense of the marvellousness of the world around and inside him – a world which he assuredly has not made and has not made itself. Such an attitude…is a form or aspect of wisdom." — St Thomas Aquinas

"The most beautiful experience we can have is the mysterious…whoever does not know it and can no longer wonder, no longer marvel, is as good as dead…"
— Albert Einstein

"Philosophy begins in wonder. And at the end, when philosophic thought has done its best, the wonder remains." — A. N. Whitehead

The Search for Truth

"The need for Truth is more sacred than any other need."
— *Simone Weil*

Since I was a young man I have kept a paper filing system to record anything that might help me understand who I was and what the purpose was, if any, of my being on the planet. These files, of which there are hundreds, are full of notes mainly from books and articles; quotations; newspaper cuttings and random thoughts. One of the thickest files is the one called TRUTH.

The subject is obviously very important as well as complex.

After reflecting on my experiences and studying the file I am impelled to make a statement.

Regardless of who we are and where we think we are going, there should be an *underlying* drive to continuously search for the truth. The more certain we are that we have sorted out our life, the more essential it is to keep searching. I sense intuitively that no matter how clever or mature we think we are, in reality we are on the lower rungs of a ladder that disappears into the clouds towards truth.

The late Cardinal Basil Hume, in an interview with *The Sunday Times* (21 December 1980) stressed that we should all be on a pilgramage in search of the truth. He also added, significantly: *"The finding is in the seeking."*

I stand in awe of the intellect and wisdom of such an erudite and spiritual scholar. Yet in another way I am confident with some of my own truths. Here is one which I have already used:

> *"Everything in Nature is alive in its own way, is on its own adventurous journey, and deserves its own well-being. Everything in Nature, from the grains of sand to the stars, is no more and no less important than anything else."*

For me this is a profound truth — so important that the human world should accept it as a foundation for a newer and better world. It is a truth I have felt in my inmost depths. This insight came from my unconscious and I sense it is a wisdom from the ages. Certainly it is a concept that has surfaced throughout the ages of man. That I cannot prove it scientifically is very unfortunate in a society that tends to ignore any truth that does not have proof. That does not alter this truth for me. It is a truth from my heart, not my head.

I will set this personal truth against a statement from Mahatma Gandhi:

"One thing took deep root in me – the conviction that morality is the basis of all things, and that truth is the substance of all morality."

If morality is concerned with a sense of goodness rather than badness – acting positively and using virtues as opposed to acting negatively and using vices – then I need to ask myself, "Is this personal statement or personal truth a moral statement?" My reply is a resounding *yes* and I wish to defend it with all my strength. Why am I so vehement? The answer is simple, at least in theory. A lifetime in the modern world has convinced me that despite what I believe is the natural goodness of mankind, *corruption* is endemic in almost all walks of life, and not least in all the corridors of power. Modern living is bedevilled with undue self-centredness. I regard this as dishonest and against the truth. There are central truths concerning how each of us lives. I have lost count of the number of times that politicians with opposing views on serious matters of concern, glibly claim to each have the truth. There seldom seems to be the time to really find the truth of the matter. How convenient to live in a (deliberately?) rushed world where we all have to move on to the next item.

Readers will remember that in the chapter on virtues, I began with what I termed the foundation virtue of *honesty*. In other words, to be honest should be the basis of our actions. I would then wish to add: in the search for *Truth*. This gives:

**Honesty is the basis of my actions
in my unending search for truth.**

Krishnamurti writes about the enthusiasm to know the truth being "the essential ingredient" for looking directly and seeing clearly who we really are.

From his comment I see the mirror in which I need to look at myself with great frequency. The questions I need to ask are concerned with whether my actions have been positive rather than negative and what was the motivation behind them. The judge is my own conscience (or heart). I know, or should know, that I can never hide from myself. My conscience is synonymous with my honesty in its purest form. Only in this way can I hope to progress towards the great truths. In other words, as I understand it, honesty is the major highway in the search for truth.

Continuously to seek the truth in a largely corrupt modern world can be a demanding and lonely challenge. John Huss deserves the final word. He was burned at the stake in 1415 for writing the following written prayer:

*"Seek the Truth
Listen to the Truth
Teach the Truth
Love the Truth
Abide by the Truth
And Defend the Truth
Until Death."*

Quotations

"Falsehood turns from the way; Truth goes all the way; the end of the way is Truth, the way is paved with Truth." — The Upanishads

"There is an inner centre in us where truth abides in fullness. It is the greatest treasure we possess." — Robert Browning

"Let us be true: this is the highest maxim of art and life, the secret of eloquence and of virtue, and of all moral authority." — H. F. Amiel

Singular Universal

I had always been aware as a young man that my actions and my experiences *outside* of myself had some inevitable effect upon my psychological *inner-self*. In other words, events that I experienced *externally* affected me *internally*.

Whether I was unusual or not, however, I saw the two – the internal and external – as *separate*. After all it was obvious that physically they were separated by my body – even if they were interdependent – good experiences causing good feelings and so on. What rescued me from this *separatist* thinking – or head-in-the-sand attitude – was a single sentence in the private diary *Markings* by Dag Hammarskjöld. The diary was the reactions of the then Secretary to the United Nations who, almost single-handedly at times, spent years trying to solve the political problems of the world. He sought his sanity in the outdoors and I found his writing compelling. This is the beginning of a poem:

> *"The longest journey*
> *Is the journey inwards.*
> *Of him who has chosen his destiny,*
> *who has started upon his quest*
> *for the source of his being."*

It was like finding a diamond. Instantly I linked all my journeys (experiences) in the outer world to their psychological effect *inside* of me. These effects were now part of my longer *journey* inwards. The object of this journey? It had everything to do with the mystery of why I was on the planet and my specific role, if any.

I now saw my inner-self as:

CONSCIOUS SELF: The self that always reacts to and is involved in the world *outside* of self; that which is characterised by action and experience; by physicality and doing.

UNCONSCIOUS SELF: The very much larger self that is the base of our spirit, our memories, instincts and so on, and stores our psychological reactions to external events.

By far the most succinct phrase I have found to describe this 'twin self' is from Nietzsche:

> *"Man is never really an individual; he is better described as a singular universal."*

In terms of understanding myself I take his phrase as follows: 'singular' refers to everyday conscious self, and the 'universal' refers to the unconscious.

The best analogy for the 'twin' selves I can find is to think of oneself as the *ocean*. Living is played out on the surface of the ocean – which of course can display all moods from calm to storm. This is conscious self. Beneath the surface waves lie the immense depths of the unconscious, containing deep currents more powerful than surface distortions. But not only are the surface and base linked or interdependent, but also they are essentially a unity.

In a world dominated by *continuous action* it is almost inevitable that the voice of the *inner-self* will tend to be either ignored or even swamped by the frenzied action on the surface. Extensive reading leads me to believe that I am not alone in this view. There follows, with comments as appropriate, examples from the writings of other authors, to support this standpoint.

> *"I look through my eyes, not with them."* — William Blake

I always find Blake, a renowned painter and mystic, full of insight and wisdom but seldom easy to understand. Here he appears confusing. I personally do look with my eyes – as keenly and with as much awareness as possible, but I sense what he is trying to put across. If you look *into* a person's eyes you hope to see the 'soul' or reality of that person. There is also the old idea of the eyes as the windows to the soul. You look out of the windows as well as into them. Blake, therefore, used his essence (or soul) to look out on to the world.

> *"Life is real only when you are. And you are real only when you are awake to your own inner presence."* [5] — John Selby

The author is an expert on meditation. I rate the quotation highly. It has a simple beauty. It is worth noting that for thousands of years there was a strong tradition in Eastern countries to explore *inner* self. This was in contrast to the Western world where the strong tradition was to explore outwards – to discover the planet and amass wealth.

> *"As you walk the inner path of awakening, recognise that it is most definitely a heroic journey. You must be prepared to make sacrifices and yes, you must be prepared to change…must be willing to change and shed the hard armour of self-centred egotism … it brings you face-to-face with who you really are."* [6] — Lama Surya Das

This seems very similar to me to Blake's *"seeing eternity in a grain of sand"*.

I have long felt few people have had the depth of understanding of inner self as Jung, and he has influenced my thinking considerably. Most importantly his concept of *the collective unconscious* made an indelible impression. This is interpreted as everything in Nature back into the mists of time, is somehow imprinted in each individual's psyche or unconscious.

"In my picture of the world there is a vast outer realm and an equally vast inner realm."— *Carl Jung*

In the quotation I suspect he might well agree that the balance between inner realm and outer realm is because, ultimately, they are the same!

"What lies behind us and what lies before us are tiny things when compared to what lies within us." — *R.W. Emerson*

This is a typical wisdom from the American writer.

"People look in vain places for peace.
They seek it in the world outside,
In places, people, way, activities…
But no peace is found in this way.
They are looking in the wrong direction,
And the longer they look,
The less they find what they are looking for."
— *Meister Eckhart*

I'm unsure whether it might be a sign of senility but in the last few years I have frequently felt that I am very much an observer of myself and my actions and reactions, as well as a somewhat detached observer of what is going on in the outside world.

"I only went out for a walk, and finally concluded to stay out 'til sundown, for going out, I found, was really going in." — *John Muir*

Muir is a hero of mine and I find this a lovely quotation.

"Where do trees, plants and flowers come from?
Just realize where you come from. This is the beginning." — *Tao Te Ching*

"What is within us is without us
What is without us is within us." — *The Upanishads*

This is one of my favourite wisdoms from ancient sources. It may be impossible to explain rationally. In no way does that worry me for I know from deep within that its words ring the bell of truth.

Summary

No individual is without their larger *unconscious* self. Nietzsche was brilliant in his idea of any person being a *Singular Universal*. My contention is that within us lies the *unity* of all Nature. It is my belief that an individual makes a massive stride in discovering 'who they are' if they accept at least the possibility that, as well as being unique and separate, they are also connected and part of that unity, even if this is generally unconsciously.

I appreciate that it is, or could be, extremely difficult to go about one's life (the *conscious* bit) constantly aware of one's *unconscious*. It may help to know that recent scientific research has clearly shown that during living, the unconscious takes in huge amounts of information about the surroundings. The conscious seems to be unaware of this event! It may also help to try not to see the human body as a somewhat rigid and separate divider between your inner-self and the outside world. There is all manner of communication going on between the two.

Quotations

"We must revolutionize this system of life, that is based on outside things − money, property − and establish a system of life which is based on inside things."
— *D. H. Lawrence*

"…there is no man who reverently, wisely and perseveringly cultivates his own spiritual life, who is not rewarded far beyond his thoughts." — *John Pulsford*

"We are only the actors, we are never wholly the authors of our own deeds or works. IT is the author, the unknown inside us or outside us. The best we can do is to try to hold ourselves in unison with the deeps which are inside us. And the worst we can do is to try to have things our own way, when we run counter to IT, and in the long run get our knuckles rapped for our presumption." — *John Pulsford*

Heroes and Heroines

"Courage is a way of saying yes to life." — *Anon*

I would define such a person as one who gives their utmost, their very best, in the most demanding of situations. These situations can be both at any time in ones life and in *any* aspect of living. Heroic actions, from the instantaneous to the lifelong commitment, should always inspire others as to what is most noble and worthwhile about mankind.

For almost all of us, there is, or should be, a need for such people and not least at such times when our journey through life becomes particularly demanding.

One benefit of modern living is instant visual access to news from around the world. A vivid example took place in the autumn of 2007:

TV screens and newspapers worldwide are full of pictures of the streets of Rangoon teeming with marching citizens led by Buddhist monks. They are protesting against poverty and a brutal regime. They carry no weapons yet they know their lives are in danger. Virtually all of these citizens and monks are heroes and heroines, an inspiration to others.

Unamuno underlines the point:

> *"We are all potentially heroes and geniuses, if we only have the courage,*
> *and do the hard work."*

> *"One who has conquered himself is a far greater hero than he who defeated a*
> *thousand times a thousand men."*
> — *Anon*

I feel strongly that each individual should search for their own heroes and heroines. When I think of my own, my mind wanders to when I was a young man. Then I tended to be concerned with whatever was my current sport. Lew Hoad (tennis); Les Jackson (England fast bowler); Herman Buhl (climber) for example. What I was admiring was their *achievements*. They inspired me to try and reach my own dreams. I knew very little of them, as human beings, apart from their obvious determination and high skill levels.

Then I discovered the giants of human endeavour in the early exploration of the polar regions. The tragic Captain Scott expedition failed to be first to reach the South Pole, and, as is well known, all died on the return journey to base. Their courage was magnificent. That they had failed to be the first to the Pole was of comparative unimportance. Beauty of conduct or behaviour; the outstanding display of key virtues such as compassion and humility, as well as determination and patience should always be admired more than success.

It was only as I grew older and more aware, that my heroes began to include explorers and adventurers who also went on to contribute to society in more conventional ways. Nansen, John Muir and Ed Hillary come to mind. Inevitably perhaps, with my deep interest in the potential of being human I also began to discover heroes and heroines from across history.

The reader should be aware that society, often in the form of the media, sets up its own heroes. Today (17 January 2008) it is Kevin Keegan for rescuing Newcastle Football club.

H.L. Mencken, writing in 1922:

> *"The chief business of the nation is the setting up of heroes, mainly bogus."*

In a materialistic society heroism often becomes cheapened and debased. Pop stars, elite sportsmen, businessmen, financiers, are often described as heroic when, at times, their actions are less than heroic. Television excels at presenting events of immediate enjoyment and then moves on to the next event. Such presentations tend to be remote from the forbearance, patience and refusal to react of true heroes like Gandhi, the Dalai Lama and Nelson Mandela.

There has also developed in modern times almost a cult of the anti-hero. There are writers who make a living by deliberately destroying or trying to destroy the credibility of individuals who have long been regarded as heroes. If this is done in the name of 'the truth of the matter' then it can be acceptable, but too often, I sense, that is not the motivation. Bad news, like the sensational, tends to make the most money.

Quotations

> *"The greatest obstacle to being heroic is the doubt whether one may not be going to prove one's self a fool; the truest heroism is to resist the doubt; and the profoundest wisdom, to know when it ought to be resisted and when to be obeyed."* — *Nathaniel Hawthorne*

> *When heroes are not needed, when they become ordinary people and their existence is not uncommon – then the times are most admirable.* — *Soetsu Yanagi*

Personal List of Some Heroes and Heroines

GENERAL	EXPLORERS & ADVENTURERS
Dietrich Bonhoffer	Birdie Bowers
Winston Churchill	Walter Bonatti
Confucius	Herman Buhl
Meister Eckhart	Norbert Casteret
Viktor Frankl	Francis Chichester
Mahatma Gandhi	Jacques Cousteau
J. W. von Goethe	Aspley Cherry-Garrard
Dag Hammarskjöld	Ellen Macarthur
Carl Jung	Douglas Mawson
Aung San Suu Kyi	Bernard Moitessier
Jiddu Krishnamurti	John Muir
Martin Luther King	Fridtjof Nansen
The Dalai Lama	Wilfrid Noyce
Michael Mayne	Robert F. Scott
Annette Mortlock	Ernest Shackleton
Laurens Van der Post	Joshua Slocum
Albert Schweitzer	Frank Smythe
Aleksandr Solzenitsyn	Antoine de Saint-Exupéry
Saint Augustine	Gino Watkins
Saint Francis of Assisi	Edward Wilson
Mother Theresa	

Summary of Wisdoms

So far I have suggested that we take with us five specific wisdoms as we journey through the undoubted complexities of living in a modern world.

These are:

Action – Reflection as the Foundation Wisdom
The quality of the experience or action to be balanced by the quality of the reflection upon those events.

A sense of Awe and Wonder
At our natural surroundings from micro to macro.
At ourselves and our immense possibilities.

The Search for Truth
A lifelong search based on the foundation virtue of honesty.

Singular – Universal
Awareness of our larger unconscious self as well as our conscious self.

Heroes and Heroines
The importance of humans, past and present, who help us or inspire us.
Awareness of the heroic within ourselves.

The next section will be concerned with four further wisdoms, only this time, direct from the natural world.

11

Wisdoms From Nature

It is a fact that we are shaped by our surroundings. For most of us that means that we are inevitably shaped by the modern or man-made world. We take it for granted, for example, that our everyday life is made easier by a whole host of technology, from living comfortably in a house, to travelling by modern transport and working in as much comfort as possible. This is regarded as *normal* living with much of it accepted as essential for civilised living. I deliberately used the word normal in the last sentence. Modern life may be normal, but it is not natural. It seems to me most important that we never forget that, as technology progresses, we remain, essentially *natural*.

The importance of our *naturalness* is that Nature holds answers, or potential answers, to how we can cope with the unnatural stresses and strains, as well as the complexities of modern living. It is perhaps salutary to realise that it is only the modern human being that does not live entirely naturally. If the present human race was generally happy and contented then perhaps there would be justification for living in this uncivilised man-made world without regard for our natural roots. Patently that is not the case.

Nature herself, of course, is extremely complex, but she does have major characteristics. If we know what these are then they may be very helpful in our journey through life *because we are natural*. In my previous book, *Beyond Adventure*, I described them as:

Pillars Of Wisdom From Nature

There are five pillars I have identified as of particular importance. These are:

Uncertainty
Energy
Balance
Unity
Beauty

The first four are briefly described in this chapter. The fifth, that of Beauty, is a later chapter. All of them should be basic to any worthwhile life. By *worthwhile* I mean the positive aspects of being human.

Uncertainty

Everything in Nature, everything 'natural', is dynamic, is moving. John Muir, who spent much of his life solo in the vast wilderness of the Rockies over a century ago, uses the word *'flow'*:

> *"Contemplating the lace-like fabric of streams outspread over the mountains, we are reminded that everything is flowing – going somewhere, animals and so-called lifeless rocks as well as water. Thus the snow flows fast or slow in grand beauty-making glaciers and avalanches; the air in majestic floods carrying minerals, plant leaves, seeds, spores, with streams of music and fragrance; water streams carrying rocks both in solution and in the form of mud particles, sand, pebbles and boulders."*

Muir's beautiful writing illustrates my key statement that:

Everything in nature is on its own adventurous journey and deserves its own well being.

The human being, like everything else in Nature, is also dynamic. Within that dynamism, and before the inevitable *physical* ending of death, the precise movements remain uncertain, no matter how careful the planning. Whatever the degree of technological progress, the journey through life is characterised by uncertainty. When I think of uncertainty I immediately think of the word 'adventure'. To adventure is to take on 'a journey with a degree of *uncertainty*'. Without that doubt there can be no adventure. It is important to emphasise that I am thinking of adventure here, not in its narrow 'adventure activity' sense, but in its broadest sense. I refer to *adventure* as accepting life itself – the journey through life with all its ups and downs – being faced in the most positive of senses.

This may be easy in theory but the practice can be formidably difficult. It may be helpful to remember that, when things go wrong, they can provide even better opportunities for learning about one's self than when they go right!

For, as Thomas à Kempis long ago wrote:

> *"A man's true qualities are revealed when things are difficult."*

It is also comforting to know that one of the great modern philosophers, Bertrand Russell, rated *vitality* as the most important of the virtues. Basic to vitality, as opposed to *apathy*, is having a positive rather than negative approach to life.

Any knowledge of the natural environment will indicate that all life-forms are characterised by *growth*. To grow is to evolve, to move onward, to progress toward maturity.

Living in a modern world can pose a major threat to having a positive and adventurous approach to self in all its aspects. A modern society has two major aims:

To increase the GNP (Gross National Product)
To increase the security of every citizen

The first aim is to make money, to make everyone financially richer. The second aim is to make everyone feel as safe as possible.

At first sight the latter seems fine, and in some ways is obviously both sensible and justifiable. Freedom to move about free from violence and terrorism, for example, is something we all desire. Yet as technology progresses at an ever-increasing pace, I sense in my lifetime, that the modern world has become more, and not less, dangerous. There are many examples. Just one will suffice here. If society is progressing in the sense of becoming increasingly peaceful then I would presume we would need less police as each year goes by. The opposite is the case.

Two quotations to consider in this context. The first is a Moorish proverb:

"He who fears something gives it power over himself."

Life is, or should be, a challenge. The uncertainty of outcome has to be faced positively, the fear tackled head-on. This means growth.

The second quotation is by J. Sainsbury, writing in a recent article:

"Organised institutionalised fear; fear of the future; fear of being fully and freely alive can seriously undermine our lives and prevent us from living life to the full. Fear can often lead to a reduction of boldness, curiosity and enjoyment of life and can also lead to many forms of illness and dysfunction." [1]

I would want to distinguish here between 'fear' and 'anxiety'. Fear I regard as natural. Not only is it a basic challenge to all life-forms in wild Nature in terms of natural as opposed to man-made dangers, but it is obviously potentially a beneficial challenge for young people, indeed any human beings, in a natural environment.

In other words it is a very powerful tool in the form of education. I know from long experience that people grow, and are exhilarated by overcoming natural fear.

I would define *anxiety*, however, as synonymous with fear but restricted to, and caused by, living in a modern world and in a modern lifestyle. The latter, so often, is about unnatural pressures and is not conducive to growth in the overall sense of *all* aspects of human potential.

Of one thing I feel certain – man has almost no limits to his cleverness and unscrupulousness if it is concerned with making money or enhancing his power and status.

This pillar of uncertainty is invaluable as a guideline to sorting out how we should face life.

I repeat, life is *dynamic*. It is not static. The implication for each of us could not be more important.

In the first instance the word 'dynamic' refers to *every* aspect of being human – physical, mental, spiritual, emotional, conscious and unconscious, asleep or awake. The entire individual, in other words, is dynamic. The reader may be tempted to think: 'so what?' The answer is formidable in its implications:

> **Every single aspect of us is doing one of two things. It is either: progressing – evolving – moving forward**
>
> or
>
> **Regressing – devolving – going backwards**

Think of the broken leg in plaster and how quickly the leg muscles degenerate through lack of use. Then apply that example to *every* aspect of yourself in terms of your daily actions or lack of them. Virtues, for example, only have a meaning if they are used or lived. Referring back to the physical, only a fool could ignore the well being of their body. Yet I would guess that it is only a tiny minority who would daily exercise their body efficiently. Inevitably the body will then degenerate, in terms of its real potential.

It should be obvious that there are massive ramifications and challenges as to how we plan and lead our lives *in detail*. To treat life both in terms of action and contemplation as an adventurous journey to be faced positively, is to face *uncertainty* with the virtue of *self-respect*.

Quotations

"Man must accept responsibility for himself and the fact that only by using his powers can he give meaning to his life. But meaning does not imply certainty; indeed the quest for certainty blocks the search for meaning. Uncertainty is the very condition to impel man to unfold his powers." — Erich Fromm

"The ultimate thought, the thought which holds the clue to life's meaning and mystery, must be the simplest thought conceivable, the most natural, the most elemental, and therefore also the most profound. To find it one needs to be an explorer."
— George Seaver

"If I have ventured amiss — very well, then life helps me by its punishments. But if I have not ventured at all — who then helps me?" — Søren Kierkegaard [2]

Energy

The concept of energy underlines all we know about the universe. It is the lifeblood of all Nature and means effort, hard work and skills.

> *"Five years ago, I had a beautiful experience which set me on a road that has led to the writing of this book. I was sitting by the ocean one late summer afternoon, watching the waves rolling in and feeling the rhythm of my breathing, when I suddenly became aware of my whole environment as being engaged in a gigantic cosmic dance. Being a physicist, I knew that the sand, rocks, water and air around me were made of vibrating molecules and atoms, and that these consisted of particles which interacted with one another by creating and destroying other particles. I knew also that the Earth's atmosphere was continually bombarded by showers of 'cosmic rays', particles of high energy undergoing multiple collisions as they penetrated the air. All this was familiar to me from my research in high-energy physics, but until that moment I had only experienced it through graphs, diagrams and mathematical theories. As I sat on that beach my former experiences came to life; I 'saw' cascades of energy coming down from outer space, in which particles were created and destroyed in rhythmic pulses. I 'saw' the atoms of the elements and those of my body participating in this cosmic dance of energy…"* — Fritjof Capra [3]

Many life forms expend tremendous energy and display magnificent skills as they journey with a natural grace through life: seabirds such as shearwaters and gannets; terrestrial birds such as swifts and swallows; fish and eels in the ocean; bees and ants at work on a summer's day. The list is endless.

In theory this message from Nature is both simple and elemental. Spare nothing in your efforts to develop progressively all your being. As you journey, accept that there will always be trials and tribulations along the way, and that further horizons will always beckon.

The implication is obvious. The potential to perform at your individual highest level exists within you. Attainment, however, demands energy and effort which is expressed through a multiplicity of skills. More than that, the modern person needs to recognise that other life forms achieve their highest levels of performance because they continuously and entirely live, work and play in a natural environment. *Their whole life is natural.* Modern man has the problem of having to devote considerable time and energy to living and working in a technological world, with its unnatural rhythms. To reach the highest levels of performance demands repeated and progressive practice, to the stage where the skills become second nature. The actions have to become as easy as walking down the road. Efficiency and rhythm in arduous and difficult situations are the result of *living* the activity and years of striving.

For human beings, excellence is reached at, or near, the edge of their capabilities. Such commitment brings its own rewards. Satisfaction can lead to deeper feelings of elation when performing with grace and rhythm in testing situations. In all the inevitable frustrations, however, of trying to improve competence in an activity, and especially in those flat periods when skills seem to stagnate, it is worth remembering that vitality and style still matter.

When I reflect I realise how very fortunate I have been. That lifelong desire to adventure out of doors rather than find recreation in the urban environment has been a blessing. The fact that it was allied to the strongest of desires to perform at or near the highest level I could manage, was also a blessing. That this demanded hard work and lengthy skills learning I accepted without question.

What I did not consider for a moment was that what I was doing – both in my work and play – was entirely *natural*. Eventually I realised that not only was everything in Nature on its own adventurous journey, but growth only came from energy in the form of effort and skills application.

I learnt also, and it still surprises me, that the body has amazing recovery powers. Those who go on expedition will know that the common element is hard work and it is commonplace to feel exhausted by the end of the day. Yet, even if, for whatever reason, sleep is hard to come by, the body is still ready to go the next day.

Quotations

"Energy is eternal delight." — *W. Blake*

"The real essence of work is concentrated energy." — *Walter Bagehot*

"It is notorious that a single successful effort of moral volition, such as saying 'no' to some habitual temptation, or performing some courageous act, will launch a man on a higher level of energy for days and weeks. It will give him a new range of power."
— *William James*

Balance

In Conrad's *Lord Jim* the butterfly collector is looking at a rare specimen:

> *"Marvellous — look at the beauty — but that is nothing, look at the accuracy. The harmony and so fragile! And so strong! And so exact! This is nature, the balance of colossal forces. Every star is so, and every blade of grass stands so, and the mighty cosmos in perfect equilibrium produces this."*

There is a fragile, almost miraculous, rhythm that must remain in precise balance between creation and destruction. That rhythm depends, among many other rhythms, on day length which in turn depends on the earth's rotation around the Sun. Therefore a cosmic rhythm has been intimately connected to the birth of butterflies for millions of years.

Everything in Nature is striving to achieve balance, from the stars in the heavens to the tiniest forms of life. Once even faintly sensed, this fact seems breathtaking. A study of the movement of tides and tidal streams, for example, whether for the British Isles or globally, reveals an amazing diversity which blends together. Studies of the winds of the world reveal the same. I used to believe that in some wonderful way the whole of the natural world was a self-regulating system in a dynamic equilibrium. In this concept of Gaia, each organism has to find a niche if it is to survive.[4] The system works through a complex series of inter-relationships at every level. Competition for survival is inevitable, but it is kept in balance as part of the whole. Co-operation is an equally fundamental concept in this respect.

Man's greediness and ruthless exploitation of the planet's resources now threatens both this balance and the future of the human race. I now believe that the universe is an evolving system which may no longer be in equilibrium.

Modern man may well be the only life form out of balance with the rest of Nature because he has free will. His decision to live in a man-made urban environment and dictate his own rhythms of life has tended not to provide the contentment he seeks. Stress is often a common characteristic. It is seen on faces, in the street, in the workplace and even in the home. Lives are often lived out of natural balance, with an almost inevitable reaction of various unpleasant consequences.

In my younger days my concept of balance had a much narrower focus. Both rock climbing and white water kayaking at, or near, my limit, made me acutely aware that success or disaster was balanced on a knife-edge. Even walking, I eventually realised, was a complex movement which only worked because of the interplay of muscles involved providing the balance necessary to stay upright.

When it comes to being aware of the balance of Nature, my memories are endless, inevitably so when so much time has been spent journeying simply and quietly in wild Nature. A particular experience, nevertheless, remains vivid. Some time in the early 1980s Annette and I were trekking Offa's Dyke, the long-distance footpath following the Welsh Border. It was early January and we were in the mid-Wales area. Dawn brought what seemed to be an almost unnatural stillness. Not only was there not a breath of wind but I sensed something deeper. I thought no more until around dusk when we were on a ridge with large and obviously mature tall trees. They were swaying dramatically in the wind, which was already gale force. I decided we should retreat to the floor of the valley and seek accommodation. That night the centre of a severe depression came through that area. Six people were killed and the devastation to the forest on the hillsides we passed the next day had to be seen to be believed. The episode reminded me of an account by Laurens Van der Post when, in a hurricane in a large boat, the author found himself in the *stillness* of the eye of the storm.

When I think now of the word balance in the context of how I live, I am in no doubt that the challenge is both considerable and very complex. It would be less than honest to admit that although now living alone and essentially a free agent, I never feel satisfied with the balance of my life. It is not helped by the awareness that although some sort of routine in daily life is essential, it can easily become a convenient rut which is not conducive to personal progress. It is not helped either by the knowledge that, because of the dynamic nature of all the aspects of myself, if I do not use them on something like a daily basis, then they will go backwards or atrophy. No wonder that I love expeditions! The balance of lifestyle is so simple. There are none of the complexities so characteristic of modern living.

Quotations

"What we need is a life of balance." — Sri Chinmoy

"Think globally – act locally!" — E.F. Schumacher

"Civilisation itself is a certain balance of values." — Ezra Pound

Unity

Unity, I sense, is the most important of all the wisdoms from Nature. Unsurprisingly, I also sense grave problems trying to explain what I mean. I accept, of course, that the individual can have strong feelings of unity, the firmest of bonds, with family, friends, pets and so on. There will be moments, undoubtedly, when in those relationships one feels non-separate.

Without that type of unity, living would be largely intolerable. For most of us, nevertheless, we tend to both feel and see ourselves as *separate*. For a start we are very obviously *physically* separate. Secondly we tend to be very aware that our feelings are unique to us as individuals even if we experience a unity of feelings with others at times. Finally, most of us live in the modern world where the cult of the individual is the tradition and 'I want, I need' is normal. When, for example, the family goes shopping, the 'wants' tend to be individualistic.

If we go back in time to the primitive tribes such as the Native American Indians they would probably have been confounded by our sense of separateness from our surroundings. Because they lived naturally and in harmony with their surroundings they knew by experience and history that they were *not* separate from the rest of the natural world.

My own belief in non-separateness from my natural surroundings comes from practical experiences *in* Nature. One such extraordinary event occurred on the solo Alaska kayak trip mentioned in the chapter 'Who Am I?' Here is another small example of a five minute experience that had massive implications in terms of my accepting 'unity' and rejecting my 'separateness': [5]

> Towards the end of a solo kayak training session on a calm Lake Windermere I suddenly flow. Fatigue vanishes and for the five minutes or so paddling to the jetty, my movement is effortless. Scientifically this is not possible, yet it occurs.

Much reflection on the incident always returned me to the matter of unity. Water, boat, paddle and I were as *one*. There was complete harmony. As a postscript, onlookers commented on how beautifully I had come into the shore. Intuitively I knew their kind remarks had come from somehow 'sensing' something special was occurring, an example perhaps of unity with complete strangers.

If the reader is sceptical about unity in this sense — of relating to, indeed linked to, the natural world, then please try and have an open mind as to its possibilities. There are no certainties in Nature except uncertainty! When you have or witness an extraordinary experience — and they can occur anywhere and any time — ask yourself:

> Has my separateness somehow been
> suspended in this experience?

Meantime I would emphasise the value of realising that there is a *unity* between conscious and unconscious self. This wisdom is particularly important because we are conditioned by politics, convention, bureaucracy, education and lifestyle to accept that conscious and unconscious are separate, and our selfish ego will always support this view. The unconscious, our larger self, is seen as a threat to the power of egoistic (conscious) self. The ego should never be allowed to dominate.

Quotations

The Roman mystic and philosopher Plotinus:

> *"Each being contains in itself the whole intelligible world. Therefore All is everywhere. Each is All, and All is each. Man as he now is has ceased to be the All. But when he ceases to be a mere ego, he raises himself again and penetrates the whole world."*

The modern American philosopher, Ken Wilber:

> *"Wisdom sees that behind all the multifarious forms and phenomena there lies the one."*

> *"I believe the present ecological crisis has its inner dimension. The next revolution, the one that will save us, will arise inside. When it does, humanity will experience itself in a new way, and when our descendants gaze at the clouds, still beautiful and pure, they will murmur to themselves, 'Ah, it's true. I am that.'"* — *Deepak Chopra*[6]

12

Act According To Conscience

Four words: Act according to conscience. So basic and yet so powerful to anyone with the slightest degree of spiritual awareness.

I came off the local hill in a gale and torrential rain with that phrase ringing in my head.

> *The theory — so simple.*
> *The practice — so formidably difficult and unceasing.*

In the chapter 'Who Am I?' I described the spiritual aspect as the most important part of being human. I also wrote that there were various words synonymous with the word 'spirit', 'heart', 'soul' and 'conscience'. In this chapter I will tend to use the last term, as it is the word most used in this context. I find it difficult to define something that physically does not exist. An analogy is probably simplest:

A 'conscientious objector' is one who has searched his *conscience* and decided he cannot accept war as the course of action. He has searched his *soul*, and what he has found is *heartfelt* and is his *spiritual* viewpoint. Whichever of these words (in italics) is used is ultimately irrelevant. In my experience conscience simply exists.

How one lives one's life, one's conduct or behaviour, is essentially decided by what one values. Those values are determined by a range of factors including upbringing and education. Of especial relevance is one's *own* experiences and what one *honestly* thinks about them. The base of one's actions stem from the base of one's values which is one's *conscience*.

This is one's freedom: to decide on what action to take.

Even in the direst of situations, such as being an inmate of a concentration camp, no one can control your thoughts and ideas, despite every attempt made to break the spirit.

Dietrich Bonhoffer was one such inmate. This is what he wrote:

> " *...only through discipline may a man learn to be free.*" [1]

I have used this quotation to indicate that the idea of freedom, other than in its spontaneous sense, has deep and complex implications which no individual of integrity can ignore.

When Bonhoffer uses the word *'discipline'* he is referring to his appalling situation and his desperate need to overcome his fear of it. That he succeeded and communicated his experience is why he is so revered. A man of courage indeed.

[1] From the poem *'Stations on the Road to Freedom'*

One can only speak or write from one's own experience. My much more limited experience nevertheless totally supports his view. Years of hard practice, developing skills, fitness and overcoming feelings of fear were necessary before I could, for example, take on a *solo* sea kayak expedition to Alaska with a reasonably clear conscience. (The difficulty was that as a family man I could not obtain insurance for the trip.)

From all the activities I have undertaken – from adventure to DIY and to gardening – the message is the same: put in the necessary hard work, learn the basic skills, and eventually you will be *free* to do, and be properly ready to do, your own creative thing within the activity.

Freedom, then, apart from spontaneity, involves the virtue of self-discipline. Blake puts it succinctly:

> *"Freedom is the greatest half-truth."*

The other half, of course, is the virtue of *responsibility*.

As George Bernard Shaw writes:

> *"Liberty means Responsibility."*

Earlier I emphasised three key points. The first was that the individual is essentially a combination of conscious and unconscious: a 'singular/universal' to quote Nietzsche. I sense it is important as well as honest to acknowledge existence of our unconscious whenever possible.

The second was that each of us is a member of the human race, and needs other people. This means inevitably responsibilities to them, and them to us.

The third was that we are all members of the planet. We cannot exist without the natural world. We come from and return to Nature. Again the message is the same. Responsibility to look after the natural world is essential and directly in our own interests in terms of survival.

Freedom, then, comes with considerable responsibilities, which need to be fully acknowledged when developing a personal values framework.

As a student at Oxford I came across two quotations which have stayed with me. I sensed they were important in trying to develop my own values. One was by William James, the American philosopher:

> *"The problem of man is to find a moral substitute for war."*

My interpretation is as follows. Despite all the worst aspects of war, human beings have the opportunity to give of their best at such a time precisely because they are challenged to their limits. Courage, for example, is rightly acknowledged as one of the noblest of virtues. Co-operation at the highest level is another, and not least in some of the prison camps.[2]

At first I thought the answer to William James's statement was sport for the latter is often seen as an acceptable and necessary alternative to war. Then I quickly decided this was wrong. Whilst sport could bring out the best in human beings – and it continues to do so in terms of skill and physical fitness, strength and endurance – it could also bring out the worst in terms of behaviour. As money has increasingly taken control of sport so unacceptable behaviour and attitudes have increased. To win at all costs demeans the human spirit.

Eventually another possible answer emerged. The moral substitute for war could be seen as the war *within* the human being. The conscience was the battleground between good and evil, between positive and negative action. And the battles, unless one is a saint, should be *continuous* throughout life. No matter how far one progresses towards maturity there will always be temptations. Which human beings, for example, are capable of giving their very best for every minute of every day when awake? That last statement, of course, is an ideal. It is known as 'living in the now' and is one of the great wisdoms which in later life I have come to accept as an ideal.[3]

In chapter ten on wisdom I explained that wisdom is within us, and like the virtues needs awakening through direct experiences in living. I was delighted when I found this quotation by Cicero:

> *"The function of wisdom is to discriminate between good and evil."*

I am pleased to link wisdom with conscience as it builds another important bridge in the complexity of being human. It is not unusual, for example, to find two people disagreeing yet both genuinely feeling they are acting wisely and conscientiously.

It is important here to comment on Good and Evil. I agree with the Dalai Lama along with many others, that man is intrinsically good. Many factors have contributed to my positive view of human nature. Annette most certainly shaped me in that respect. Wild Nature has also made a massive contribution – something so beautiful, so awe-inspiring in all its moods, so diverse and so immense, had to be essentially 'good'. To *feel* part of that natural environment through elemental experiences, was the finest proof I could ever need. The 'feel-good' factor should never be ignored.

The Chinese philosopher Mencius puts it so well:[4]

> *"The tendency of man's nature to be good is like the tendency*
> *of water to flow downwards."*

If the human being is essentially good, as I believe, then I have to accept that he is also capable of evil. Man is capable of the greatest good and the greatest evil, and all points in between. History makes this very clear. Life is a continuous battle between the two, the good and creative versus the bad and destructive. I am tempted here to say the former is typified by wild Nature, and the latter by the modern man-made world.

It is certainly true that the man-made world is characterised by a myriad of temptations. Not only that but there is considerable encouragement to succumb to these temptations. It is regarded as normal, for example, constantly to upgrade your style of living regardless of your responsibilities to the environment and the rest of the human race. The unnecessary four-wheel drive vehicles crowding our roads are an example. They make a fashion or status statement and appear to be mainly owned by people without a conscience. Most of us, I suspect, succumb to a variety of such temptations. On the other hand life would lose its meaning if man did not have to choose between good and evil. Indeed it may well be that freedom, in any sense other than the spontaneous, can only become a reality from a positive outcome to this internal struggle.

As I am writing this, my head keeps filling with thoughts of should I give up eating meat! Sketchy research by me seems clearly to indicate that I should. My conscience agrees and yet I know this is going to be a difficult battle.

A key principle of one of my heroes is most persuasive:

> *"For ethics also is nothing else than reverence for life. Reverence for life affords me my fundamental principle of morality, namely that good consists in maintaining, assisting, and enhancing life, and that to destroy, to harm or to hinder life is evil."*
> — *Albert Schweitzer*

Summary

If one acts positively according to conscience then one grows towards maturity. It is a wisdom that goodness attracts goodness and that one is shaped, not only by one's surroundings, but by one's actions. Every single good act moves one onwards towards such feelings as peace, happiness and to the ultimate wisdom of the unity of everything.

If one acts negatively – and we almost all do frequently – then one goes backwards, or regresses. One moves towards extreme self-centredness or egoism which negates development of all that is good within human potential.

Quotations

"You shall be free indeed when your days are not without a care and your nights without a want and a grief. But rather when these things girdle your life and yet you rise above them named and unbound." — *Kahlil Gibran* [5]

"A Peace above all earthly dignities, the world has achieved brilliance without conscience. Ours is a world of nuclear giants and ethical infants."
— *General Omar Bradley*

"We have in us the will that is free to destroy slowly the evil principle in us and to exist as an instrument of the good, if we only knew it, this is our eternal happiness."
— *Cecil Collins*

13

Transcendent Experiences

Looking back over my lifetime, a tiny number of experiences stand out because they were 'out of the ordinary' and possibly 'extraordinary' (the technical term is *transcendent*). Two things about them initially make them different. They had a deep effect upon my feelings. They also defied rational explanation. In other words I could not explain them purely in intellectual terms. I also somehow sensed they were very important. I now feel I have glimmerings of understanding as to their significance.

That understanding has come about because it has long been a personal habit to accept the cardinal wisdom of:

> *"Quality of action or experience needs to be balanced by quality of reflection upon that action or experience."*

Unless I had used this wisdom, had not reflected deeply and just moved onto the next action, I would have missed the significance of what were some of the most *valuable* events in my life.

I am dividing these unusual experiences into two very broad categories. The first are those concerned mainly, but not all, with occurrences in the natural environment. The second are concerned with the most important of all words – LOVE – which will be covered in Chapters 17 and 18.[1]

Experience: It is winter 1954. I am 19 and on a 48-hour pass from Catterick Camp back to my parents' home in Derby. It is my first year of National Service and I have been playing much basketball for my regiment. I decide to attend the weekly Friday evening practice session for Derby Town, hoping to be able to join in. Eventually they let me play and I can sense they are not thrilled by a stranger wearing glasses. In the twenty or so minutes on court, every time I take a shot I score. To their surprise (and my amazement) I quickly realise it does not matter where I shoot from – either distance or angle – they just go in – many not even hitting the backboard or the hoop! From then on every time I am at home I play for the town. Never before or since have I ever had such a 'cannot miss' shooting phase.

Reflection: Even physically the human body is unbelievably complex, and every single microscopic cell of the quintillion we are made of is unique and alive. If one adds the even more complex *psychology* of the human being to the occasion, then I find it unsurprising that this happened only once in years devoted to the sport. More positively, what happened in those 20 minutes was that 'I' – an amazing amalgam of all those bits and pieces – performed as a *unity*. I was going, all of me, in one direction. The favourite term is *flowed* because what seemed to be almost impossible – the scoring of a basket with *every* shot, not only happened but felt almost effortless.

Experience: A few months later, I am playing a match against Nottingham. Another unusual and brilliant event occurs. Basketball is, or was, known to be the fastest game on your two feet. In this match the five of us on court play as though we are one person. We win easily.

Reflection: The same result as the previous one except that this time five people were a *unity*. 'play as a team' is always a basic to any team game. For that to become *reality* is a wondrous feeling. It never happened again and it had never occurred previously.

Experience: It is the summer of 1957. I am leading a 6-man expedition to an area east of Narvik in Arctic Norway. The aim is to ascend as many new peaks as possible. The area is remote and has not been visited by climbers. About a month into the expedition and I am leading my partner on a steep 700 metre face. Pitch 10 is a 30 metre vertical rib with what appear to be minimal holds. It looks like the crux of the climb and I can see it will be at least one or two grades more difficult than the pitches below. Normally a careful and cautious climber, I decide to 'really go for it'. The pitch turns out to be very hard, yet somehow I *flow* up it.

Reflection: There was that *unity* again, only this time it was between me and the rock. The climbing genuinely felt almost effortless and was what Maslow termed a 'peak experience'.[2] For me, my bold action was out of character, especially as there were only two of us on the cliff, and at least two days away from any rescue. This was the only time in fifteen years or so of climbing that such an experience occurred.

Experience: Summer 1970. Carmarthen Bay. I am helming my 2-man open racing catamaran on a glorious sunny and windy day. I am sailing across the wind – the fastest point of sailing – heading east and going like a train. What makes it exhilarating is that I am reaching across the 6-foot high waves where they first break before they run up the beach. Picking the right waves I surf them and then pull back off them before the depth becomes too shallow for the boat. I know I am playing a dangerous, indeed silly game, but I cannot resist. It is a joy to use my kayak surfing experience along with my new enthusiasm for sailing. In any event the worst that can happen is that we will finish in a jumbled heap on the deserted sandy beach with a damaged boat.

Reflection: Over what must have been about an hour, exhilaration was the keynote. Somehow everything was right – boat, crew, weather and sea. At the risk of boring the reader, we *flowed*. It was as though all the aspects of the situation merged into that magical *unity*. I can remember it as though it was this morning. Nothing similar ever occurred in the catamaran sailing except for a night crossing of Morecambe Bay.[3]

Experience: Autumn 1982 Lake Windermere. I am preparing for a solo kayak trip to Alaska. It is the final mile or so of a ten-mile daily training trip. A beautiful evening and a flat calm lake. As befits a training trip I am feeling physically very tired from the hard paddling. From nowhere the final ten minutes into the shore at Ambleside becomes *effortless*. Somehow tourists on the beach have sensed something 'magical' has happened as they compliment me on my beautiful paddling. I am happy but bemused.[4]

Reflection: This is what I wrote in *Beyond Adventure*: "*When you have spent years…trying to perfect the skill of paddling which is in itself very complex, and you suddenly 'flow' effortlessly, it is as though you were projected instantly into another very elusive and wonderful world, What was especially significant was that it did not in any way feel restricted to a matter simply of physical involvement and technical skills or reduced to any of the scientific and psychochemical 'explanations' – of body chemistry, for example, concerning substances such as endorphins or decomposing adrenalin. I felt as though the whole of me, consciously and subconsciously, was merged into this experience. In that sense, I would say in those moments my entire being was in complete harmony, I had experienced a unity within myself. To ignore the lake, however, would be to miss something of even more importance. As I paddled through the water, for the final ten minutes or so, movement was effortless despite my being very tired, The word flow describes exactly how it felt. Logic dictates that to move a paddle through water, as with all physical actions, effort must be involved in order to make progress. Once again such experiences appear to defy the laws of science. 'Defy' is perhaps the wrong word in this context; 'are beyond' would perhaps be a better phrase. In any event, the key feature of this experience, as in all the others, was the feeling of oneness. In those precious moments, my separateness from the situation had vanished.*"

Experience: 1983. The 650 mile solo sea kayak expedition in Alaska as described in chapter six 'Who am I?

Reflection: Maslow describes this type of transcendental experience as a 'high plateau'. He says it can be achieved, earned and learned by long, hard work. Many years later I began dimly to understand using the phrase 'that part of me that was the ocean had somehow been switched on'. In other words *I was nature* – even if most of that was in my unconscious. (I could have equally said *each of us is nature* – with the same rider, for that is what I believe).

The *unity* this time could not be more immense – indeed virtually 'mind-blowing'. I have not had a further 'high plateau' experience, and have yet to meet someone who has. This may well be because of my narrow obsession with outdoor adventure and a very limited social life.

Experience: Summer 1991. A beautiful June morning and I'm off to do a solo rock scramble in Middlestead Gill above Thirlmere in the Lake District. Arriving at the start I notice directly in front of me at the foot of the rock face, a single tall plant with a magnificent deep blue flower. It impresses me, which is most unusual as I always ignored flowers. I then concentrate on the climbing. As I scramble over the top of the climb, to my surprise there is another flower identical to the one at the start of the climb. This time I study the shape of the flower – something I have never done before. Its appearance is striking. I return home in some excitement – not because of the climb but with a strong urge to identify the flower. Annette, my wife, a keen botanist, quickly identifies it as *Aquilegia vulgaris* (the Eagle flower). I later discover that this flower, common in Wordworth's day on the Lake District hills, is now a rare find in the wild.

Reflection: That experience led to finding wild flowers becoming my major passion and recreation for about two years, and a love that I know will last the rest of my life. But where did this new interest come from, as it was not only quite unexpected but very out of character. I was an adventurer and had a contemptuous attitude about becoming interested in flowers. Such interests were for the ladies. Mountains and rocks were for climbing as I was a man.

My intuition leads me to believe the following. The solo Alaskan kayak trip had fundamentally changed my attitude away from being a self-centred, egoistic adventurer to being more of a pilgrim adventurer. In other words I still loved adventure but now accepted that in wildness – in Nature – there was something more profound than individual self. The sentence I used to explain the Alaska trip was "somehow the button within me marked *ocean* was pressed." With the flower incident, somehow, from deep within my unconscious something said "you are still too egoistic as an adventurer. I am going to teach you a lesson and your button marked *wild flowers* will be pressed!" This seemed possible because the *high plateau* experience in Alaska had convinced me that the whole of Nature resided in my *unconscious*.

Whatever the cause or origin of this new passion, it led to a major step forward in terms of my maturity. It took me *out* of my self-centredness and egotism in an elementary way. As I have become older I have realised that there was a major weakness in terms of my personal adventure. Because of the need to control my fear, along with the often intense *physical* and skill demands of the action it was inevitably *self-centred*. With this new enthusiasm as my major activity the wild flower became the centre of my attention. I had been taken out of myself in my form of recreation. I continued to adventure with enthusiasm but I sensed a markedly less arrogant approach to wild Nature. After all wild flowers were on their own adventurous journey and I was often presented with difficult challenges both to find and to then identify them. They were also often strikingly beautiful. By being more aware and looking much more carefully at what there was in wild Nature, I sensed that I was moving strongly towards an implicit acceptance that I was part of the *unity* of Nature. I was losing my separateness.

Experience: 1997. Summer at home in the Lyth Valley in the Lake District. I am hanging out clothes on the line in the early morning sun. I feel a sudden jolt in the small of my back. I turn around, and face a group of beautiful *Viola cornuta* – large pansies from the Pyrenees. Somehow I know they are reproving me for not acknowledging their existence as I went past them.

Reflection: The jolt in the back was psychological but it happened and it was powerful. In the fifteen years or so of my enthusiasm for flowers this was the only time I felt flowers communicating directly with me. Sometimes I regret it was only a single occasion. Deep down, however, I am content because in some unfathomable or inexpressible way, I sense that my love of flowers is reciprocated.

Experience: Over the years I have given a considerable number of lectures to a wide variety of audiences. One lecture stands out as extraordinary.

It is in the 1980s to a group of about thirty teachers at a Local Education Authority Outdoor Centre. The subject is to do with beauty and adventure in wilderness and it is profusely illustrated with slides. Something intangible happens to the atmosphere – almost a sense of awe and wonder. I know somehow that everybody in the room has been deeply affected.

Reflection: A group of individuals who all loved wild Nature experienced the *unity of nature* during the lecture. In recent years there have been other times when I have sensed this unity with the audience. It is profoundly moving.

Experience: The raven is well known both for its intelligence and its ability to play. Among some of the native peoples of North America, it was a principal god. I empathise with that viewpoint. The raven seems to epitomise the spirit of the wilderness.

On one occasion, sea kayaking in west Scotland, I set up camp on a tiny island at the entrance to Loch Moidart. In the evening, I climb to its highest point. As I look out towards Mull and brace myself against the strong westerly wind, I am suddenly aware that, upwind and just below me, a raven hovers with wings spread as it too faces westward. As I am enjoying this moment, for I am used to seeing ravens at a distance above me, it suddenly disappears like a bullet to the east. It seems impossible that it could have seen me, as I was directly behind, above and downwind. Somehow, I know that it had become aware of my presence. The following morning, I set off to kayak round the westerly headland of the island. The weather has deteriorated and the sea is rough. After some misgivings, I decide to carry on. As I round the low headland, to my astonishment there is a raven sitting no more than 20 metres away, watching me intently. I have no proof, but I know it is the same raven, and that it is getting its own back. "We can both play this game, of spying on each other." [5]

Many years later, I have an even closer encounter with a raven. Having completed an interesting way up a Lakeland fell in winter, I sit on the top in the lee of some rocks. The weather is poor, with strong winds and rain. A raven lands no more than five metres away. They are quite common in the Lake District, but I have never expected to see one so close. I glance at the silent, dark bird and could not resist calling "Quork, quork" in a loud voice. To my delight, not only does it reply, but our 'conversation' goes on for two or three minutes. It was almost as if we are both saying, "so what if it is bad weather, let's enjoy meeting each other for this moment".

Experience: I have never regarded television as reality. Watching a Nature programme, for example, can never be the same as experiencing Nature directly. Nevertheless on two occasions 'reality' has burst through the screen as though the screen did not exist. The first was an interview with Virginia Wade, the tennis star. It was early morning and she was due to play her semi-final that afternoon at Wimbledon. It was as though she was in my lounge – her physical power and vitality left me in no doubt that she would win.

The second was the funeral of Princess Diana. I could not resist having a quick look on the TV during the service. I burst into tears.

Reflection: I used to cry extremely rarely so my response initially seemed amazing. Now I accept that it was an expression of the *unity* of everything in spiritual or psychological terms. From what I read of this tragedy I suspect I was one of millions of people who were psychologically engulfed by the occasion.

Implications of these elemental experiences [6]

Of the dozen or so unusual personal experiences mentioned here, the high plateau experience of the solo kayak trip has had by far the most radical effect on my attitude to, and eventually understanding of, how I relate to my natural surroundings as well as how I relate to myself. It literally changed me from the self-centred adventurer concerned with the size and difficulty of an adventure to someone who wished to spend his life as a pilgrim, ideally still taking adventurous journeys but as a humble observer. Put another way I became very much aware of my 'universal self' as distinct from my singular, or egoistic, self. What I found fascinating was that *practically* that expedition remained a normal type of trip with all the attendant highs and lows, easy days and hard days, and attendant dangers. It took years to begin to understand its immense significance, which included the vital importance of humility.

That significance is startlingly simple and yet profound;

<blockquote>The baseline of our existence is unity, not separateness.</blockquote>

All the diverse group of personal experiences mentioned, along with a host of other peoples' recorded in my files, have this same characteristic – they display that despite our feelings of a separate conscious self living in an individual physical body, beneath this and within our unconscious, there is a unity with everything natural.

Most of the human race currently live in societies where separateness is taken for granted, and the cult of individuality is dominant. What this means in practice, very often, is that apart from close relationships, the rest of the human race *in practice* is seen as separate from oneself and even as a resource, where appropriate. The same is even truer of wild Nature and the Planet. They tend to become so often a resource for the benefit of the human race.[7]

If I can use an analogy. Treating (most) human beings as a resource and Nature also as a resource is, in construction terms, akin to building one's life on a foundation of shifting sand. If anything characterises the modern world it is its *instability* as well as its *separateness* from Nature. If on the other hand modern human beings constructed a society on the principle that in essence everything is a unity, then the human world, I surmise, would make much greater progress towards *stability*. It is somewhat ironical that global warming, and other planetary devastation by humans, along with the increasing violence of natural disasters, are making it essential that the human race acts as a unity before it is too late.

There is a need to heed the words of Maslow:

> *"Very important today…is the realisation that plateau-experiencing can be achieved, learned, earned by long hard work. It can be meaningfully aspired to.*

*But I don't know of any way of bypassing the necessary maturing,
experiencing, living, learning. A transient glimpse is certainly possible
in the peak experience which may, after all, come sometimes to anyone."*

Quotations

*"The central perception of the perennial philosophy is that there is a fundamental reality...
that transcends the ordinary world, yet exists in it.[8] However separate in appearance they
may be, the individual, the universe and the transcendent divinity are essentially one. This
spiritual reality is the source of all consciousness and can be known directly...because we are
secretly joined with it already."* — Michael Murphy

*"True solitude is not loneliness. It is a great oneness. One with everything – the cool grass,
the deer, the glade, the wood, the countryside, this thin envelope of gas which gives our world
life, the planet, the galaxy, the universe. It is not a loss but a gift of wholeness. A wholeness
with everything; body, mind, spirit, and the whole level of attention. A wholeness in the
one moment of time poised in eternity."* — John Wyatt

"We are not in a relationship with the earth: we are the earth." — Matt Cawood

14

The Search For Beauty

"What is beautiful is a joy for all seasons and a possession for all eternity."

Oscar Wilde

In *The Unknown Craftsman* Soetso Yanagi writes:

> *"I would like to believe that beauty is of deep import to our modern age. Without question, the intention of morality, philosophy, and religious belief is to bring hope, joy, peace and freedom to mankind. But in our time religion has lost its grip. Intellectualism has undermined spiritual aspiration in most people. At this juncture I would put the question, might not beauty, and the love of the beautiful, perhaps bring peace and harmony? Could it not carry us forward to new concepts of life's meaning? Would it not establish a fresh concept of culture? Would it not be a dove of peace between the various cultures of mankind?"*

I not only strongly support Yanagi's view but wish to put it in a personal context:

The journey through life should be a continuous search for beauty.

Everything in Nature is beautiful in its own way, or as Confucius writes:

> *"Everything has its beauty but not everyone sees it."*

I am convinced that the more beauty we can see, or are aware of, the more mature we are. In other words, if our underlying goal is fulfilment or maturity, then every experience of beauty is growth towards that goal.

When I suggest life is seen as a search for beauty, I refer to three aspects:

> *Beauty in one's surroundings – from micro to macro*
> *Beauty in terms of all human contact and relationships*
> *Beauty in terms of one's own thoughts and actions*

I am conscious that this somewhat radical viewpoint on the importance of beauty in our lives was not my view at all when a young man. The reader may recall that in the first chapter on school days I remembered a particular beautiful red sunset among all the climbing action. At the end of the chapter I then wrote:

> *"...[the sunset] was probably the start of an increasing awareness of the immense potential of beauty."*

That memory was of an extra-ordinary experience. Such experiences were the subject of the last chapter. The contention in that chapter was that unusual experiences – those that are somehow beyond purely rational explanation – all indicate that in essence, or spiritually, we are not separate. In other words that in Nature there is an underlying unity. If I am also correct in the interpretation of my Alaskan experience in particular, that Nature in its entirety rests in my unconscious, then the importance of intense feelings of beauty should be both obvious as well as profoundly moving. I sense the truth in my statement that:

> *"In the moment of intense deep feeling concerning beauty, you and the object of contemplation are a unity. Your separateness, your sense of self, your sense of 'I am' is somehow suspended."*

Here is a graphic example from Arthur Koestler in his biography *Arrow in the Blue*. He was six years old and had just been diagnosed with an abscess on his appendix. He recalls:

> *"I was to be operated on the next day. I was taken to the hospital in an ambulance. It was a bright, clear, winter morning; as we crossed the lovely courtyard of Vienna's Imperial Palace, small flakes of snow began to whirl down from the sunny sky. Through the window next to my pillow in the ambulance, I watched hungrily the dance of the white crystals in the air, and while I did so a curious change of mood came over me. I believe that in those moments I became for the first time aware of the gentle but overwhelming impact of beauty, and of the feeling of one's own self peacefully dissolving in Nature as a grain of salt dissolves in the ocean. At the beginning of the journey I had watched the faces of passers-by in the street with impotent envy; they laughed and talked, their morrow would be like yesterday; only I was set apart. Under the snow-flakes in the courtyard of the palace, I no longer minded; I felt reconciled and at peace."*

Although Koestler does not use the word 'unity', I know from my Alaskan experience that he refers to the same thing I experienced. The feeling of 'peace' he mentions is a major clue. Fragile and vulnerable self – the 'I am' – is immersed into something beyond words which is wonderful, awe-inspiring, immense and peaceful. He was frightened until that experience. I too was frightened in Alaska – not overtly, but deep down, at the danger inherent in the challenge I had taken on.

I could see this clearly when I thought about my rest days. I kept myself very busy doing a hundred and one jobs. I was *too* busy. Conveniently it gave me minimal time to dwell upon bears and other possible problems!

Koestler's experience is extraordinary. It is the type of experience retained by the memory with startling clarity, no matter how long ago it occurred. It is important to realise that feelings of beauty as powerful as this example are likely to be very rare. This should not in any way undermine the case for Beauty and the search for it being a central feature of our living.

I have become convinced that there is an *instinct* for Beauty or an inbuilt *sense* for Beauty. Like the instinct for adventure, indeed all instincts, it needs to be used. If it is unused then it may well disappear altogether as with our natural instinctive sense of direction. I would prefer to be positive and think that at the very least it resides in our unconscious. John Lane in the introduction to his recent *Timeless Beauty* notes:

> *"Writing this book has led me towards an astonishing conclusion: That for a timeless period our species was instinctively tuned to the beautiful."*

If, as I know, we are shaped by our surroundings, then this idea makes eminent sense. For thousands of years our ancestors lived alongside and were in tune with, wild Nature, where beauty and mystery were normal.

Plato believed that Beauty was the only spiritual thing we loved by instinct.

I find his comment valuable. If the spiritual is the most important aspect of being human and is the basis of our values and our virtues and vices, then the concept of beauty could not be more important. It is probably the best way – the most beautiful way – into our spiritual depths and an understanding of our true self. In further support of this concept, I believe that the word 'beauty' is either strongly linked to, or synonymous with, *truth, wisdom and love.*

I wish to turn now to more practical considerations as to how best to try and appreciate beauty in everything natural.

In the first instance it may be helpful to realise that the opposite of beautiful is ugly. Indeed we need ugliness as a strong comparison. The opposite of natural is artificial. 'Man-made' is artificial. I would suggest a walk in a 'built-up' area is likely to produce much more evidence of ugliness than a walk in the country. The latter may be ugly, or be exposed to ugliness, but that is generally due to man-made actions!

I accept, of course, that what is beautiful and what is ugly is an individual matter. Nevertheless, my contention remains: that wild Nature at least, is *intrinsically* beautiful. The man-made world does have beautiful aspects but they are not intrinsic and, I would guess, are the exception rather than the rule.

In the second instance the *attitude* of the individual, as usual, is crucial. If a person is emphatically self-centred and egotistical, and/or predominantly concerned with becoming a success in modern materialistic terms he or she is unlikely to grasp the importance of beauty in its instinctive and spiritual sense. They will be people who are into 'having' and 'wanting' rather than, to use Schumacher's term, 'being'.

The reason for this is surprisingly simple. We are shaped by our surroundings. The impetus or driving force of the modern world *in reality* is money, status and power, and these ends often justify corrupt means. Unscrupulousness and cleverness, rather than integrity and honesty, are far too often the key to success in this world. The modern world encourages and is typified by the vices. Somewhere in my notes I have reference to the contention that of the seven deadly sins, six at least are characteristic of this culture.

Apart from the virtues, and accepting them as ideals, in the search for beauty, a meditative mood; measured slowness; lack of distraction; patience; calmness and attentiveness are all most helpful. The innocent and open approach of the young child also comes to mind as being helpful.

Leonardo da Vinci wrote:

"The eye…is…the window of the soul."

I interpret that seeing clearly means both *inwards* into beauty as the source of the spirit, and the much more obvious *outwards* at the beauty of the object. I sense that this is not only synchronicity but that the going outward and going inward are the same things. They are *unity*. I would say that this experience is an example of life as a *circle*. The Upanishads put it more eloquently:

What is within us is without us.
What is without us is within us.

Whilst referring to the appreciation of beauty there is an important difference between what I would term 'surface' beauty and 'source' beauty. I came across a vivid example. In a biography of a famous politician, the biographer described his subject's ambience as 'charming' and many of his speeches 'beautiful'. The content of the speeches however was vacuous and lacking in integrity or honesty. It would be dishonest not to recognise the beauty of the speech in terms of its delivery, but equally it would be dishonest not to criticise the substance, or lack of it, if the motivation for the speech was self-enhancement. I find this type of beauty shallow, even evil, and a major contrast to beauty in wild Nature. There is a depth in Nature which is truth in its deepest of senses. And, if aware, one is filled with a sense of awe and wonder, or mystery. This is probably why I sense that wild Nature needs to be experienced as much as possible, in contrast to the dishonesty and machinations of the modern world.

Early in this chapter I referred to seeing beauty in three ways: in the surroundings, in other human beings, and in terms of one's actions and thoughts. Using the term 'beauty' with reference to the surroundings is traditional. Using the word with regard to dealings and relations with others is much less conventional. I see no reason, however, why it cannot be used and I like its simplicity. Every time I come into contact with another person my attitude can be seen as somewhere between extreme beauty and extreme ugliness. The lout who attacks the hospital nurse attempting to help him is behaving in a manner of extreme ugliness. The bus traveller who smiles and says 'thank you' to the driver as he gets off displays a moment of beauty.

The use of the word 'beauty' in terms of one's own thoughts and actions is probably even more unconventional. Yet I sense both that it fits well, and that the reader knows what I mean. It perhaps indicates something about present society that 'an ugly thought' seems to be much more common than 'a beautiful thought'.

How much beauty there is in a person's life obviously depends on a considerable number of factors. I know from experience that severe fatigue and depression can lead to feelings that there is no beauty relevant to your life. In positive frames of mind however, progress probably comes down to sorting out a personal framework of values, and then trying to live up to it in detail.

I try to think like this every time I wash up! When I remember, not only is the crockery 'alive in its own way' but it's also beautiful (or should be) and deserves its own well-being!

I also try constantly to remember a policy of *minimal destruction* – to my better self, to others, and to everything around me. I know that this approach, what Buddhists term mindfulness, can work against ugliness.

Quotations

"I returned, and saw under the sun, that the race was not to the swift, nor the battle to the strong, neither yet bread to the wise, nor yet riches to men of understanding, nor yet favour to men of skill, but time and chance happeneth to them all. Beauty is truth, truth beauty…that is all ye know on earth, and all you need to know." — Keats

"I am inclined to think that the worst feature of modern life is its failure to believe in beauty. For human life beauty is as important as truth – even more important – and beauty in life is the product of real feeling. The strongest condemnation of modern industrial life is not that it is cruel and materialistic and wearisome and false, but simply that it is ugly and has no sense of beauty. Moral conduct is beautiful conduct. If we want to make the world better, the main thing we have to do is to make it more beautiful. Nothing that is not inherently beautiful is really good. We have to recapture the sense of beauty if we are not to lose our freedom. And that we can only do by learning to feel for ourselves and to feel really. This is not a side issue. It is the heart of the problem of modern civilization." [1] *— John MacMurray*

15

Music

"The best of music, best of art and best of literature are all inspired by love"

Anon

I am working at my desk in my office one winter morning in my tiny house in Scotland. Classic FM is playing through the sophisticated stereo system in the adjacent lounge. There is a change in the music. I am immediately attracted – sufficiently to go into the lounge, sit comfortably and just listen. After five minutes or so the track ends. I am awestruck. I am filled with wonder and joy. So moving is the piece of music that I intuitively know that I can spend the rest of my life listening to such heavenly sounds.

Through local friends I discover it was the Adagietto from Symphony No. 5 by Gustav Mahler. In reading about Mahler, one of the first things I discovered was that you did not need to know anything about classical music to enjoy this piece. That made me smile – on two counts. First, I was almost completely ignorant concerning such music. Second to describe my reaction to the Adagietto as enjoyment would have been the understatement of the year. It had expressed in some magical way the very depths of my soul. I then discovered that this piece was famous, not least because it was the theme music of the film 'Death in Venice'. More importantly I learnt that of all the great composers Mahler was considered by many to have the greatest ability in terms of expressing the full range of human emotions. His life had had more than its share of tragedy as well as joy.

This had me fascinated. I needed to try and understand why I had been so incredibly moved. At first the explanation seemed obvious. Based on the premise that our feelings stem from either a base of fear or love, then it was the latter. My love for Annette was very much on my mind at that time. Then, eventually, and I suspect intuitively (from my unconscious) I realised that it was more than that. It also expressed all that I felt about wild Nature. In other words my (universal) love for wild Nature was expressed in this short piece of music. The words of Thomas Carlyle are apt:

> *"Music is well said to be the speech of angels; in fact, nothing among the utterances allowed to man is felt to be so divine. It brings us near to the infinite."*

As are those of Hermes :

> *"...the Powers which are in all things sing within me also."*

And Thomas Carlyle again:

> *"See deep enough, and you see musically; the heart of Nature being everywhere music, if you can only reach it."*

It made sense when later reading more extensively about Mahler's very tempestuous and socially demanding life, that he escaped from this lifestyle by spending substantial time in a hut alone in the mountains of Austria. The latter could well have been an instrumental factor in shaping his music.

As music is native to the human mind and as it is an important aspect in many peoples' lives, I will reflect upon my own attitude to, and enjoyment of, music. I sense there is something to learn about the mystery of life and especially those ideals of *beauty*, *truth* and *love*.

In my youth, popular music and jazz dominated. The former expressed my dreams of romantic love. The best examples not only became embedded in my memory, but have remained in my collection. The latter – the jazz – was essentially swing and the big bands – Duke Ellington, Count Basie, Stan Kenton, the Dorseys and so on. The sound and power of the pulsating rhythm of such bands I found compelling – and I still do. In these later years of my life I play such music only occasionally instead of constantly, as I did in my youth.

In Annette's final few weeks at home a bed was made for her in the lounge. When there were no visitors she loved to listen to her favourite classical music, much of which was from compilations. This type of music, with the exception of some Bach, was new to me. My abiding impression at this saddest of times was one of peace. I now, some years later, would add the word beauty.

After she had departed and I lived alone in the North West Highlands, I gradually found that music seemed to take her place. Not that this was in any way possible, but appropriate music, I found, was an immense comfort. For someone alone and psychologically lost this was hardly surprising as much of my life was now inevitably dominated by memories of our times together.

At first I concentrated on extending my collection of popular music, although I was beginning to play Annette's classical compilations with increasing frequency. I also began to listen more to Classic FM radio. Then, by chance, when in Edinburgh, I went into the HMV store on Princes Street. In the classical section I found the manager and said I had no expertise but sought music that could be described as extremely beautiful.

She was brilliant. I was soon armed with a dozen CDs and headphones with which to listen to them. I was so lucky. I walked out with 11 of them. They ranged from solo voices, such as Angela Gheorghiu singing sacred arias to some new classic compilations of relaxing music. I was becoming aware that I had the whole world of classical music to explore in my search for beauty.

Part of most evenings at home were then devoted to listening to music. Despite an excellent sound system I decided to use high quality headphones as well. I don't think I was fully aware at first of the importance of what I did in terms of understanding the mystery of my life. As I relaxed with headphones I became fully immersed in the music.

The music and I became as one.

Here was this unity again, my non-separateness. This time, however, it had one major difference from the transcendent experiences which also expressed this unity. The latter could not be produced on demand. They were always unexpected. With the music I could experience unity whenever I wished! Here was something which I would have hoped would convince anyone with an open mind, that an experience of unity was relevant to anyone with a love of music.

"I lost myself in a Schubert Quartet...partly by ceasing all striving to understand the music, partly by driving off intrusive thoughts, partly by feeling the music coming up inside me, myself a hollow vessel filled with sound." — Joanna Field

Among the music I listened to was Opus 36 from Symphony No. 3 by the Polish composer Gorecki. Like the Adagietto from Mahler this piece is well known. Its theme is the horrors of the Second World War and the concentration camps. A more solemn, and mournful piece of music, I suspect, would be hard to find. Mahler's Adagietto I could play daily, Gorecki's work only weekly as it was so sad.

It took a while to appreciate a crucial link, for me at least, between the two pieces. They were both *beautiful*. Indeed I can now happily play the Gorecki piece daily. It was one thing to write 'everything in Nature is beautiful in its own way if you can see it'. It was far more meaningful to *experience*, and eventually enjoy, the beauty depicting such horror. It reminded me of Annette's face in her last few days – so beautiful and yet not being consciously aware, except very dimly, of the significance of that beauty.

There was something else about beauty and music that has occurred as I have been writing this book. Much of the time at my desk I have classical compilations of re-laxing music playing quietly. From the time I started playing them I made a note on the cover of each as to which tracks especially moved me, and others which caused a gentle stirring of my emotions. (The idea was that one day I would make my own compilations). Over the next few years I inevitably replayed the same discs – perhaps four or five times annually. To my surprise I found I was adding further tracks in both my categories, and this process has generally repeated itself. In other words, I was finding much more beauty in a given CD. It was an example not only of eve-rything in Nature being dynamic, but, more importantly perhaps, my awareness of beauty was markedly increasing for this type of music. This must be a natural, as well as a pleasing, process. I am none the wiser with reference to any technical un-derstanding of the music.

There is something else I have started to find as I have entered this world of classical music, which is contributing to my understanding of my existence. It has something to do with the search for truth and the spiritual nature of man. Since I was a young man I have always loved Bach's Toccata and Fugue – almost the only piece of classical music that I revered when I was young. As I became increasingly interested in Albert Schweitzer I became interested in his passion for playing Bach. After his demanding days running his hospital in remote Labarene in Africa, he would find solace playing Bach. I had found something in common with my hero. In recent years I had become used to playing Bach when working at my desk. Whilst much of his work I found beautiful, the overriding feeling was one of *peacefulness*. I then read some of Schweitzer's comments on his favourite composer where he speaks of a lack of self-consciousness by Bach when composing.

I wondered from this whether Bach, like some of the other great artists, deliberately lost his conscious self in order to allow his much larger unconscious self to take over when he was being creative.

I also came across a quotation from Edna St. Vincent Millay in which her love for Bach was due to his music being "so pure, so relentless and so incorruptible". My mind immediately linked the word *pure* to the great virtue of *Purity*. To listen to Bach can be to lose oneself in Purity.

I was reminded of several interviews I had seen on TV with famous conductors. Some impressed me with their humility. A striking example was an interview with the conductor Gustavo Dudamel at the end of a performance of Shostakovich's 10th symphony. This young man emphasised the crucial importance of humility in his role. This was not just as the bridge between composer and orchestra, but that he saw himself as one of the orchestra. His whole demeanour suggested strongly that these were not empty words. The quality of the performance was spellbinding to the point where the visiting expert said she had never heard a better performance of the 10th symphony. I would go much further. Listening to the applause from the massive audience, and watching the relationship between orchestra members and conductor, I have no doubt this was an extraordinary (transcendent) experience for everyone – a genuine example of *unity*.

I then read an article in *The Times* (21 October 2007) celebrating Sir Colin Davis's 80th birthday. Above all was emphasised his *"unswerving committment to truth"*, and his hope that all young musicians would have this committment. My reaction was the wistful hope that *all* young people should take the same central path through life, wherever it may lead.

I am conscious that I have made no comment on the music of wild Nature. That I love it I am in no doubt. To read that John Muir thought that the most beautiful sound in the whole of Nature was the cry of the loon was one thing.[1] It was quite another to kayak solo at dawn in Alaska through flocks of these birds deep in their own conversations. These experiences were utterly memorable as well as beautiful.

Yet the beauty was different from the sound of Mahler's Adagietto, although hardly less moving. Comparisons of Nature's music and man-made music would however, be immature. Most of man-made music has been inspired by listening to Nature. John Muir knew about the music of Nature in considerable detail, loved it, and could write eloquently of it:

> *"Purple morning and evening. The evening lark song is 'Queed-lix boodle.' Today is Tuesday with us mortals, but it must be Sabbath day in the lark calendar, for they have been holding meetings extraordinary, and their songs were sweet and pure as the light which inspired them. Lark song is very absorbable by human hearts. It is about the only birdsong of these plains that has been made with reference to our ears. Yet how grand must be the one general harmony of all nature's voices here – winds, waters, insects, and animals. Music belongs to all matter."*

Quotations

> *"My compositions spring from my sorrows. Those that give the world the greatest delight were born of my deepest grief's."* — F. Schubert

> *"Music puts our being as men and women in touch with that which transcends the sayable and which outstrips the analysable. It has long been, it continues to be, the unwritten theology of those who lack or reject any formal creed."* — George Steiner

> *"The thought of the eternal efflorescence of music is a colourful one and comes like a message of peace in the midst of universal disturbance."* — Romain Rolland

16

Mystery and God

"The divine essence is Love and Wisdom."

E. Swedenborg

Thoughts of writing this chapter have daunted me. How dare I write about the unknowable when I have read so little of the standard religious texts. And yet I remember vividly a teacher on one of my one-term Outdoor Adventure courses. Unusually amongst my students, he was a strong practising Christian and there was an air of religious zeal about him. After listening to all my sessions on values he said something like: "You do realise that all your values are in the Bible" and then added: "Of course you can find anything in the Bible if you look hard enough!"

A memory surfaces of my first day at Oxford University. I remember being distinctly worried as to whether I would cope with this highbrow academic world. After two years of National Service in the ranks, at the age of twenty, I felt I now knew something of life. On the other hand it was hardly suitable training for a three-year degree course in Modern History. Even worse, fate had decreed that my final six months in the army were to be spent in Brighton. What else was a man to do other than do his job well and enjoy his spare time. My job was to test daily the regiment's sports equipment. This involved swimming offshore in flippers every day, and then with a face mask diving down to ten metres! (It seems hard to believe now. I was even given the responsibility of spending £50 on whatever I decided as the regiment's sports equipment). In my spare time I sought my adventure in a similar manner to most of my fellow soldiers: girls and modern dancing.

Unsurprisingly then, Oxford appeared very alien. Student 'Oxford' accents made me wince in the corridors and quadrangles of my college of Keble. The knowledge that Keble was recognised as the most religious of the Oxford Colleges made me feel even more like a fish out of water. It was the practice of the then Warden, Eric Abbott, to ask each freshman two questions: "Did I want to sing in the choir?" and "Did I want to serve in church?" As he looked at me, my single button green jacket, cut away collar and slim jim tie adorned with a range of jazz instruments he answered his own question: "No Colin you don't want to do either do you". I hastily concurred, feeling embarrassed. I doubt they ever had a student who, at that time, had both such a profound ignorance of, or interest in, matters concerning the spiritual. The idea that one day I would write a chapter on such matters would I am sure bring a smile to his face. In his quiet and benign way, along with his wisdom and advice when my climbing partner was killed, he probably initiated the beginning of my interest in this most interesting and challenging aspect of being human.

Before I move to the present and attempt to inform the reader as to where I am currently with my own spirituality or beliefs, I sense it important to give my views on certain key words.

I have long had difficulties with the term 'religion'. The strict meaning of the word comes from 're-ligare' meaning 'to tie again to a common source'. Another definition I have seen describes it as 'basically an attitude or approach to life on the part of an individual'. I concur with both of these meanings. Unfortunately the word 'religion' seems to be conventionally accepted in the narrow sense of 'man-made' religions. This is why, throughout my writing, I have used the word 'spiritual' rather than 'religious' to describe this most important aspect of being human. I see the word 'spiritual' as being 'natural' rather than 'man-made'. It also has the advantage of pertaining to anything, not just humans. It is normal, for example, to speak of 'spirit of place'. Many religions, in practice if not in theory, seem to be much too human-centred for my liking, as well as, to often seem narrow and prescriptive.

Since I was a boy I have also had difficulties with the word 'God', as well as the term 'the Lord'. I now know that it was a word devised by many wise men to describe the profoundly indescribable, but my difficulties remain. My problems are the images it produces in my mind – a singular, superior male. Whilst the word God makes me feel uncomfortable, not least because it seems to emphasise my separateness, I have no objections whatsoever if others choose to use this term. My preferred term however, is either *sacred mystery* or *transcendent mystery*. It would have been simpler to just use the word mystery but this seemed too broad. In the first instance it can refer to something evil. In the second instance it can refer to mystery that is of shallow consequence as compared to the deeply spiritual. There are, of course, other words which, for me, capture the spirit of God or sacred mystery. "Truth" is one. I love this quotation where Gandhi puts the emphasis on the latter:

> *"The little fleeting glimpses that I have been able to have of Truth can hardly convey an idea of the indescribable lustre of Truth, a million times more intense than that of the sun we daily see with our eyes."*

I also like the words of Max Lerner:

> *"Cutting across the difference in doctrines between the world's great religions – of Moses and Jesus, of Lao-Tzu and Buddha, of Confucius and Mohammed there remains the truth that God is what man finds that is divine in himself. God is the best way man can behave in the ordinary occasions of life, and the farthest point to which man can stretch himself. "*

I take this to mean goodness in terms of behaviour and that the essence of goodness is to be found in both our heart (or conscience) and, at the higher level, a perfection (in God) beyond man's rational understanding or attainment.

Lloyd Geering, the New Zealand spiritual writer, uses other words:

> *"God may be seen as an ultimate point of reference or an eternal principle."*

As does Don Cupitt:

> *"God (and this is a definition) is the sum of our values, representing to us their ideal*

unity, their claims upon us and their creative power..."

Bertrand Russell, the philosopher says:

"If life is to be fully human it must serve some end which seems, in some sense, outside human life, some end which is impersonal and above mankind, such as God or truth or beauty."

I would interpret that as seeing God, Truth and Beauty as synonymous – or at least in the deepest senses of the last two.

From at least middle age I have regarded wild Nature as a church without a roof – the finest of all churches and a sacred place to visit as often as possible.

Many who have journeyed long in the great realms of Nature speak of profound experiences of beauty, synonymous with religion in its most fundamental sense. John Wyatt, for example, describes his feelings concerning a high view over Lakeland fells,

"I stood there for perhaps half an hour before I started back... It was as if I had been, by divine choice, privileged to approach the golden gates of paradise. It left me breathless, elated, awed."

Near to Cape Horn, the solo sailor Bernard Moitessier, writes of the sea *"so beautiful it really breathes"*, and of his first view of the Southern Lights (the Aurora Australis) as *"perhaps this voyage's most precious gift to me"*.

Up in the wilds of Alaska, the explorer Robert Marshall writes of a brilliant day:

"...we felt genuine exultation in seeing the flawless white of those summits and the flawless blue of the sky"

Whilst further south in Colorado, John Muir is similarly inspired by the morning after a severe storm:

"In vain as I crossed the open meadow did I search for some special palpable piece of beauty on which to rest my gaze...But no such resting-place appeared in the completed heaven of winter perfection...It is all one finished unit of divine beauty, weighed in the celestial balances and found perfect."

Up in the Polar region Nansen and his crew watch the Northern Lights. They make a profound impression:

"No words can depict the glory that met our eyes...surpassing anything that one can

dream'…and…reaching such a climax that one's breath was taken away."

Volumes could be written of those who have experienced the beauty of Nature, from the tiniest flower to the view of Earth from outer space. John Muir perhaps captures the magic of all such experience:

"These beautiful days must enrich all my life. They do not exist as mere pictures – maps hung upon walls of memory to brighten at times when touched by association or will, only to sink again like a landscape in the dark; but they saturate themselves into every part of the body and live as always."

Inevitably as a climber I was affected by the beauty of the mountains, crags and moorland. I suspect, however, that most of the effect was on my unconscious. I was too consumed by the challenge of the adventures themselves. Changing my recreation to kayaking, and especially sea kayaking was a major step in becoming spiritually aware. Three significant factors were responsible for this increased awareness. The first was that the sea is a major natural environment. This is also the case with major mountain ranges of course, but my climbing was mostly in Britain in the smaller ranges of hills. The second factor was that in a tiny open boat on the sea one was much more immediately affected by, or at times threatened by, sudden weather changes than when climbing. It is common knowledge that Britain does not have a climate. It has weather. The third factor, which is of considerable importance in terms of my spiritual awareness, is that most of my later sea kayaking was in solitude. Solo experiences are generally recognised as being much more psychologically intense than when with fellow human beings. It does not take much imagination to realise that solo sea kayaking, and not least on long expeditions, or in dangerous and committed conditions on wild coastlines or crossings out of sight of land are often extreme psychological experiences. In terms of spirituality these adventures were very significant. At times I was made to realise my insignificance and to realise I was probably less than a matchstick on the immensity of the ocean.

I am reminded here of a powerful phrase in the writings of the solo sailor Bernard Moitessier:

"It is here, in the immense desert of the Southern Ocean, that I feel most strongly how much man is both atom and god."

I relate strongly to his words. On a tiny open boat out of sight of land and in threatening weather, it is easy to feel no more important than a speck of dust. There have been times, however, when I have felt on top of the world. Having said that I would hastily add nothing like as high as 'God' conveys in terms of those experiences. I prefer to see 'God' residing in my deepest unconscious, or as perfection or my ultimate ideal. It is something – a sacred mystery – which even in my wildest dreams – I could never achieve. This 'beyond words phenomena' is the 'truth' towards which I continue to struggle. The most I can hope for is to have glimpses of 'the infinite' or 'eternity'. The high plateau experience of Alaska provided one of those glimpses. It left me with the deepest feelings of awe, wonder and humility. There was something so obviously beyond, and way beyond the trivialities of self-centredness and egotism.

No wonder I regard wild Nature as sacred. I find it comforting that 'sacred' means not only 'holy', but also has a second meaning of 'a place of refuge' or sanctuary. I know that I am at my most content when I am self-reliant in wild Nature and staying over in such places in a bivouac or tiny tent. Those feelings are among the strongest of my current memories not least because Annette had similar feelings. Her sudden death emphasised in the most powerful of ways that the spiritual aspect of being human is not only the most important aspect, but also that it never dies. I now know this is true – from deep within my heart – and I rejoice.[1]

The brightness of Annette brings to mind a quotation from the compelling writings of the Vietnamese monk Thich Nhat Hanh:

> *"We have to remember that our body is not limited to what lies within the boundary of our skin. Our body is much more immense. We know that if our heart stops beating, the flow of our life will stop, but we do not take the time to notice the many things outside of our bodies that are equally essential for our survival. If the ozone layer around our Earth were to disappear for even an instant, we would die. If the sun were to stop shining, the flow of our life would stop. The sun is our second heart, our heart outside our body. It gives all life on Earth the warmth necessary for existence. Plants live thanks to the sun. Their leaves absorb the sun's energy, along with carbon dioxide from the air, to produce food for the trees, the flower, the plankton. And thanks to plants, we and other animals can live. All of us – people, animals, plants and minerals – 'consume' the sun, directly and indirectly. We cannot begin to describe all the effects of the sun, that great heart outside of our body."*

This quotation emphasises the truth that in essence, or spiritually, there is a unity between everything that is natural.

In the same way that I feel the unity between Annette and me, so strongly in my memory, I also feel the unity between wild Nature and me. What I find brilliant about this quotation is that, for me at least, it breaks down the idea of our separateness, so entrenched in our psyche because we have a separate physical body. When I ask people if they are aware that they have two hearts, inevitably I get puzzled looks (at minimum!).

This unity is well expressed by Alan Watts:

> *"There is simply one all-inclusive happening in which your personal sensation of being alive occurs in just the same way as the river flowing and the stars shining far out in space."*

I feel this sensed unity is my spirituality made conscious. Everything natural has its own spirit. When I walk past a tree I am conscious that the tree is observing me even if it is in some indefinable way. 'Spirit of place' is a well accepted term – even in the modern world. Spirit does not physically exist. My feelings of the unity of everything also do not physically exist. Yet I know they are totally real or true within my psyche and I can embrace the following quotations:

> *"…I think one's whole life is a search…with God…a reunion with one's origin. I always feel that origin and destination are one; they are the same thing in the human spirit, and the whole of life consists of making your way back to where you came from and becoming reunited with it in greater awareness than where you left it; by then adding to it your own awareness, you become part of the cosmic awareness."*
> — *Laurens van der Post*

And these brilliant words from Empedocles:

> *"The nature of God is a circle of which the centre is everywhere and the circumference is nowhere."*

In other words 'God' is in everything natural, which includes each raindrop, blade of grass and snowflake, and stretches to eternity.

I follow Krishnamurti's words in searching for the meaning of God or *transcendent mystery*:

> *"I maintain that truth is a pathless land, and you cannot approach it by any path whatsoever, by any religion, by any sect. That is my point of view, and I adhere to that absolutely and unconditionally…"*

I am essentially at ease with this solo spiritual journey because I know from experiences that there are fellow travellers who have joyously shared my feelings of unity – hearts have met and indestructible bridges have been built.

Summary

My spirituality, in terms of conscious awareness, has been shaped by three main factors. The first has been a life lived as far as possible in wild Nature in a self-reliant way. At first that spirituality was largely unconscious as I was too self-centred and egoistic. Solo sea kayaking led to a revolution in my attitude – from adventurer to pilgrim.

The second factor was deep reflection on the sudden demise of Annette. This was particularly concerned with what Annette had meant to me after many years shared, along with trying to understand the meaning and implications of the unselfish way she lived her life.

The third factor was beginning to glimpse the reality of what universal love meant to me personally in terms of my feelings.[2]

The sacred mystery ('God') is the ultimate reality in which all we experience is grounded; the essence glimpsed is all that is beautiful, true and good.

Each person has a unique spirituality. In addition I would support the monk Thomas Merton that everyone should find their own God and have their own name or phrase to describe this most profound aspect of being. I would humbly suggest that, as I sense there is no certainty in Nature, then the efforts to understand the mystery of it all should be continuous.

"I know that the Eternal Mystery is beyond all concepts, but the feelings and ideas which pass through me are my symbols of that mystery, and that we should all have a symbolical view each according to his chemistry and dreams" — Cecil Collins

Quotations

"The fairest thing we can experience is the mysterious. It is the fundamental emotion which stands at the cradle of true art and true science. He who knows it not and can no longer wonder, no longer feel amazement, is as good as dead, a snuffed – out candle. It was the experience of mystery – even if mixed with fear - that engendered religion. A knowledge of the existence of something we cannot penetrate, of the manifestations of the profoundest reason and the most radiant beauty, which are only accessible to our reason in their most elementary forms – it is this knowledge and this emotion that constitute the truly religious attitude; in this sense, and in this alone, I am a deeply religious man."
— Albert Einstein

"Do you need a proof of God? Does one light a torch to see the Sun?"
— Oriental wisdom

"The power that holds the sky's majesty wins our worship." — Aeschylus

17

Love

Love above all things is personal.

A.N. Whitehead

In this chapter I want to trace back my view of, and my feelings concerning, this word 'love'. It is only in recent years that I have come to accept that there is no more important word in any language. John Selby expresses my thoughts clearly:

> " *It is not a belief. It is the positive life force and integrating power that creates and holds all reality together.*" [1]

As a young man my view of love was conventional. Love meant romantic love, that magical experience so searingly well-expressed by the best pop songs of the 1960s. I realise now I did have other forms of love: for my new bike as a 14-year-old; for cricket and tennis and then, above all, for climbing. Mainstream jazz was also a strong addiction and a live band was a magnet. These were all loves utterly different from romantic love, and upon reflection, I would have probably preferred to use the word 'enthusiasm'.

Meeting Annette, when I was a student at Oxford, brought romantic love brilliantly into my life. From the moment I saw her – at a mid-week tennis club dance to which I had gone reluctantly (!) – I knew she was special. It seemed almost a miracle that the attraction was mutual. Very quickly, or so it seemed, we became inseparable except when I was climbing. Even 'falling in love' (and the lamp-posts did seem to be pink!) could not deter me from my view that the driving force in my life was my ambition to be a top climber. So powerful was this force that I remember initially not wanting even to get married.

That love of climbing had received a very powerful boost from the tragic death of Bernard Jillot, my best friend and climbing partner when at Oxford.[2] I was now to climb for him as well. This had happened only a few months prior to meeting Annette.

Annette also loved the outdoors and being in mountains. There was thus every reason to share our young lives together. In many ways, however, it was a marriage of opposites. Annette was blessed with a happy and spontaneous personality who seemed to enjoy life in all its diversity. Being unselfish and making others happy were also some of her defining characteristics. I, on the other hand, was a tense person, who tended to be socially ill at ease. I was always searching for physical challenge, and much of that searching was to do with adventure and expeditions.

Inevitably, as I now understand the wisdom, the lamp-posts regained their natural colour, or in the words of M. Scott Peck: [3]

> "…*that the feeling of ecstatic lovingness that characterises falling in love always passes. The honeymoon always ends. The bloom of romance always fades.*"

John Berger in '*The White Bird*' (one of Annette's book collection) I also found help-

[3] *The Road Less Travelled*, (1979)

ful. In it he describes being in love as an *"infinitely extensive mood"* but that *"it cannot develop without changing its nature"*.

This is what happened after a few years in my relationship with Annette. Being a romantic I was deeply saddened by the disappearance of those magic feelings. I fervently hoped that throughout our time together those romantic feelings for her would one day reappear. Annette, I sense, somehow retained her love for me throughout our 42 years together. It would be less than honest, however, not to admit to giving her a very hard time at times with my self-centredness, my undue pride in the control of my emotions and my love of adventure. At no time, however, did I ever want to hurt her. In many ways she brought up our 3 daughters single-handedly, allowing me to commit myself to the concept of adventure for young people, as well as my own expeditions. I suspect our own expeditions – as a young family and later in life just the two of us – were instrumental in keeping us so very strongly together. She was the ideal expedition companion as well as the ideal life companion. I now realise that our relationship, from my viewpoint at least, had moved from romantic love to the highest form of friendship.

Whilst we were both *individually* exploring our inner journey, our ideas on such matters were openly discussed occasionally when time permitted. We were also bound together very strongly in our agreement about the immense potential value of wild Nature in seeking answers to the great mysteries of life. Along with this view we both shared a fervent desire to leave the world a better place for the next generation.

Love of wild Nature

This type of love almost certainly began in my teens, if not earlier and has continued throughout my life. Among all the memories I still remember with delight and not a little awe, various parts of the geologically complex coastline of Pembrokeshire. I am thinking here neither of the kayaking and sailing nor of the climbing but what might be termed coasteering. As a form of relaxation from the Centre Courses at Woodlands, I would take a rope and abseil (rope down) to high tide level on an exposed section of coast. Armed with local tidal knowledge, a careful study of a large scale map; a weather forecast, and, not least, much solo climbing experience, I would explore along the coast and aim to climb out somewhere different from the start of the day. This world – the splash zone – where the sea meets the land on an exposed coastline is special. This is particularly true, if solo, as well as often in winter and in the presence of roughish seas. I still miss those days full of adventure and wilderness.

Certainly in the later stages of my life my love for wild Nature could not have been stronger. This was very evident to me from the intense anger I felt at the Exxon

Valdes oil spill on the then pristine coastline of South East Alaska.

In chapter fifteen – those *extraordinary* experiences with their underlying element of the *unity* of everything in Nature, I seldom (if at all) mention the word 'love'. Yet I could have done. If I love *all* of wild Nature then this would seem a big step in the direction of what is known as 'universal love'.

Love of human beings

When I think of the 6 years I was responsible for the Oxford Outdoor Centre I can say with honesty that for most of the time, the 30 young people on the courses, and all the staff involved, seemed to me as though they were all part of a mainly happy and contented family. Whilst this was in no way feelings of universal love I can now see that it was along the road to that ideal. It is almost trite to say that those experiences were generally of a very positive nature for all concerned and had a sense of purposeful challenge and worthwhileness. Highly relevant was that the Centre, like most such centres, was remote from the city and their homes, and was located in the countryside.

When I compare this experience to the rest of my working life I can begin to see why I cannot *feel* love for perpetrators of evil actions nor for people in power that abuse that position for self gain or egoism. What I am saying is that the modern world is so bedevilled by vices and bad behaviour that inevitably many humans succumb to these temptations. I believe humans are inherently good but have been shaped in negative ways by these surroundings. It is this fact that makes me unable to practice universal love.

Love of self

I perhaps should have started this chapter with the question *'Do I love myself?'* I do not mean in the narcissistic sense.[4] My response to that question – and it has not in essence changed since I was a young man – is NO WAY! I have always had a sense of unworthiness, an acute awareness of my vices. I do have respect for some of the things I have done and even a sense of pride, perhaps, but not love. It is hardly surprising that I find contentment most when in wild Nature as opposed to social situations. Yet Nature of course is dynamic and my feelings are changing, becoming more positive concerning the latter. It was a significant step when I added 'Forgiveness' to my list of key virtues. I eventually accepted the wisdom of forgiving myself for my vices, although they will never be forgotten. The journey to understanding self must now, I feel sure, be a positive journey to accepting universal love as a concept and, as far as possible, a way of life.

I like Arthur Koestler's comments on this matter: [5]

> " ...*self-love is a virtue – if it is as fierce and humble, exacting and resigned, accepting and rebellious, and as full of awe and wonder as love for other creatures should be. He who does not love himself, does not love well... and hatred of evil is as necessary as love if the world is not to come to a standstill.*"

When Koestler writes "*self-love is a virtue*" I see this as looking at my thoughts and actions against my list of virtues. In the first instance is the need for ruthless *honesty* in the mirror. Secondly, I need then to look at the relevance of other specific virtues such as *self-discipline, self-reliance, vitality* and not least, *humility*. My motivation must also be honestly questioned although at times there may be many reasons, both good and bad which may tend to merge into it. I also always need to remember I am human and therefore I will make mistakes. Importantly I need *vitality* – to move on, and I should never forget my sense of *humour*. As my *awareness* of self grows, hopefully so will my *respect*. Love of self remains a distant ideal. I suspect that the most I can hope for, as I grow more mature, is that there will be infrequent times when I can sense that light.

Love of beauty in wild Nature

I wish now to take a different approach to Love. One of the extraordinary personal experiences not mentioned in the chapter on transcendental experiences happened as follows:

Two of us are returning from Holyhead on Anglesey across Morecambe Bay to the Lake District in a tiny open catamaran.[6] By nightfall, after 13 hours of slow sailing in light winds, we had reached the main channel into Liverpool. We were about 10 miles offshore. Unbeknown to us it was approaching high water at Liverpool Docks and a stiff breeze from the east had sprung up. The next hour or so was a time of near terror. The main channel was very busy with boats up to liner size coming out of or going into the city, some ablaze with lights. We were crossing the dark channel at right angles – a game of Russian Roulette, especially as our only light source was a head torch. At one point we both felt we were doomed. A liner ablaze with lights seemed to be coming at us no matter which way we changed direction. Once across the shipping lane, this was what I wrote in '*Beyond Adventure*':

> "*My crew, Mike Waites, who had spent some years in the Merchant Navy and had shouldered the responsibility of reading all the lights in order to try and determine a safe course, retired to sleep on the trampoline deck. The next few hours until dawn were very special. At the other extreme of deep emotion, instead of suppressed panic I felt unbelievably happy. At first this did not make sense as I was very tired and the situation was still dangerous. The wind was now fresh offshore and the boat was moving fast*

through sheets of spray. A capsize would have brought severe problems and pushed us further out to sea. Yet the feelings of deep contentment could not be explained entirely by the relief at crossing the shipping lane. Somehow, almost in an ethereal way, as night in the outdoors has often seemed to have some magical quality, the fatigue and dangers appeared irrelevant amidst so much startling beauty. A huge moon in a starlit sky, the long ribbon of yellow light from the Lancashire coastline far away to the east, and the green phosphorescence from the spray and the wake of the rudders all combined to make the deepest and most indelible of impressions. Even now, it is as though it happened yesterday. At the time, I had no thoughts of the merging of man and nature. It was simply seen as an experience of extraordinary beauty and power. Now I realise that I must intuitively have felt an integral part of this magical scene."

Asked to use one word to describe this experience I could use the word *unity*, as I have with all the other elemental experiences. Instead I want to use a word that I feel is inextricably linked to unity, and that is the word '*beauty*'. The recent chapter on beauty suggested that in the moment of experiencing the beauty, the separateness of self was suspended, and the individual became part of the unity. I also suggested that we have an *instinct* for, or innate *sense* of beauty, or feelings for beauty.

If it is an instinct, then it is *universal*. What I am suggesting is that Beauty and Love are at least considerably intertwined and may well be synonymous. I love beauty rather than merely liking it, and am aware that, at least in wild Nature, there is beauty, as well as truth, in everything if I can but see it.

Kathleen Raine sees the link:

"Beauty is the real aspect of things when seen aright and with the eyes of love."

Universal love and the virtues

Moving now to the last few years and indeed to the birth of this book I want to continue this search to understand love beyond its romantic and filial senses.

In 2002, with both of us retired, Annette and I completed three one-month trekking expeditions; to Crete at Easter, to the Cordillera Cantabria mountains in Spain in early summer and to the Ariège region of the Pyrenees in late summer. During the last journey Annette picked up a stomach bug from a severely flooded public camp-site. On return to the UK, it was checked out and a cancerous growth in the bowel was discovered.

An anxious time then followed, for six weeks or so, to await the report from the specialist consultant. Our anxiety was only helped by Annette's very high state of fitness and the knowledge that the consultant had an excellent reputation.

The appointment at the Westmorland General Hospital finally arrived in November. I met her in the car park as she returned from the interview. The beautiful morning was matched by her smile. The verdict she reported was great news: an operation, radiation treatment; a recovery period and within twelve months she would be fully fit for our next expedition.

What happened next was probably the single most startling moment of my life, and certainly the most daunting. As powerful as any bolt from the blue, I was psychologically poleaxed by the flash of words that said *Annette is going to die*. As the words hit my brain I felt a terrible and inevitable certainty.[7]

My physical reaction to this message was almost as startling and very out of character: I burst into a flood of tears. Annette, thank goodness, presumed my reaction was one of relief and happiness at her good news.

Within six months Annette had gone.

There were two key aspects from her last few weeks in the hospice. The first was that the nurses were deeply moved by Annette's *compassion*. The second was her insistence that she was in a bubble of happiness. I was moved beyond all expression of language by her manner. I knew somehow, that my desire for the rekindling of that romantic love I had felt so strongly for her in our youth, had been rekindled. I was acutely conscious of its immense depth and power. I have wondered whether this was because my unconscious self knew there were only a few days left before she slipped away. The other, later, reflection was that this might not have been romantic love but universal love; or if in some way they were synonymous. Or again, the possibility that love itself has to mature within *conscious* self. I suspect this may be the answer and, in terms of my relationship with Annette, my love had reached maturity. It is also worth noting that, in those last days of her life, I was dimly aware of the almost ethereal beauty of her face when in repose. All those reflections, of course, came later. The reality of that time for me was deepest misery and frequent floods of tears.

Once the funeral was over I realised the wisdom of 'radical problems demand radical solutions'. With the considerable help of Vember, Senja and Tiree, our daughters, I sold up and, against much advice to go south, went north to live in West Scotland. The tiny village of Strathcarron lies between Inverness and the Isle of Skye. I was surrounded by mountains, close to the west coast and the sea and very much back in wild Nature.

After many months wandering alone in wild places my desolation gradually began to lift. The beauty of this part of the world, along with the brilliant friendship of a local couple, began to work its magic. I was constantly buoyed by two thoughts: One was that I should consider myself extremely fortunate to have spent most of my life with Annette. The other was that I knew she would be very disappointed in me if I did not face her demise in a positive manner. (It would be true to say that I often sense her presence – no doubt smiling at my attempts to try and understand it all!)

After about a year I sat down and wrote at length to myself, knowing that it might help to clarify my jumbled thoughts. I had gone from thinking I knew enough about life, adventure and wilderness to write two books and lecture extensively, to realising that I knew nothing about death, at least the death of the loved one.

In reading about death I came across the following quotation from Johann Wolfgang von Goethe:

> "Death is a commingling of eternity with time; in the death of a good man, eternity is seen looking through time."

These words had a powerful positive effect upon my depression; they reinforced my conviction both that the spirit does not die and that it is synonymous with eternity.

I liked also the words of John Milton:

> "If death is a journey to another place…what good can be greater than this? … Above all, I shall then be able to continue my search into true and false knowledge."

I knew from reading Annette's expedition diaries and her notebooks, that she was always seeking to understand, but had little time for it in her busy life. I also liked the idea that in her spiritual life she would continue the search unhindered.

Wandering in North West Scotland, with my mind inevitably full of memories of her, I happened to link her with my ten key virtues. These virtues were at the base of my student teaching, lectures and books. To my surprise she seemed to have all ten. This seemed most unlikely as I had long been convinced that to be human is to admit fallibility. In other words we are all a mixture of virtues and vices.

I checked with her friends and, with one exception, they agreed with me about her lack of vices. Even the exception voiced what was hardly a major vice: "*she talked too much*"! I suspect at least part of this vice was in fact the virtue of vitality and her longing to communicate her own joy of life and share it with others.

Of the utmost significance to my understanding of love was the immediate reaction over the phone from her headmistress, "Everyone, in both junior and senior schools, pupils and staff, *loved* Annette".

Later my mind flashed back to the scene when I arrived at the crematorium; the area was packed. I now know the headmistress was correct. Annette personified this universal love. She was naturally happy with both animate and inanimate nature and socially at ease with everyone.[8] Despite being very gifted in many different ways, her life was essentially lived unselfishly.

I was to read the wisdom that 'how you die depends on how you lived your life". It seemed totally appropriate that she departed in a state of happiness. She also said she felt 'safe'. Maybe it was that life loved and protected her, and took her back to itself.

She could have written the words of Dostoyevsky: [9]

> "Love all God's creation, the whole of it and every grain of sand. Love every leaf, every ray of God's light! Love the animals, love the plants, love everything. If you love everything, you will perceive the divine mystery in things. And once you have perceived it, you will begin to comprehend it ceaselessly more and more every day."

It is also very relevant here to note that Love and God have, from ancient times, and from both Eastern and Western religions, been regarded as synonymous. Annette was a Quaker, and unlike myself, was content with the word 'God'.

In the last section I said that Annette both seemed to possess all ten key virtues I had used in my writing at that time, and that she personified this universal love in the way that she lived. Most people who met her seemed to love her, which seems to point strongly in that direction. A personal set of memories also seems to point in that way. In our last few years on expedition we would often seek mountain areas that were off the beaten track. This meant, whilst on expeditions, arriving at remote mountain villages where almost any visitors would be unusual. At that time anywhere near, even remote, habitation especially in Spain, was officially: NO WILD CAMPING. Accommodation also in such places was often non-existent. Tired at the end of expedition days I always sent Annette into the village to sort out the problem. She never failed despite language barriers.

In Crete staying in a mountain village for a few days, several locals said did I know how lucky I was to be with Annette. And in several mountain villages on several expeditions the old ladies would come up and touch her. It may be that she was just an 'old' lady with a large rucksack and they admired her fitness, but I seriously doubt that was the only reason. She seemed to have an indefinable yet endearing presence which I particularly noticed on the later expeditions when in the presence of strangers. I now wonder if it is possible that these unworldly spiritual folk somehow knew she was close to her God and was going back soon. In other words they were touching the divine.

To return to 'universal love' and the matter of how this relates to the virtues it is worth looking at St. Paul's idea of love, which he said had nine elements:

patience	humility	unselfishness
kindness	sincerity	good temper
generosity	courtesy	vitality

Eight, if not all nine, of these were on my list of ten virtues. I must stress here that I am searching for the *truth* of the matter. If the reader feels I am placing Annette on a pedestal then I can only concur, because she *deserved* to be. I am in no doubt that she was a remarkable woman who epitomised all that was best about being human. That has become very clear to me since her demise. The wisdom, unfortunately, is correct; you only really appreciate something when it has gone.

If the reader remembers my chapter on virtues he or she will remember there were twenty-six of them. Having now looked at them in comparison to Annette's personality and how she lived I am more than ever convinced that 'universal love' does exist and that I was incredibly privileged to have spent most of my life with her. She has led me to see that:

Universal love is the universal or all-encompassing virtue.
Universal love is the circle of life as it should be led.
The specific virtues are segments of that circle and only need to be articulated and practiced in a man-made world.

In this world the vices rather than virtues are given prominence because materialism rules rather than spirituality.

"All noble qualities feed and exalt love. They are in turn by love fed and exalted."
— *Mark Rutherford*

"The virtues are nearly all justified by our lack of love." — *St. Augustine*

"Why love among the virtues is not known, is that love is them all, contract in one."
— *John Donne*

What convinces me even more in this matter is yet another virtue (the twenty-seventh!) which I have not yet mentioned. It came to me suddenly – from my intuition – in 2007. It was:

Naturalness

In one way naturalness can be seen as **the** pillar of wisdom from Nature. Everything else, apart from modern human beings, lives naturally and I regard that as beautiful.

As a possible key virtue on my list I had to dismiss it as an idea. As we are shaped by our surroundings, we are almost inevitably affected by the vices so characteristic of the modern world. The constant bombardment of advertising from an early age, for example, often leads to 'wanting' and 'must have' as a normal attitude to life.

Annette was an *exception* in this respect. People loved her because of her *naturalness*. She had much about her that personified those elusive virtues of purity and honesty.

For me at least, I now realise that Annette personified *universal love*. And as a result of my time with her, reflection upon it, and subsequent reading I accept implicitly that:

Love is the driving force of everything in nature.

Quotations

"Within me is the happiness of an expression of my inner god – that joy and that love have flooded my limbs and senses, my mind and intellect, this universe right in front of me, my past without beginning and my future without end. Certainly I understand nothing of this play of love, and yet it is always taking place within me. The light that pleases my eyes, the cloud-glow of dawn and dusk that pleases, the greenery of grass and foliage that pleases, the image of a loved one's face that pleases – all this is a succession of waves brimming with love's divine play. And within it frolic the shadows of the whole of life, joy and sorrow, light and dark." — Rabindranath Tagore

Tschu–Li describes universal love as:

"The spirit that endows all things with life."

From the Bible:

"Love bears all things, believes all things, hopes all things, endures all things, love never ends" — 1 Corinthians:13

Teilhard de Chardin reminds us:

"Love in all its subtleties is nothing more, and nothing less than the more or less direct trace marked on the heart of the element by the psychical convergence of the universe upon itself." [10]

"Love is the general name of the quality of attachment and it is capable of infinite degradation and is the source of our greatest errors; but when it is even partially refined it is the energy and passion of the soul in its search for Good, the force that joins us to Good

and joins us to the world through Good. Its existence is the unmistakeable sign that we are spiritual creatures, attracted by excellence and made for the Good. It is a reflection of the warmth and light of the sun." — Iris Murdoch

"Does the Universe exist to be explained or lived? Knowledge does not end in explanation, for things are endless and relative and much knowledge is the same as little knowledge. No, The Universe exists to be lived, joy can only come through love which is the highest wisdom because love is willing to live life as mystery even as darkness, thus all mysteries open up before Love" — Cecil Collins

18

Friendship

"To love purely is to consent to distance."

Simone Weil

In the previous chapter I mentioned that after the loss of Annette I moved to the North West Highlands of Scotland and eventually wrote to myself to help try to clarify my jumbled thoughts. What I wrote I initially entitled 'Chasing Rainbows' because I felt I was trying to reach the beautiful yet always out of reach. The script attempted to address three questions:

Who am I?   Where am I going?   How do I get there?

The major part of the essay addressed the final question, and there was no thought of publication.

Using email attachments I sent it to about thirty friends around the world – different ages, backgrounds and yet all with a love of Nature. Many were adventurers but there were also some artists and gardeners. My plea was: could they help me to understand? And in return for confidentiality they could respond to my ideas and their presentation in any way they liked.

Almost everyone responded, often in great detail. I then looked as carefully and as *honestly* as possible at what they had written. Amendments were made to the original draft. I also read more about values – from a wide variety of sources and not least biographies of people like Gandhi, Schweitzer and certain adventurers and explorers. From this reading I made and filed further notes.

The whole response process was repeated. Chasing Rainbows mark II went out in January 2007 and by Easter all replies had been returned. Mark III went out in November the same year.

I learned valuable things from this unusual procedure. The first was considerable humility and an increased awareness of these friends – most of whom were not close friends when the process started. It was one thing to accept that everyone was unique. I found for some odd reason that I was surprised that this was also true of their viewpoints. The diversity of viewpoints, sometimes on the same matter also surprised me.

An example of the latter were the responses to the large number of quotations in the second edition. I knew I had gone 'over the top' in any conventional literary sense. I felt it would be easier to prune quotations for the next edition if I had some agreement on what to prune.

Comments on the quotations varied from obvious exasperation at their excess (along with a severe literary telling-off!) to individuals praising the idea and even offering me further quotations to consider! I eventually realised that quotations should be a *major* aspect. Wise individuals throughout the ages have expressed the importance of all that is good about being human. I admire and have learnt deeply from such people and I regard it as a privilege to quote from their writings. I feel that they add their often considerable strength to my viewpoint.

This comment, of course, is also relevant for those who have helped me by responding to my writing. I like this *shared* aspect. It seems particularly appropriate as unity is a major concept of this work rather than separateness. I am, however, under no illusion of the central importance of my own experiences. There is simply no substitute for them. In my case it is also crucial that I can begin to see the truth of my own experiences. If I do not reflect on them accurately – at least as far as I am able – or if I do not bother to reflect at all, then I minimise my growth towards maturity in terms of understanding my life. I also would be unable to write this book!

What follows next is difficult for me in the context of accurate reflection. Of all the responses, two had an immediate and profound effect upon me. Each had an accompanying letter asking if I minded if they replied very frankly to what they had read. Both gave some excellent constructive criticism. This was true for many of the other respondents. What was different about these two replies was their ambience. They contained great *naturalness* and *spontaneity*. This may well not surprise the readers when I tell them they were very young. They were also young women. I sense that it is likely, if one dares to generalise, that young people naturally tend to be more spontaneous than those who are much older.

What was exciting for me was the joy I felt not only when I first read them, but whenever they cross my mind. My intuition said they were sublime *sparks of this elusive universal love*. It felt like it was heart to heart contact. The reader should know that I did not know either of them nor what they looked like.[1] That last point seems important to me when I realise that my joy might be due to the fact that I am an old man, who has lost his wife and is also a romantic. Having thought about this further I have all but dismissed this reason. The final and probably most important point is that I tend to rely on my intuition rather than rational thinking. In this situation it said, in effect, these two people are *soul mates* for you.[2] They are with you *in spirit* and *universal love* can be a *joyous reality*. Reading their responses was a transcendent experience for me – a wonderful sense of that *unity* again.

It is helpful to quote Stephen Levine here:[3]

> "*As we tune in more and more to our heart, to ourselves, we discover that there is also a silent transition of heart between people. The heart recognises that words are often an excuse for people to communicate while the real communication is taking place. Instead, words sometimes even block the heart: by keeping the reception only in the mind, instead of allowing it to be sensed from that place where we can experience another person within ourselves … when we experience that deep connection of intuitive mind to intuitive mind, the separation between beings melts away and communication has less to do with words.*"

I find these words profound and, in my own use of words, would prefer "heart to heart" rather than "intuitive mind to intuitive mind." [4]

George Steiner, in his remarkable book *Real Presences*, also indicated strongly the possibilities of a transcendence, where normal feelings of separateness may be suspended:

> *"Speech can neither articulate the deeper truths of consciousness, nor can it convey the sensory, autonomous evidence of the flower, of the shaft of light, of the birdcall at dawning...It is not only that language cannot reveal these things: it labours to do so, to draw nearer to them, falsify, corrupt that which silence...that which the unspeakable and unspeaking visitations of the freedom and mystery of being — Joyce's term is 'epiphany', Walter Benjamin's is 'aura' — may communicate to us in privileged moments. Such transcendental intuitions have sources deeper than language, and must, if they are to retain their truth-claims, remain undeclared."*

I love these remarks and in particular the phrase 'transcendental intuitions'. For me, my reaction to these two youthful responses were extraordinary experiences. They involved the deepest of my feelings.[5] This to me was that *unity* again, only this time it was not in wild nature, but through words and pieces of paper with strangers.

Thoughts, of course, can be very powerful in their effects, whatever their origin. If they come from the rational aspect of being human, then they are pallid when compared to the immense power of deep feelings. Gibran is, as usual, helpful:

> *"For thought is a bird of space, that in a cage of words may indeed unfold its wings but cannot fly."*

The two examples I have given concerning my 'understanding' of the concept of universal love were radical. They woke me up — in the best possible way. My problem now is to find suitable words to describe other experiences, that if they have not given me the immediacy of joy, they are *along* the road to joy, giving me a strong sense of well-being. One category of these I feel through many of the other responses to *Chasing Rainbows*. I can sense the heart of the responder through the veils or between the words.

Another category is what the Greeks called 'filial' love. Having three daughters and six grandchildren has naturally become an important part of my life. The way my daughters took charge of the arrangements for Annette's funeral was unforgettable and our relationship grows ever stronger. As for the young children, they are a joy to be with, and they respond well to my adventurous disposition. There is something eminently beautiful in experiencing life as essentially a circle rather than a full stop.

Then there are friendships outside the family. There are heartfelt links with people with whom I have shared adventures and other experiences worldwide. There are friends locally. I find this especially important as they have a *physical* presence. I have begun to appreciate the real importance of genuine friendship – and not least through the physical gestures on meeting. Such a friend gave me a simple book on a recent birthday. In it I read with delight:

> *"And when someone hugs us, the soul bird, deep down inside, grows and grows until it almost fills us. That's how good it feels when someone hugs us."* [6]

The last possible type of friends are, as the wisdom has it:

> *"Strangers are friends we have not yet met."* — Anon

Two such memories surface. They were both fleeting, involved powerful handshakes and the eye contact was 'to the soul'. If I ever met them again, I am sure we would immediately acknowledge the strongest of friendships. The first was in the Pyrenees. This is what I wrote in '*Beyond Adventure*':

> *"Even fleeting moments between two strangers can sometimes be seen as beautiful moments. One early morning whilst on a Pyrennean expedition, I found myself on a col leading down to the head of a remote valley. I was in deep shadow and my mood matched the gloom. With a heavy pack, danger obviously lurked on the steep trackless slope beneath. To my amazement, I saw a figure coming diagonally up the slope, using a long wooden pole across his body for balance. When he reached me, he looked me in the eye, and then we spontaneously shook hands. The shepherd, in that single powerful grip and without words, seemed to say, 'This is a magnificent wild place of which we are both a part'. It was a moment of synchronicity and certainly of beauty."*

The second was at the Royal Geographical Society in London in 2005. I had just given a lecture on the potential of expeditions for young people. A young man came up and said "Thank you. That lecture has changed my life".

I have now realised there are four stars in the book. One is wild Nature. Another is Annette. A third is a young lady I have yet to meet. A fourth is an even younger lady whom I have now met. To me, joyously, they are all part of that wonderful unity of Nature to which I feel so thankfully I genuinely belong. Love can indeed open the gates to eternity.

I also have little doubt that Annette is smiling as she thinks, "At last, Colin, you are beginning to understand."

Quotations

"I define love thus: The will to extend one's self for the purpose of nurturing one's own or another's spiritual growth." — M. Scott Peck [7]

"Love is the purification of the heart from self; it strengthens and enables the character, gives motive and a nobler aim to every action of life, and makes both man and woman strong, noble and courageous; and the power to love truly and devotedly is the noblest gift with which a human being can be endowed; but it is a sacred fire that must not be burnt to idols." — Miss Jewsbury

"We need a moral philosophy in which the concept of love, so rarely mentioned now by philosophers, can once again be made central." — Iris Murdoch

[7] *The Road Less Travelled,* (1979)

19

Truth And Living In The Moment

"...the really 'final' truth that, carried to extremes, opposites meet."

C.G. Jung

For a long time I carried this difficult truth in my head, sensing it was true but that it might be rationally inexplicable. Being aware that I was not clever in any intellectually academic sense did not help. Then, probably from my intuition, a possible answer, or example, appeared, or at least a way of explaining the statement:

What has gone is the past.
What is to come is the future.
Where these opposites meet is the present moment or the now.

The answer, then, and it may also be the final wisdom, is to do with the Present Moment. I smile at this (possibly through ignorance as I am no scientist!) because friends suitably qualified in the sciences were insistent that technically 'the now' does not exist. This may be true but I do not mind because in terms of living my life and understanding my life I know intuitively what 'the now' means! I thus came to:

The key to how to live my life lies in how I live each moment of my life.

The words of Michael Mayne come to mind:

"Listen to your life. See it for the fathomless mystery that it is. In the boredom and pain of it no less than the excitement and gladness, touch, taste, smell your way to the hidden heart of it because in the last analysis all moments are key moments, and life itself is grace."

The same author then refers to the playright Dennis Potter. As the latter lies dying of terminal cancer he describes:

"…the nowness of everything as absolutely wondrous."

If all feelings are ultimately based on either the emotions of fear or love (or a mixture of both) then Dennis Potter would appear from his words to be entranced by love. This makes some sense if one can view one's death in a positive sense rather than in a fearful, negative sense. As death approaches, then one would, perhaps naturally, become more aware of, each moment in time. What is important in terms of my own understanding is that Annette slipped away in a bubble of happiness. If the reader will now bear with me, I will return to this subject towards the end of the chapter. I sense it may be useful to the reader if I go back to the early days of my journey through life in terms of 'living in the moment', and then progress to my understanding of where I am at currently.

Looking at my climbing, and other forms of adventure I can now see that 'living in the moment' was a key attraction of these demanding sports. When Rilke writes:

"One lives so badly because one always comes into the present distracted."

I can respond by saying 'yes, that is so often true of much conventional living but it is not true of serious adventuring'. Indeed, I can go further. If I am distracted at the critical moments when in dangerous situations, then I may well become disastrously unstuck. The knife-edge between life and death can be the most exciting place in the world if you have freely chosen to be in that situation and have prepared yourself well to overcome the challenge. These are the times when the human being can give of his or her best; when the adrenalin flows in order to help performance. All other life-forms naturally face danger in this way, and such times give the participant the best opportunity for growth. Life is lived to the full because there is no acceptable option. Nietszche was correct:

"The secret of reaping the greatest fruitfulness and the greatest enjoyment from life is to live dangerously!"

Immediately after a near disaster or an 'on the edge' situation, all of one's senses tend to be enhanced by the joy of being alive and one's world seems a wonderful place.

In climbing, I loved the movement – often feeling that it was the best and most natural of all human movements. I also loved the beauty of the situations, and the beauty of my performance when climbing well. In contrast I was fearful of falling off and especially of being irreparably wrecked. This worried me more than dying. In extreme situations my fear could be predominant over my love. For that reason it was a relief to take up white water kayaking. Certainly I did not like trapping my legs deliberately and encasing my lower half in the kayak – a most unnatural position – but the idea of drowning was infinitely preferable to being wrecked by long vertical falls to land on boulders. Unfortunately I eventually discovered that white-water rivers could have boulders beneath the surface that posed severe danger if, in the event of a capsize, I failed to eskimo roll quickly. Even worse was the thought of being trapped in an upturned kayak in such situations. It was hardly surprising that I eventually turned to sea kayaking and the ocean depths!

Seminal moments in terms of changing my attitude to living in the moment occurred during the 'high plateau' experience of the solo kayak Alaska trip. The first was as mentioned previously: caused when facing dangerous conditions on the final day when capsize was a strong possibility. I was, I discovered, at peace with the possibility that I might well die because I *loved* what I was doing. It was my chosen way of life whenever possible.

The second was the whole 'high plateau' experience – the feeling of being linked 'unbrokenly' to the ocean in psychological terms. The only explanation had to be that I *was* Nature: For one incredible experience that part of my unconscious marked 'ocean' had come into my *conscious* self.

The experience a few years later of falling in love with wild flowers – which became my major passion – confirmed my belief that in my unconscious resided the whole of Nature, and another aspect – wild flowers – had now come into my conscious.

The chapter on extraordinary experiences emphasised that all those experiences underlined my *unity* – my non-separateness – from the rest of wild Nature. In all this process of fumbling towards some understanding I needed to take account of my working life. Discovering that *all* rather than some young people for example were naturally adventurous and could grow apace in a positive sense when faced with natural challenges was initially a great surprise. It was important for me to realise that I was no different from others in that respect. Then later, I discovered that "everything (else) in Nature was alive in its own way, deserved its own well-being, and was also on an adventurous journey".

Eventually, therefore, I reached a point where my egocentric self (my conscious self) diminished considerably and became of minimal importance (it will always remain, however, my dangerous enemy.). I accepted my Universal or unconscious self was the true self or 'real me' because I *was* Nature. I felt it was totally valid for me to love this *universal* or natural self.

I need now to return to the matter of Annette's last few days and her insistence that she was in a bubble of happiness. One message from that saddest of times could not have seemed more important. She loved life and lived life to the full. She loved not just wild Nature as I did, but she loved people – of all kinds and all ages. Wherever she went she was loved. A strong statement but one I know to be true.

Several friends said she had lived the life of at least three normal people. Above all she lived her life *unselfishly*. This was why the message was so important for me – the unselfishness of her living in all aspects of being a mother. It is pertinent to note that she had a policy of looking to others for their virtues rather than their vices.

She had always, ever since I met her, lived life with considerable zest. She naturally tended to *live in the moment*. I could make an analogy with young children – it could be like that – the spontaneity, the honesty and the joy – yet she was a highly intelligent and mature woman.

Annette would have appreciated these words from Fred Rohe as she loved fell running when she had a spare moment, and sometimes talked of 'floating' and 'flowing': [1]

> "…from the experience of running meditatively I learn that potentially my entire life can be lived meditatively and it seems to me I should learn to live it so. To me this means I will be calmly, courageously, alertly, intelligently, energetically present for each moment of my living until life is done with this body."

Summary

Over my life I have very slowly learnt to try and live in the moment in a non-egotistical way. I find it a formidable ideal. Annette was a beacon in this respect, and has remained an inspiration. I have read extensively on the subject of living in the now. Whilst most of it has been helpful it bears no comparison to the experience of living with someone who lived it naturally. Love and Goodness; Truth and Beauty lived in her presence.

Quotations

'Our everyday life, that is the Tao." — *Joshu*

"Nowness, or the magic of the present moment is what joins the wisdom of the past with the present." — *Chögyam Trungpa*

"Time is eternity; and we live in eternity now." — *Herman Melville*

20

Natural Examinations

Some values of wilderness challenges in terms of fulfilment of individual potential.

Y ou attempt something. You succeed or you fail. You have been examined. But is it really as simple as that? Of course it is not! Success and failure, as Kipling so famously noted, are twin imposters. They are the surface criteria so popular in our materialistic and very shallow societies. If our overall aim is fulfilment in all positive senses of our potential then what matters is the degree of effort we put into the challenge, along with the motivation behind our efforts.

In this chapter I explore three experiences in wild Nature in some detail to try and begin to assess their value in terms of my own positive growth. Is this exercise necessary? In one way it is not. I know each of these experiences was worthwhile, rewarding and unforgettable. On the other hand our modern lives are almost bedevilled by the vast array of choices of what we can do for recreation. Education is also swamped by too many subjects and too little time.

I am convinced these types of outdoor activities are invaluable for almost everyone.

I have always had an intense dislike of examinations. This may well be to do with a strong sense of inadequacy in terms of my academic abilities. The one examination I have embraced throughout my life has been taking on a *natural* challenge. These have been my adventures and expeditions. Whilst I would not normally use the word examination (too many negative vibrations) there can be no doubt that having set myself a challenge, I would generally be rigorously examined in the process.

Earlier in the book I emphasised the importance of the foundation wisdom that:

> **The quality of the action or experience needs to be balanced**
> **by the quality of the reflection upon that**
> **action or experience.**

Reflecting in depth and with the hindsight of old age is not something I have ever done until I started to write this book. As the person who was in these situations I have a genuine interest to try and see in what ways these challenges have contributed to my journey towards my maturity.

The first experience I will look at is as a member of the 1960 expedition to climb Trivor in the Karakoram Himalayas.[1] In the context of all my expeditions this is the one that not only gave me the least satisfaction but also, in terms of my virtues and vices, the one I would prefer to forget. Ironically, unlike some expeditions to the larger Himalayan peaks, there was little friction between team members and we also climbed the mountain. Essentially what happened was that I was overawed by the sheer scale of the mountains. Having climbed the previous year a difficult snow and ice route on the largest face in the Alps (the Italian face of Monte Rosa) I thought I knew about mountain scale. I was not the first novice in the Himalayas to have this problem. As usual, experience is everything in really knowing about something.

This fear was compounded by three other factors. It was common knowledge among mountaineers of that time that there was a one in ten chance of not returning from such expeditions because of the high degree of objective danger – the type of danger a human being cannot control such as avalanches and storms. The second was that my best friend and climbing partner, Bernard Jillott, along with another friend from Oxford, had perished in a horrific accident on Haramosh whilst I had been climbing in Arctic Norway two years previously. The final factor was that although I loved climbing I was essentially a rock climber. Apart from the previous year in the Alps I was unfamiliar with the world of snow and ice.

At first on the expedition, none of this was important. From the initial advance party stage, Don Whillans and I were in the lead and expected to go all the way to the top. I had huge confidence in Don's abilities as a mountaineer. I was aware that I was climbing with a legend, someone who could climb almost anything and yet who would not hesitate to back off if this was dictated by his common sense and long experience. Then the situation changed dramatically. At camp IV – a long way from base camp – Don became ill with possible symptoms of polio. The doctor prescribed rest at the camp until, hopefully, he improved sufficiently to retreat. From the tent door we could see the summit although there would be two more camps before it could be reached. I knew I did not want to go on without Don. Although I knew the other two – Jack Sadler, the American, and Wilfrid Noyce – were both gifted and experienced mountaineers, I *intuitively* did not have confidence in them. I returned to Base Camp and persuaded Wilfrid that he, and not I, should go on to the summit. There was no reason why I should not have gone – physically and technically I was fine but my underlying fear at what might happen was too strong. The stark reality was that I was a coward. In another sense my weakness was probably a blessing for Wilf. I suspected he was sad that he had not been the first to climb Everest and I always felt that if anyone deserved to have done so, then it was Wilf. At least now I had given him the chance for a new Himalayan peak.

The other vice I would rather forget about from that expedition could be termed in various ways but comes back to self-centredness. Lack of *empathy* and *awareness* were characteristic of my attitude to expedition member Oleg Polunin. His sole purpose on the team was botanical exploration of the approaches to the mountain. In those days my contempt for flowers was total. As far as I was concerned we had a big and unknown mountain to climb and it needed his efforts as well as ours at least in order to become properly established on the long approach to the summit. It is one of the sadnesses of my life that when years later I became an avid botanist and even used his flower guides to the Alps and Mediterranean, I could not contact him and apologise for my earlier infantile attitude, because he had died.

The next experience I want to look at took place a few years after the Himalayan expedition. This was a day kayak trip on the river Wye on the Welsh border. The section of river was the sixteen miles between Builth Wells and Glasbury-on-Wye.

This is a classic canoe trip in a beautiful mountain valley. It is graded white water at grade II with one rapid of grade III.[2] There are seven main rapids extending up to a half mile in length. As an experienced white water kayaker I used this river section regularly when running the Oxford Outdoor Centre. My challenge was decidedly unusual. I decided to try and paddle the section *against* the river from Glasbury to Builth, without getting out of the boat. It was to be an upriver journey.

Without going into technicalities I knew this would present me with a severe challenge. The key was the grade III rapid known as Hell Hole. Most of the river funnelled down a narrow twisting channel which was impossible to paddle up. To do the trip meant waiting until the river rose in spate high enough to allow me to paddle up the rapid at the side of the twisting channel. Unfortunately the river in spate meant higher volumes of water flowing against me over the whole sixteen miles.

To complete the challenge, the final half mile or so to the finish at Buith Wells bridge was a continuous rapid without eddies.[3] This meant no places to rest when I was at my most fatigued.

The challenge was completed in one of the winters between 1966 and 1970. It took around eight hours. I was in my early thirties and was on my own.

In reflecting on the trip *at the time* I would have kept it very simple. It was a memorable journey that was probably unique in the history of canoeing on the Wye. Now I wish to explore deeper to see in what ways it might be of value in terms of my positive growth. The analogy I will use is that previously mentioned: of reviewing the action on the surface *first* and then exploring the *depths*, as though I were the ocean.

Physically I was stretched to my limits. Like the best of adventures the biggest challenge was at the end: the final rapid. I arrived at this point severely depleted in terms of physical energy. By the end my back was so stiff with lactic acid that I had to lie down on it whilst awaiting transport. These demands were essentially of endurance but each rapid also demanded power and skill to overcome it.

Mentally there was no question of a constant need for alertness. Whilst this was a very narrow focus (on each piece of water) I knew that I had to conserve my energy at all times. In other words I had to read the water precisely in order to see the best route. *Skill* was then needed to execute the movements. As the day progressed and fatigue became an increasing factor the need for alertness remained paramount.

Emotionally I loved canoeing and the challenge of being 'on the edge' of my capabilities. Fear was in the background mostly, except on one occasion on the crux of a particular rapid when I realised I might have got the angle of attack slightly wrong and I could easily be washed back down to the foot of the rapid. This would have meant at best a waste of energy. At worst I might have capsized, failed to eskimo roll, and been in trouble. Kayaking alone on rapids is frowned upon for obvious safety reasons. What matters in this context is that such matters were in my mind. I was not unaware in that sense.

With regard to *Spirituality* I initially described this aspect of being human as not only the most important aspect, but as "The base of our values and the source of our virtues and vices".

It is at this point that I need to reflect beneath the surface of myself. I now know that the source of this challenge was my unconscious in the form of my instinct for adventure and it was expressed through whitewater kayaking. I *valued* this activity as something I loved at that time. When it comes to the matter of the virtues and vices I have previously put forward twenty-six virtues as ideals towards which I should strive. I know that to a very large extent the virtues used in living define the quality or calibre of any human being.

This unusual kayak experience needs to be addressed against those virtues if I intend to know myself further in an "inner journey" sense. If the reader was asked to make an assessment of me, several virtues would seem almost self-evident. *Determination, Self-Reliance, Concentration, Awareness* (narrow focus on river), *Vitality* (Enthusiasm), *Simplicity* could all be obvious examples. Others may be less so. *Respect* was necessary for the river environment, underlined by the awareness that solo kayaking is considerably more dangerous than with others, accentuated by the river being in spate. *Patience* was also important. At all times I needed to conserve my energy because I knew, or sensed, that it would be a very close-run thing as to whether I would have enough energy for the final rapid. *Responsibilty* was also involved because I knew soloing was dangerous and unconventional and yet, using my own judgement, I decided the challenge was acceptable for my level of competence. *Creativity* too was very evident in the idea of the journey itself. Kayaking was traditionally down rivers rather than up rivers! It is also possible that *Purity* was involved. By that I mean that my motivation was not in any way clouded by the egocentrism of "hey look at what I have done". Fellow kayakers would have rated the idea as daft or "typical Colin"!

Two other virtues were also relevant. The use of *Self-discipline* was necessary to control fear. This was only on brief occasions where my actions were not as good as I hoped and capsize threatened. Having said that, despite familiarity with the river, that it was in spate and that I was alone (I saw no-one all day), probably meant that I used more of this virtue than I perhaps realised. The other virtue was the use of *Honesty*. I use that word in two senses. The challenge itself was not only simple as a concept but also demanded *exactness* in terms of my precise line up the rapids. I regard exactness or accuracy as an aspect of Honesty or Truth. The other way in terms of use of honesty is in my reflections on the experience. I would be less than honest, for example, if I did not say that that the more virtues I can find in this exercise the better I will be pleased. They will all support my deep feeling that natural examinations are deeply worthwhile experiences!

The virtue involved that most pleases me is that of *Empathy*. Sitting in an eddy just before tackling the crux of a rapid, I suddenly saw a large shadow beneath the kayak: a salmon. Intuitively I sensed my affinity with this magnificent fish. In order to successfully complete my journey I had to think like a salmon. Not only that but I had to try and use my skills as efficiently as the fish. I had to rest similarly in the eddies, then execute my movements as I went up each rapid. Each rapid, in spate, generally had a complex of possible routes, and yet only one was likely to be the best way; the one that required the least energy. What the salmon did naturally, had taken years of hard practice for me to emulate (apart from leaping up falls!). My thoughts went deeper. I knew these salmon had travelled from places like Greenland to swim up the Wye, and spawn at what was the end of a very long journey: a journey which made mine seem minuscule. How could I not feel a high degree of *Humility*. There was no place here for *Arrogance*. There was also the somewhat amusing thought that my contrived and unconventional upriver challenge was completely natural for the salmon!

Little mention has been made here of the twenty-six vices. Most I sense were not present. The major exceptions are the obvious ones of *Self-centredness, Selfishness* and egoism. I cannot deny the existence of the first two. The latter was essentially killed by realising how important the salmon was, both in terms of putting my journey in perspective and that in some inexplicable way I had a link with the salmon. In light of my much later awareness of the unity of all things natural I suspect this trip was an important experience. It was also important in terms of a build up of self-confidence for much more dangerous and demanding solo expeditions to come.

In finishing with this experience, a few comments concerning the specific wisdoms mentioned earlier in the book. That of *action/reflection* at the time lacked any depth of reflection. The *search for the truth* was relevant only in a shallow sense, though perhaps very important at that time. This was: I had an idea of a challenge. Taking it on revealed the truth of the matter. The practice worked out. *A sense of Awe and Wonder* was not relevant except perhaps with the thought of where the salmon had come from. (A six-metre flood on this section of the Wye gave me that sense as seen from the bank!) The *concept* of *singular/universal* or conscious/unconscious was relevant, as recently (2006) scientific research has shown that the unconscious takes aboard a very considerable number of messages about the surroundings, regardless of what the conscious is doing. I have no way of knowing what information was stored and how it may have contributed to what I now believe. With reference to the pillars of wisdom from Nature three of the five mentioned earlier in this book were very prominent. *Uncertainty* was a constant. It was an adventure in a natural and beautiful setting. *Energy*, effort and skills were also in constant demand as was *balance*! There were, however, no conscious experiences of *unity*, except possibly the seeing of the salmon, nor of *beauty*.

In terms of the virtues then, fifteen of the twenty-six originally listed, were to a greater or lesser extent, involved in the journey. Significantly almost all of the eleven other virtues were not relevant because they were not directly applicable to a solo journey. In other words these eleven virtues were those concerned with human relationships.

The third natural examination I wish to review takes place in the summer of 1998, nearly forty years later. I am aged 62 and Annette is slightly younger. For this exercise I am using days six and seven of a twenty day Pyrenean expedition.[4] Day six turns out to be an interesting and physically demanding affair. In eight hours we cover only about 12 kilometres but climb around 1400 metres up the Spanish side of Monte Perdido (3355 metres). The start of the day, from a wild camp, is spent heading west across indistinct trails at the head of the Pineta Valley. After a failed attempt to find a little used track over the frontier ridge, we continue west to join the main track. Long hours follow of uphill toil in hot sun and bring us to a magnificent tiny campsite at 2530 metres. From the tent door we overlook the Pineta Valley and another world below. The site, on gravel, is very exposed but the weather seems set fair.

An early start the next day sees us enter another world of snow, rock, and ice-encrusted lakes. Once the route is found, we scramble up a loose, dangerous gully to a nick in the rocky frontier ridge. This is the Breche de Tuqueroye (2666 metres) complete with a metal box emergency shelter. Annette's biggest Pyrenean adventure is about to begin and she can sense it. From the nick in the ridge our unmarked way into France lies down a steep and exposed 300 metre snow and ice slope. Walker's 6-point crampons are put on, and our trekking poles are exchanged for our light-weight ice axes. The dramatic descent begins. We are extremely fortunate. This north-facing slope has had a slight thaw and it is just possible to break the surface with my boots before using the axe to enlarge the steps. Annette follows me down, step by step, and with infinite care. She is unused to such places. I know that our equipment is not really suitable for such a place. Eventually, and with considerable relief, we reach the foot of the slope. Camp that night – overlooking Gavarnie and with views across to the Brèche de Roland – is an enjoyable affair. A big adventure under our belts; some wonderful flowers to add to our list and tomorrow a rest day and fresh food in the town below.

In reviewing this very different experience from the kayak trip up the river Wye I want to concentrate on the virtues not relevant to the latter. First, however, I will briefly look at the aspects common to both journeys. Physically, mentally and emotionally these two days were demanding. Annette and I loved the Pyrenees, not least for their wildness, their beauty, and their alpine flowers. We accepted without question the hard work and simple living involved. The descent from the ridge was a heart in the mouth affair for Annette. *Concentration* at such times was normal. *Self-reliance* was interesting in this situation. I was self-reliant in that I took it as read that if she slipped I *had* to save her. (She was inexperienced in ice axe breaking.) This was also my use of *Responsibility*. Annette had to use her *Self-reliance* when making each move, although psychologically she knew I was there to help if necessary. Naturally both of us were using *Awareness* to our fullest extent. This narrow focus of awareness is directly comparable to the awareness of the rapids as I went up the river Wye. When I think of awareness in terms of a broad awareness – full environmental awareness would be a better phrase – then in a personal sense the difference for me between the two experiences (thirty odd years apart) is almost startling. On this later trip I doubt I could have been more aware of my surroundings. I had literally spent months expeditioning in such places as a pilgrim – looking as keenly as possible at all around me, and not least for the alpine flowers. I saw *beauty* everywhere and a sense of awe and wonder was commonplace. Similarly was the matter of *unity*. I felt part of this wild Nature, much more so than when back in the man-made world.

Concerning virtues so far unmentioned, I wish to look at those to do with the individual in a social context. I could simply state that as Annette was the ideal expedition companion then she exhibited all eleven of them. By so doing, and because of my utmost respect for her in expedition mode, I followed her example. In other words she brought out the best in me by the example she set. As others who knew her well have confirmed, she was the epitome of goodness and naturalness. A few examples may help to illustrate the point. Both of us were compassionate and altruistic when required. On that descent from the frontier ridge, and other dangerous situations, I knew Annette did not have my mountaineering experience. I accepted I was responsible for her safety at all times. *Friendliness*, *Kindness*, and *Gentleness* were characteristics of her, as was *Tolerance*. To a degree she shaped these virtues within me – as far as was possible as I tended towards their opposing vices at times.

Gratitude was not a virtue I ever thought about on expeditions except for being grateful every time a dangerous situation was overcome! I sense it was almost a subconscious virtue in that, intuitively at least, I was grateful for all the positive events on an expedition such as a flat area to camp on; sun after a storm; finding water or an exquisite flower. *Forgiveness* was rarely in use because of the strength of our relationship. Justice or *Fairness* was a given because we knew and accepted the importance of always working as a team. A particular example was the constant need for both of us to show *Patience*. Annette was a very keen macro-photographer of alpine flowers. This is technically and *creatively* a very demanding activity where time, unlike timing, is of no importance. I, on the other hand, was the one who always wanted to move on. These were two awkward and opposing objectives of our expeditions. We accepted them. Courage was not a feature, but I suspect some of our actions were a severe test of *Self-discipline*, when fear lurked strongly and had to be overcome psychologically and then action had to proceed. As far as *Humour*, whilst it was not a strong characteristic of either of us, we could both appreciate it. The camp overlooking the Pineta Valley for example, had a wondrous and spectacular view. It was also ridiculous as a campsite. Even half a gale would have blown it away!

In trying to summarise this chapter I am conscious that this has been a very crude analysis of the deeper values of such experiences. Virtues and vices for example are not only dynamic but often merge into each other. Nevertheless, having done this analysis it has confirmed my intuitive belief that such experiences have magnificent potential to help the individual grow towards full maturity in all positive senses. It would be fascinating to take experiences from the man-made world, such as conventional sports, and try to evaluate them using similar criteria.

21

Looking Back

Throughout the book, and from the last chapter in particular, it is very evident that I have great enthusiasm for the value of suitable experiences in wild Nature in terms of developing positive potential. In chapter two, The Instinct for Adventure, I wrote the following:

> *"As I write this in 2007 I am acutely conscious of how, deep down, I am very angry and frustrated at what has not happened in adventure activities with young people in the UK. By now it should be normal for all young people in this country to have Outdoor Education as a key part of their education – and in that programme the adventure should be at the level of the needs and abilities of each pupil."*

That anger and frustration is directly due to the fact that education out of doors generally, and *Adventure* and *Expeditions* in particular, have become bedevilled, if not almost strangled, by a plethora of rules, regulations and risk assessments.

Writing this chapter today I happened to read over lunch *The Times* main article (17 January 2008) entitled "Caution! The State has gone haywire". The article reports the establishment of "the new anti-nanny quango, the Risk and Reformation Advisory Council" which will assess whether the Health and Safety Executive has gone "over the top". A few examples are given that are almost beyond belief. These include the dangerous game of conkers; the dangers of hanging baskets; the refusal to allow some parents to borrow armbands for their toddlers' swimming pool session because "they might contain germs"; and not least the coastguard who recently resigned because he was censured for not wearing a safety harness. He had rescued a girl from falling off the crumbling top of a sea cliff, and thereby saved her life. It was his professional opinion that, *in the situation*, he did not have the time to first go and get the required pieces of equipment!

It is no wonder I am both angry and very sad at the same time. Throughout my working life in Adventure Education, from Manchester Grammar School in 1972, the six years at the Oxford Centre, and the College in Ambleside until I retired in 1992, there was, as far as I know, no Health and Safety Executive. If it existed, then it had no part in Outdoor Education. During this period National Qualifications for the different adventure activities were developed and eventually demanded by the Authorities. As this took place, I know I was not alone in viewing them as 'amateur pieces of paper'. Those of us working with young people at that time *knew* that the activities were dangerous. We took pride in what we regarded as our *professional* approach. Yes we provided, and were responsible for, exciting and worthwhile adventure activities but it was total common sense to bring all the young people back at the end of the day's experience. The majority of teachers and instructors involved were themselves adventurers. In other words they *knew from experience* what they were doing. In general their skills and competence were several grades higher than those whom they taught. When I ran the Woodlands Outdoor Centre, for example, I had *complete* confidence in my staff. I sensed that they had confidence in me. I shared the dangerous activities, such as expeditions. Canoeing was my particular role, which was mirrored by a caver, a climber and so on. When I just wrote *"complete confidence"*, that phrase needs to be qualified. 'Complete' is too strong. Like 'perfection', in terms of human action, it is inaccurate. By definition *all* human beings make mistakes. In other words accidents can and do happen. This is especially true when working or playing in wild Nature because it is dynamic.

What particularly incenses me is that for most of my working life I was working on the edge of what was acceptable in Adventure Education. In every aspect of society there needs to be people in this frontier situation. This is what leads to progression rather than regression. In the book I have given a few examples of being 'on the edge' where I was directly responsible for the young people. These were never enjoyable occasions for me personally. There was always the threat of 'what if something goes wrong?', and knowing that society, or at least the media, would have a field day. Fortunately my conscience was clear and my arbiter has always been my conscience. In all those years it became evident that this was a magnificent form of education that was loved by young people. Amongst many other things being learnt, such as the virtues thriving rather than the vices, was that, suitably trained, even ten to twelve year old boys and girls are eminently capable of one week expeditions in wild country *without* adults.

It is not appropriate here to try and work out what went wrong in our society, though I feel sure the clamp imposed on the freedom of the outdoors for young people in my lifetime is but a tiny part of a general decline in civilisation. I do sense it has emanated from, and been fuelled by a climate of fear or anxiety. I also would be less than honest if I did not report that my attitude to being British has taken a severe downward spiral. Once very proud of my country as a young man, I now take no pleasure in that fact. That comment needs a little explanation. It comes from experiences. One was giving a keynote lecture on Values, Adventure and Young People in Australia. I was astonished to find that the majority of my audience were ex-poms. Whilst they had their own reasons for emigrating there was a strong agreement about the need to get away from UK bureaucracy and red tape. I was later to find similar echoes in Canada and New Zealand. Another group of experiences was to do with finding other people both in outdoor work and education generally who were principally interested in protecting their position and were dominated by self-interest. Politics, if not internecine warfare, I was to find, was a common feature of higher education.

Above all, perhaps, I sense that many, if not the majority, in positions of power within society both at local and national levels, tend towards the vice of cowardice rather than the virtue of courage. When I think that history clearly displays that there is no nation on earth that begins to compare with the British in terms of adventure and exploration, and yet accepts almost unbelievably restrictive practices around education out of doors then something is radically wrong and reeks of hypocrisy.

It may be apposite to repeat the words of Professor Whitehead from the 1930s. First that he saw five characteristics of any civilised society. These were *Beauty, Truth, Peace, Art* and *Adventure*. I wrote earlier that at least three of these were characteristic of experience in wild Nature (and not least for young people). Secondly his classic statement:

> *"A race preserves its vigour so long as it harbours a real contrast between what has been and what may be; and so long as it is nerved by the vigour to adventure beyond the safeties of the past. Without adventure civilisation is in full decay."*

22

Towards A Better World

"Nothing in this world is as powerful as an idea whose time has come."

Victor Hugo

Some ideas are proposed here as a basis for a more worthwhile, a more civilised and a more equitable world. As you would expect from this author, experiences in wild Nature, adventures and expeditions, would make a major and essential contribution. I am sufficiently optimistic to believe that the following *hypothetical* main article in *The Times* could become a reality!

A RADICAL CONCEPT

In the light of the severe decline in civilised behaviour characterised by a selfish, materialistic outlook on life; along with the dishonesty endemic from the top to the bottom of our society, radical actions are obviously needed. Bearing in mind also the very real threats of obesity and mental stress endemic in our modern world and that there is much honesty and wisdom to be gained from experiencing the reality of wild Nature, then, in the first instance, I make the following recommendation:

ALL MEMBERS OF PARLIAMENT SHOULD UNDERTAKE A SELF-RELIANT EXPEDITION IN WILD COUNTRY IN THE UK WITHIN THE NEXT TWELVE MONTHS. [1]

The following conditions will apply:

A minimum of one-week duration in vacation time.
A journey that is physically demanding and containing natural dangers.
Numbers in party from one to four; members of similar outdoor experience.
Simple living – tents or bivouacs only.
All equipment and food to be carried.
Journeys to be approved by local 'wild area' panels, made up of citizens with suitable outdoor experience.
A diary to be kept by each member and the journey to be evaluated.
These to be made available to public scrutiny.
No publicity.

MPs represent the citizens of this country. If there is sufficient support for this idea from the public, then a referendum will be organised to see if this expedition idea could become a reality.

If this becomes the case, then the idea will then be extended to all councillors, teachers and headteachers. If there is then a consensus in favour of this type of experience, then, in due course, expeditions will be extended to all pupils in both primary and secondary schools.[2] It should then naturally follow that 'education out of doors' will become an essential element of education.

In an ideal modern world this concept would become an important and integral part of our life. Families, for example, would be eligible for government grants to go on expedition. Eventually all peoples and cultures would accept the need to live in harmony with their natural surroundings. They would also accept that hard work and honest toil are basic to the growth of everything in Nature. Everyone would also agree to accept the implications of the following principle:

To live with
an awareness of, respect for, and love of self [3]

balanced with
an awareness of, respect for, and love of others

balanced with
an awareness of, respect for, and love of the environment

Comments on such an article

The reader may think the author is ridiculous to compose such an article – even in theory. I could not be more serious. All my experience across the age ranges; all my own adventures and expeditions, have completely convinced me that such a preposterous idea needs to become a reality. Such is the decline in civilisation; the cult of the individual *without* the responsibilities; the ever widening gap between the 'haves' and 'have-nots' and the destruction of wild Nature for greedy 'live now, pay later' reasons make such an idea essential. Radical problems demand radical solutions. Modern living divorces human beings from their natural roots. Wild Nature, as I have tried to indicate in this book, is vastly more than an environment in which to merely have fun, to study and to use as a resource.

From my deepest unconscious, from where my instinct for adventure is located, comes the intuition that:

Wild nature resides in each individual, and this is mostly within our unconscious.

We need to explore through natural journey experiences what this means.

From these same personal depths came:

> **Everything in nature is alive in its own way; is on its own adventurous journey and deserves its own well-being. Everything in nature, from micro to macro, is no less and no more important than anything else. This includes human beings.**

Our human world needs to be built on this statement. It means an attitude of minimal destruction to everything natural around us. It means maximum awareness and humility towards wild Nature. The natural world is an expression of, or synonymous with, what we term God, or *Transcendent Mystery*.

It means we could create a new way of living taking these and many similar principles as our framework for what we do with our lives.

For this to happen we need to be enthusiastic about our amazing potential in all positive senses of being human. We also need all members of our society, and not least the politicians and other people in positions of power, to base their decisions on that foundation virtue of honesty. In that process there is an urgent need to move away from human and self-centred actions to those that are eco-centred.

There is a need also to build a society based more on universal love rather than fear and anxiety; a society that encourages the use of the virtues rather than the vices. At an individual level there is a need to look openly and honestly at those basic questions of *Who am I? Where am I going?* and *How do I get there?* These are difficult questions at the best of times. In the rush and stress of modern living they can become formidable and very easily put to one side. To do this is not only cowardly but will hasten the further decline of civilisation. These are strong words. They are necessary because far too often the individual tries to hide from their deeper self by ignoring his or her responsibilities. A life so lived is an all too convenient lie. Each of us has responsibilities and links to all other human beings. Each of us also is indelibly linked to the natural world. We should embrace and enjoy the responsibilities involved.

There is nothing more important to discuss and contemplate than the great questions concerning our existence and how life is best lived. I find it very sad, as well as a graphic illustration of the decline of society, that such questions are seldom a feature of conversation. Thoughts and ideas are the basis of how we live in practice. Each of us, to a great extent, chooses how to live our lives. This needs to be based on a *personal values framework* that is both coherent and simply expressed to those around us.

We do have the potential to leave the world a better place than is currently the case. For this to happen demands radical action at all levels and demands a positive and open response from each individual in terms of how they intend to journey through life.

23

Epilogue

In my lectures, especially in the last ten years, I have on occasions lost track of time in my own enthusiasm for the subject. The effect on audiences has been noticeably more intense, almost as though more warmth has been generated in a cold room. Eventually I sensed that wild Nature was speaking *through* me. In other words, I was a conduit. This made me feel both humble and embarrassed. Close friends advised me that feeling like a conduit was both acceptable and not that unusual. I remained unconvinced. That is until recently when the obvious finally fell into place. Early in the book I mentioned that as a result of unusual experiences in general, and the high plateau of the solo kayak Alaskan experience in particular, I could only conclude that I *was Nature*, even if most of Nature resided in my *unconscious* rather than in my *conscious* self. In other words, in lectures where I forgot time it was my *unconscious*, something *within* me, trying to communicate directly to the audience.

Why do I mention this now? The answer is to do with living in the *now*. In those lectures, those involving my unconscious were far more effective because the audience were receiving 'the depths' of the speaker. 'Speaking from the heart' would be an appropriate phrase. Finally I will come to the specific point here which is: 'in writing this book how much have I lived in the now?' There is no doubt that I have been consumed by the process. It has been an adventure and remains so with all the polishing and amending necessary before going to publication. I have enjoyed the challenge of what has been an intense *indoor expedition* (except for when the sun shone!).

In other words, I have lived the book, trying to write something daily, from the heart and as naturally as possible. The rest of my life has been comparatively unimportant except to preserve my sanity! It has been very much 'a journey with a degree of uncertainty' and not a little fear: especially the thought at times that I would not begin to do justice to the immensity of my subject. There have been occasions also when writing, when I didn't know where I was going until it was written – an exciting learning process! Overall, however, I have loved doing it and felt privileged in the process. The wisdom of Tagore seems apposite. He believed not only that knowing himself was not the final truth but also that letting himself be known was also of great importance.

I feel like adding a rider to this wisdom: "Yes, providing that 'myself' essentially means my unconscious self (wild Nature) rather than merely my conscious and egoistic self."

An important and necessary part of 'the rest of my life' during this writing process has been climbing a Lakeland hill around dawn on alternate days. The early, dark and often cold starts along with the effort involved going up steep hills is hugely outweighed by the benefits. The beauty of a wild hill, in all its moods, never tires. Psychological satisfaction is considerable. More often than not, I also return with further ideas for the next chapter. There is a simple beauty in the balance of indoor and outdoor expeditions. Even then there is something else so easy to forget and yet so important to me. On the hill the *whole* of me is involved *naturally* – much more of a natural *unity* of self than when sitting at a desk. The human being is designed not to sit but to move simply in a natural environment.

One of my reflections on the hill recently concerned the importance of books in my life. The ones in my house – and there are many – I regard as friends. A few of the authors I know, and others I have known. The majority I do not know and yet many I feel I do know. They span the ages. Yet I treat them as friends. If the most important part of being human is the intangible *spirit*, then it is the spirit of the authors that share my living space. I believe implicitly that there can be heart to heart contact, even across the ages, because of the underlying unity of everything in Nature.

Two of the books I am currently reading are biographies of particular heroes. I love what they are about and find them inspirational. From Albert Schweitzer:

> *"A philosopher – he sees the Truth as something which is beyond the power of abstract thought either to discover or comprehend, and finds that the more systematized any philosophical system so much the more fallacious it can be shown to be."* [1]

> *"I wanted to be a doctor that I might be able to work without having to talk…but this new form of activity I could not represent to myself as talking about the religion of love, but only as an actual putting of it into practice."* — Ibid.

And from Edward Wilson, the doctor on Scott's last expedition; as quoted by his biographer George Seaver:

> *"To make love the ruling power of my life, the only power. To be kind, gentle, considerate and unselfish…never to consider myself and my own feelings but only other peoples'…to put myself out, especially for the sake of those who are not attractive."* [2]

And:

> *"He saw Beauty not only in the tenderness of springtide and the glory of summer, but also in the frailty and transparency of fading leaves, sickness, old age, and even death. He saw it also in moral excellence and mental achievement. Beauty and Goodness were for him but aspects of the same eternal Truth which is another name for Love. 'Love comes to me by one channel only – the recognition of some beauty, whether mental, moral or physical; colour or form or sound; so long as it represents to me a type, however lowly, of my conception of what is perfect – there is beauty."* [3]

I know little of art but I love the paintings of Hokusai, and especially his famous 'The Wave'. I admire the following which he wrote at the young age of seventy five:

"*From the age of six I had a mania for drawing the form of things. By the time I was fifty I had published an infinity of designs; but all I have produced before the age of seventy is not worth taking into account. At seventy-three I have learned a little about the real structure of nature, of animals, plants, birds, fishes and insects. In consequence when I am eighty, I shall have made more progress; at ninety I shall penetrate the mystery of things; at a hundred I shall certainly have reached a marvellous stage; and when I am a hundred and ten, everything I do, be it but a dot or a line, will be alive.*" [4]

And, finally, from Dogen Zenji:

"*Enlightenment is like the moon reflected on the water. The moon does not get wet, nor is the water broken. Altho' its light is wide and great, the moon is reflected even in a puddle an inch wide. The whole moon and the entire sky are reflected in one dewdrop on the grass.*"

24

Postscript

Most of 2008 was taken up waiting impatiently for publishers responses to the manuscript. It was almost with relief that, in the autumn, a decision was taken to self-publish. I could hardly complain as my work was confronting the attitude of 'money is the bottom line of everything'. Confidence in what I had written remained undiminished.

My impatience at the waiting for much of the year was stupid. Various developments, apart from improving the script, took place that were to have positive effects concerning eventual publication and promotion of the values expressed.

The first of these developments was Tracy Dixon writing the Introduction to the Author. From the moment I saw what she had written, I knew we were kindred spirits with regard to the values of wild Nature. It also brought some feelings of relief. I was only too aware of how easy it would be for my ideas to be ignored or dismissed as the irrelevant musings of an old man who had no place in a youthful action packed modern world. Now I had a strong bridge. Even better was that her new post was with The Outward Bound Trust. Not only had I spent quality time in recent years with friends at Outward Bound New Zealand, but, as a student, I had both met and been inspired by Kurt Hahn, the founder of Outward Bound. I also remembered that in the late 80s I had given the Hahn lecture to the Round Square Conference. This international group of schools, that included Gordonstoun, were committed to the educational philosophy of Hahn. In that particular year, their conference was held at St. Anne's School in the Lake District. My subject was the philosophy (values) of Outdoor Education as practiced at my College. I was delighted to find that Hahn's aim of education was the development of the whole person in the pursuit of truth.

Significantly perhaps, as an idealist, I was disappointed by the response to the lecture. Despite ample time for discussion, none of the 90 or so heads and staff took issue with any of the values I expressed. That was the good news. The bad news was that only one of the schools comprehensively practiced these values (and that closed within a year!). It was obvious that the demands of examinations and all the conventional measureable requirements of the modern world held sway. In my ideal world I would have both the Round Square Conference schools and Outward Bound International – with all its Centres world-wide – taking a lead and promoting the values implicit in The Spirit of Adventure.

The second development concerned the idea of lectures. It may have been memories of the 1970s when I had lectured extensively around Britain on the importance of adventure for young people, that triggered the thought that I now needed to do two lectures to roughly coincide with the publication of the book. One of these would be a public one. The other would be for those involved in education out of doors.

With regard to the latter it seemed sensible to contact the Institute for Outdoor Learning to see if they would host the lecture. One autumnal afternoon Karen Frith, the Chief Executive, duly arrived at my home to discuss the matter. In what seemed no time at all she had to leave. In reality four hours had flashed by and I sensed another strong bridge was being built. This was quickly confirmed by another meeting after she had read the book. The traditional loneliness of the writer was now fading rapidly. In its place was the joy of the unity of enthusiasm for what promises to be an exciting project.

To return to the matter of the public lecture, I eventually settled on a lecture title:

**Outdoor experiences and the future,
or demise, of civilisation.**

The more I thought about the implications of this radical title the more convinced I became of the almost unbelievable *potential* importance of the wild Nature experience. Whether that potential becomes a reality however, depends on the attitude and awareness of each individual involved.

I will try and explain what I mean using the following example. A young person experiences an adventure in wild Nature; subdues their fears; uses effort and skills and finally overcomes the challenge. The resultant 'feel good' factor is both natural and justifiable. This is the best way – through direct experience – that the young person learns genuine self-respect, along with the increased desire to face further challenges.

The attitude of the young person after such an experience can literally affect the rest of their life. The choice lies between two extremes: separation as an approach to life or unity as an approach to life. The former might be termed the conventional modern view whilst the latter might be termed the truly natural view. How much does this matter? As a basis not only for how one approaches life but also how one lives the detail of their life I cannot think of any more important decision to make.

The obvious separatist view is not only dishonest but has led to the disaster that is the modern world. My criterion here is the positive potential of being human in all senses. This view, this disaster of a modern world, is built on money, status and power and the cult of the individual *without* responsibilities. It is also, consciously or unconsciously, the acceptance of the vices of selfishness and arrogance. When I reflect over my life I see innumerable faces of individuals, not least in education, bureaucracy and in positions of authority who appear to enjoy their separateness. How many of them, I wonder, would genuinely accept that they are no more and no less important than a pebble or a daisy. I feel immensely saddened at how this self-centred and egoistic attitude has caused mayhem throughout history. In the short timespan of man on earth, countless numbers of humans have been maimed and destroyed; other life forms decimated; and pollution has effected every corner of the planet and beyond. The phrase *homosapiens* must be the sickest joke of all.

We do not have to accept this approach to life. The alternative – accepting that it should be one of unity – in the first instance the unity of the conscious egoistic self with the deeper unconscious self – and then with the rest of Nature, has to be the true and common sense approach. To accept that viewpoint in practice, however, I suspect, can be a formidable challenge. Certainly for me it took until middle age. The solo kayak experience in Alaska – the high plateau experience – at last transcended that deeply entrenched feeling of "of course I am separate". Once I had begun to realise that unity was the basis of my existence; and that universal love, as personified by the way Annette lived, was the driving force behind evolution, I began at last to grow up and appreciate the joy as well as the sadness of human existence.

The rest of wild Nature, naturally and wonderfully, evolves – keeps progressing. Modern man, unless he honestly accepts the underlying unity of all life, cannot be part of that progression. His separatist world – the world of wanting, constant re-crimination and bickering, is a world of regression…the evidence is there for us all to see.

A walk up the hill, uplifting in every sense on a beautiful autumn morning. I decide to see if can write a few final paragraphs. As usual I have a jumble of thoughts, including "too many words already". No matter. I need to try.

Whoever it was that suggested the human race links hands across the globe and then the individuals at each end insert the fingers of their spare hand into a light socket may have been a cynic. In terms of destruction already perpetrated by the human race such a suggestion, however, carries strong echoes of truth.

In light of the urgency of the current situation it seems essential that:

- Each individual looks honestly at how they can practically, as well as psychologically, relate back to their unity with Nature (to make conscious what lies within their unconscious).
- All organisations involved with using wild Nature for providing experiences – educationally; recreationally or commercially, do so with honesty rather than dishonesty; with humility rather than arrogance; and awareness rather than ignorance of the wonders and implications of the natural world.
- Lead organisations and centres concerned with the outdoors promote the deep values implicit in outdoor experiences:
  - beauty – truth – wisdom – freedom
  - the virtues and not the vices
  - the unity

To accomplish this is perhaps the biggest challenge of all.

Appendices

Appendix A

Annette (1939–2003)

The unexpected demise of Annette led to the birth of this book. It seems highly relevant to give the reader a pen picture of her.

From 2004 to 2007 an exhibition was held alongside the Quaker Tapestry in Kendal, Cumbria. It was entitled:

"The Expedition Diaries of a Remarkable Quaker Lady"

It was an interactive display of exquisite diaries, paintings and photographs. Between 1991 and 2002 she went on expeditions with me to the mountain ranges of Europe, especially the Pyrenees. During this time she trekked 3,786 miles and made 268,690 metres of ascent (although she had no interest in such figures!). It was her habit to work on her diaries every night when on expedition, regardless of fatigue from what were generally physically demanding days. The purpose of the diaries was for her old friends to enjoy her experiences.

A teaching colleague and close friend of Annette, wrote the following about her:

"Trying to describe her is like trying to catch sunlight in a string bag.

"When they approach death, great artists see life more clearly.

"Her (heightened) awareness of transcendence and her absolute directness of vision.

"Quaker. Nature – knowledge of plants, animals, geology, bee keeping, woodland, W.I gardening, fruit picking, jam making, cooking. Books. Teaching school and Brownies. Travel and expeditions. Environmentalism. Philosophy. Dyeing with natural vegetable colours. Spinning. Weaving. Laughter. Non-judgmental. Facilitator. Tolerant. Flowers. Painting and photography. Welcoming.

"Annette had a gift for friendship wherever she travelled. With her sparkling spirit, infectious and often irreverent laughter, boundless energy, optimism, enthusiasm and eternally outward gaze, she had the touch that opens new horizons. Always open to people and experiences, wherever she was became home, with a welcoming brew – which may have been delayed by yarns about her life and tales of her family – and a kindly touch, while her eyes danced with the fun of life. She radiated warmth and generosity. Generous with her thoughts and ideas, multi-talented, she always saw the potential in anyone's skills or talents, however small. Living each day with love and energy, the joy, compassion and creative imagination of this remarkable and exceptional woman made her a healer. She had the ability to lift the spirits of others and make them see possibilities in themselves previously undreamed of.

There was the memorable 'orchid walk' when the rare and common orchids on Whitbarrow and the butterflies showed her knowledge of, and delight in, Nature. Many were the ways in which Annette shared her sheer joy and enthusiasm for life. It was infectious as was her lovely and loving smile, as was the laughter which rang out and lightened many a loaded situation. Christmas time brought us to the plantation where we dug up our Christmas trees so that they could be replanted afterwards. All life was precious, beloved and accorded its own due of sacredness.

A healer, bringing compassion and imagination to sorrow, pain or fear, she led the way both metaphorically and physically, not for self-seeking, but simply because she was braver than others, whether it was exploring new ideas or new routes. A nervous friend, 'enjoying' a vertiginous walk in the high Pyrenees, was encouraged to find a way round a nose of rock, where the down view was simply thin air, by an exhortation to 'keep an eye on my green boots and just follow them round!'.

She was one of the first pioneering generation of students of Lancaster Universities' MA course "Values and the Environment", bringing her enthusiasm and relevant wilderness experience to the venture, as ready for intellectual as for physical adventure and to combine the two. It was natural to her to relate theory and practice. Her dissertation was on the idea of "friluftsliv" that Arne Naess makes a central concept of his ecophilosophy. Never content with half-measures, Annette spent a vacation in Norway to experience friluftsliv at first hand and to interview one of Naess' collaborators which resulted in a fascinating, entirely original piece of research. She was as inspiring a student as she was a teacher.

Rising early and living each day with love and energy, she was a shaft of bright sunlight, an understanding and humorous friend who could always shed a new light on things and show just how exceptional life can be, welcoming and enjoying all the rich diversity in Nature and in the human heart. With creativity, she opened the doors of perception for her own beloved daughters and her pupils with joyous playful vision. There were always so many things on the go, but never any sense of tension, just her beaming smile and laughter, always laughter…one of the outward expressions of all her special inner qualities. The effect she had on all who knew her was totally self-less; she was not interested in exerting power over others, but in releasing them from any constraints by empowering their imaginations and hearts."

Appendices

Appendix B

Author Background

Since my Oxford days as a young student I have had an urge to try to understand something of the great philosophical questions concerning human existence. Long have I been convinced through practical experiences with young people, that adventure was instinctive. To be curious, to explore, seems natural as an instinct because our earliest forebears living in the wilderness, of necessity faced dangers daily. It is only in my later years, however, that my urge to understand the mystery of existence I can now see clearly, is the *same* instinct – to journey further *'inwards'* rather than the more obvious 'outwards'. Indeed I now find the inner journey becoming increasingly exciting as I have more glimmerings of understanding.

I write essentially from a background of *practical* experience. By that I mean essentially 'the whole of me' which as my life has been mainly concerned with adventure in wild Nature then inevitably it has to have a significant element of my *physical* nature. That fact, the *physical* involvement in the experience, I regard as a considerable source of strength for my ideas. Whatever I read or think can mostly be tested in the honest reality of the natural world. It is worth remembering the classic statement by Thoreau:

> *"In wildness lies the preservation of the world."*

Since time immemorial leaders of men, as well as hermits and lone travellers, have sought to understand the great mysteries of life by journeying and living simply in wilderness.

The other practical base that has helped my understanding very considerably is my late wife Annette. For over forty years I had the exceptional good fortune to share her love of both the natural world and the human race. The way she lived her life was both inspiring and exemplary. Most unusual is a human being gifted in so many ways and yet with a lifestyle so unselfish. It was no surprise to find, after she had gone, that the word 'Love' was very frequently used to describe her by those who knew her.

The third source for the development of my ideas has come from a lifetime of reading widely, and discussions through conferences and correspondence. This source – other people – has been invaluable. Other people's experiences, however, at best, can only be the mortar between the bricks of one's own experience. I can learn from and be inspired by other people – their actions and their ideas. I now know that can never be a substitute for my own practical experience. In this way only can I hope to gain the reality of wisdom.

As Cargas says:

> *"The message the mystics have for us is that while there is indeed a very real world 'out there', there is a more real world within each of us. The meaning of this cosmic centre is: each must learn individually. I am the living text for me, the only text I cannot learn*

the lesson from what another has experienced or has written. Some can help me on the periphery, but the heart of the matter is in the heart of my soul."

Apart from my enduring interest in the questions concerning human existence, three broad strands have interwoven through my life. They are work, play and family life. Work, apart from the initial four years at the Royal Wolverhampton School and then Manchester Grammar School, focussed almost entirely on what I defined as Adventure Education. Even at Manchester Grammar School, my life in the final year was largely involved in leading a large schoolboy expedition to Arctic Norway. The six years running the City of Oxford Outdoor Centre in Wales was followed by teacher training at what was then the Charlotte Mason College at Ambleside in the Lake District. This period of my life coincided with what was the heyday of adventure activities for young people in Britain. These were exciting times for me. I often felt I was on the crest of a wave. Apart from my normal work, I was writing, starting associations, helping create courses in Ireland and establishing community projects. In addition I was lecturing on Adventure and Values the length of Britain and giving keynote lectures abroad.

Outdoor play, or recreation, remained a major part of my life whenever time permitted. The decision to give up climbing after sixteen years of commitment shocked me. I loved the activity but felt I had reached a plateau in terms of improvement. I then took up other forms of adventure – white water river canoeing; catamaran sailing; sea kayaking; and finally trekking and steep walking.[1] It was in my nature to take up one of these activities at a time, and then pursue it towards the limits of my abilities. Each of these enthusiasms was to last many years. This gave me time to develop advanced skills and to begin to appreciate the particular attractions of each form of adventure.

Completely unexpectedly, there was also a period in the early 1980s where my major passion became searching for and identifying wild flowers. For a year or so this became my sole form of recreational adventure, before it became a major and integral part of my wilderness exploring and trekking.

Life with Annette and the family almost inevitably took much of a backseat with the demands of my work, especially as I was seen as something of a leader in what was taking place. This lack of time with Annette was not helped by the demands of my recreative climbing and canoeing. My levels of adventure meant Annette was not involved. She never had the time, even if she had the inclination, to train hard. In any event, being mum to three girls was a full-time job in itself. This was made even more onerous for her as, until she retired, she was also a teacher. Extreme one-sidedness in terms of Annette bringing up our young family almost single-handed, was only infrequently balanced by more than my fleeting involvement. This often took the form of one-week expeditions by the whole family when the youngsters were still very young. A favourite area were the islands off the west coast of Scotland.

---

[1] An unconventional activity taking ways up hills, following natural features and avoiding recognised paths and scrambles.

All equipment was carried and a tent shared. In terms of time they were of short duration. In terms of value they were very rich periods for all of us – a life shared in wild Nature. I still have vivid memories of Annette carrying Tiree, the youngest, on her front; a large and full rucksack on her back (for balance!). Great memories also remain of Vember and Senja. For example after a gruelling coastline trek in bad weather we were all shattered. Soon after a brew the youngsters went back out of the tent and spent hours playing, jumping off the large sand dunes!

To summarise my background I guess the word *adventure* would dominate. I just hope that the self-centredness implicit in that word has largely been banished by how I see myself in my advanced years!

Acknowledgements

My grateful thanks to:

Marian Armstrong
Jeanni Barlow
Monica Baynes
Max Biden
Linda Bourne
Senja Bownes
Geoff Cohen
Rob Collister
Jillian Cooke
Geoff Cooper
Tiree Dawson
Andrew Dimberline
Tracy Dixon
Alan Dougherty
Margaret Ellis
Jackie Fay

Eleanor Forster
Ray Goldring
Rawdon Goodier
Elizabeth Hilton
Roger Hubank
Gaike Knottenbelt
Lavahouse Associates
Liz Lemal
Jenni and Jim Levi
Hilary and John Luker
Jim Marland
Vember Mortlock
Ross Morton
Franck Powell
Kev Reynolds
Heather Rhodes

and never forgetting flowers and wild Nature...

Information on Authors Quoted

I take humble pleasure from including this briefest of introductions to those from whom I have quoted. These individuals speak truly to me from the annals of history, as well as from the present day. I am immensely grateful:

Adams, J.	(1735–1826)	US President and one of the Founding Fathers.
Aeschylus	(525–465)	Philosopher and father of Greek Tragedy.
Amiel, H. F.	(1821–1881)	Swiss diarist.
Aristotle	(384–322)	Greek philosopher and scientist.
St. Aquinas, T.	(1225–1274)	Italian philosopher and theologian.
St. Augustine of Hippo	(354–430 A.D)	Philosopher and theologian. Key figure in Western Christianity.
Aurelius, M.	(121–80)	Roman Emperor. Writer famous for his meditations.
Bacon, F.	(1561–1626)	Statesman and lead figure in natural philosophy.
Bagehot, W.	(1826–1877)	Economist, journalist and famous essayist.
Barclay, W.	(1907–1978)	Leading Christian writer and lecturer.
Berdyaev, N,	(1874–1948)	Russian religious and political philosopher.
Bhagavad Gita	(c. 500 b.c)	Classic text of Sanskrit literature.
Bonhoeffer, D.	(1906–1945)	German pastor; famed opponent of Nazism.
Bradley, O.	(1893– 1981)	American General.
Buddha	(563–483)	Founder of Buddhism; "the enlightened".
Bulwer-Lytton, E.	(1803–1873)	English author and playwright.
Butler, S.	(1835–1902)	Iconoclastic author, painter and musician.
Carlyle, T.	(1795–1881)	Scottish historian, essayist and sage.
Carrel, A.	(1873–1944)	French biologist, surgeon; Nobel Prize for medicine.
Chapman, J.J.	(1862–1933)	American writer, poet and reformer.
Chardin, T. de	(1881–1955)	Jesuit priest, writer, philosopher, palaeontologist.
Chaucer, G.	(1345–1400)	First great English poet of the English race.
Chesterton, G. K.	(1874–1936)	Notable English critic, novelist and poet.
Cicero, M.T	(106–43)	Roman orator, statesman and man of letters.
Coleridge, S.T.	(1772–1834)	English romantic poet.
Collins, C.	(1908–1989)	English nature writer.
Collis, J.S.	(1900–1984)	Acclaimed English visionary artist and writer.
Colton, C.C	(1780–1832)	English cleric and writer.
Confucius	(551–479)	Founder of Chinese philosophy of the same name.
Conrad, J.	(1857–1924)	Polish-born British writer.
Cortazar, J,	(1914–1984)	Belgium-born Argentinian writer.
Disraeli, B.	(1804–1881)	Famous British prime minister and novelist.
Dogen	(1200–1253)	Key Zen figure in Japanese history.
Dostoevski, F.	(1821–1881)	Acclaimed Russian novelist.
Douglas, N.	(1868–1952)	British author, scientist and diplomat.

Dryden, J.	(1631–1700)	English poet and playright.
Eckhart, M.	(1260–1327)	German mystic and writer.
Einstein, A.	(1879–1955)	World class physicist and humanist.
Emerson, R.W.	(1803–1882)	American philosopher.
Empedocles	(c. 450 b.c)	Greek philospher, poet, doctor and statesman.
Epictetus	(55–135 a.d)	Greek stoic philosopher and moralist.
St. Exupery, A.	(1900–1944)	Famous French writer and aviator.
Field, J.	(1900–1998)	Pseudonym for Marion Milner, American psychologist and artist.
St Francis of Assissi	(1181–1221)	Founder of the Franciscan order. Patron Saint of ecology
St. Francis de Sales	(1567–1622)	French prelate and spiritual writer.
Fromm, E.	(1900–1980)	Social psychologist and humanist philosopher.
Gandhi, M.	(1869–1948)	Indian leader venerated for his non–violent approach.
Gary, R.	(1914–1980)	French novelist, aviator and diplomat.
Gibran, K.	(1883–1931)	Lebanese philosopher, artist and poet.
Gide, A.	(1869–1951)	French novelist, diarist and man of letters.
Goethe, J.W.	(1749–1832)	German poet, scientist, dramatist and philospher.
Gracian, B.	(1601–1658)	Spanish Jesuit writer and philosopher.
Guru Arjan	(1563–1606)	Inspirational Sikh mystic and writer.
Hammarskjöld, D.	(1905–1961)	Swedish statesman; Secretary General of the UN, 1953–1961.
Hawthorne, N.	(1804–1864)	Central figure in American Renaissance.
Hesse, H	(1877–1962)	Visionary German born Swiss writer, philosopher and poet.
Hofman, H.	(1893–1973)	German born American abstract expressionist painter and writer.
Hokusai, K.	(1760–1849)	Legendary Japanese artist.
Hopkins, G.M.	(1844–1889)	Victorian poet, Jesuit priest and professor of Greek.
Hugo, V.	(1802–1885)	French author, poet and leader of the French romantic movement.
Hume, B.	(1923–1999)	Revered head of the English Catholic church (1976–1999).
Hutcheson, F.	(1694–1746)	Major figure in Scottish philosophy.
Huxley, A.	(1894–1963)	Philosopher and lead intellectual.
Huxley, J.	(1887–1975)	Biologist and humanist; Director General of UNESCO.
Huss, J.	(1369–1415)	Bohemian religious reformer, preacher and martyr.
Inge, W.R.	(1860–1954)	Yorkshire prelate and theologian.
James, H.	(1843–1916)	American novelist; brother of William James.
James, W.	(1842–1910)	Pioneering philosopher and psychologist.
Jefferies, R	(1848–1887)	English naturalist and writer famous for *"The Story of my Heart"*.
Jewsbury, Miss	(1812–1880)	Renowned English novelist and essayist.

Jung, C.G.	(1875–1961)	Swiss psychiatrist famous for his writings on the psyche.
Keats, J.	(1795–1821)	Famous English romantic poet and writer.
Keller, H.	(1880–1968)	Acclaimed blind American writer.
Kempis, T. á	(1379–1471)	German religious writer.
Koestler, A.	(1905–1983)	Hungarian born writer and journalist; refugee and prisoner.
Krishnamurti, J.	(1895–1986)	Indian theosophist and guru.
Lao Tzu	(6th century)	Chinese philosopher; the inspiration for Taoism.
Latimer, Bishop	(1490–1555)	Notable English protestant martyr.
Lawrence, D.H	(1885–1930)	English novelist, poet, essayist; radical thinker.
Lerner, M.	(1902–1992)	American newswriter, author and public critic.
Lewis, C.S.	(1898–1963)	Famous Irish born writer, academic and christian apologist.
Lincoln, A.	(1809–1965)	American president.
Lindbergh, A.	(1906–2001)	Pioneering aviator and author.
MacMurray, J.	(1891–1976)	Notable moral philosopher, writer and critic.
Main, J.	(1926–82)	Revered Canadian Benedictine monk and writer.
Mansfield, K.	(1888–1923)	Leading New Zealand writer and poet.
Maslow, A.	(1908–1970)	Writer; father of humanistic psychology.
Marshall, R.	(1901–1939)	American writer and explorer. Founder of the Wilderness Society.
Mayne, M.	(1929–2006)	Dean of Westminster; writer.
Mencius	(371–289)	Confucian philosopher; profound influence on Chinese thought.
Mencken, H.L.	(1880–1956)	American journalist and writer; *"The Sage of Baltimore"*.
Merton, T.	(1915–1968)	Trappist monk; prolific writer of international reputation.
Millay, E. St V.	(1892–1950)	American lyrical poet and playright, Pulitzer Prize winner.
Milton, J.	(1608–1674)	English poet and writer; *"Paradise Lost"*.
Moitessier, B.	(1925–1994)	Round the world sailor, writer and nature lover.
Muir, J.	(1838–1914)	Scottish born American naturalist, scientist, explorer and writer.
Mumford, L.	(1895–1990)	American author, editor, lecturer on social problems in cities.
Murdoch, I.	(1919–1999)	Outstanding British writer, philosopher and novelist.
Nansen, F.	(1861–1930)	Norwegian polar explorer and statesman; Nobel Peace Prize.
Nietzsche, F.	(1844–1900)	German philosopher, especially existentialism.
Norris, K.	(1880–1996)	American poet and writer.
Orage, A.R.	(1873 –1934)	English writer and editor; friend of Gurdjieff and Ouspensky.

Ortega Y Gasset	(1883–1956)	Spanish writer and philosopher.
Ouspensky, P.	(1878–1947)	Russian philosopher, disciple of Gurdjieff.
Peck, S. M.	(1936–2005)	American psychiatrist and best selling author.
Penn, W.	(1644–1718)	English Quaker and reformer; founder of Pennsylvania.
Plato	(428–348)	Like Aristotle, a famous philosopher.
Plotinus	(205–270)	Neoplatonist philosopher; prolific writer and sage.
Pope, A;	(1688–1744)	English poet, writer and satirist.
Post, L. van der.	(1906– 1996)	South African farmer, philosopher, war hero and conservationist.
Potter, D.	(1935–1994)	English playright.
Pound, E.	(1885–1972)	American poet and critic.
Pulsford, J.	(1815–1897)	Clergyman, editor and writer.
Radhakrishnan, S.	(1888–1975)	Indian philosopher and statesman. President of India.
Raine, K.	(1908–2003)	Poet, critic and poet laureate.
Rilke, R.M.	(1875–1926)	German lyric poet and writer.
Rooseveldt, F.	(1882–1945)	American president.
Ruskin, J.	(1819–1900)	English writer; art critic and sage.
Rumi, J.	(1207–1273)	Persian born Muslim mystic and poet; leader of Sufism.
Russell, B.	(1872–1970)	Leading philosopher and mathematician.
Schopenhauer, A.	(1788–1860)	German philosopher.
Schubert, F.P.	(1797–1828)	Austrian composer and musician.
Schumacher, E.F.	(1911–1977)	International economist and acclaimed writer.
Schweitzer, A.	(1875–1965)	German medical missionary; theologian, musician and philosopher. Probably the noblest figure of his time.
Seattle (Chief)	(1786–1866)	Leader of Amerindian tribes.
Shakespeare, W.	(1530–1601)	English playright, poet and actor.
Shambhala		In Tibetan Buddhism a mythical kingdom modelled on an actual place.
Shaw, G.B.	(1856–1950)	Irish dramatist, essayist and critic.
Shelley, P.B	(1792–1822)	Major English romantic poet.
Smiles, S.	(1812–1904)	Scottish writer and reformer.
Socrates	(469–399)	One of the great figures of ancient Greek philosophy.
Stevenson, R.L.	(1850–1894)	Scottish novelist, poet and travel writer.
Stravinsky, I. F.	(1882–1971)	Russian composer.
Suzuki, S.	(1904–1971)	Japanese zen master based in America.
Swedenborg, E.	(1688–1772)	Swedish philosopher, scientist and theologian.
Tao Te Ching	(428–348)	Ancient Chinese philosophical text ascribed to Lao Tzu.
Tennyson, A.	(1809–1892)	English poet; poetry laureate.
Thoreau, H. D.	(1817–1862)	Famous American naturalist, writer and poet.
Tagore, R.	(1861–1941)	Indian poet and philosopher; Nobel prize for literature.

Unamuno, M.	(1864–1936)	Spanish essayist, novelist, philosopher and poet.
Upanishads	(c. 800–400)	Ancient Sanskrit writings which underpin much Hindu philosophy.
Vinci, L. de	(1452–1519)	Famous Italian painter, sculptor, architect and scholar.
Watts, A.	(1915–1973)	English born American philosopher (Buddism) and writer.
Weil, S.	(1904–1943)	French philosopher, christian mystic and writer.
Whitehead, A. N.	(1861–1947)	Philosopher, mathematician and writer.
Whitman, W.	(1819–1891)	American poet, essayist, jounalist and humanist.
Wilcox, E.	(1850–1919)	Writer and poet; mystic Rosicrucian.
Wilson, E.	(1872–1912)	English physician, painter and naturalist, famous Polar explorer.
Wyatt, J.	(1925 –2006)	First warden and chief ranger of the Lake District National Park, UK.
Yanagi, S.	(1889–1961)	Philosopher and founder of the Japanese Folk Craft movement.
Yeats, J. B.	(1870–1957)	Irish impressionist painter and cartoonist.
Yeats, W. B.	(1865–1939)	Irish poet and dramatist.

Current Authors Quoted

Bennett, W. J.	American writer, speaker and government official.
Bierce, A.	American writer on philosophy, psychology and history.
Capra, F,	Lead physicist and writer; five best sellers.
Cargas, H. J.	American professor of literature.
Cawood, M.	Australian nature writer and farmer.
Chase, A.	American journalist and editor.
Chopra, D.	Renowned Indian writer on Spirituality; physician.
Compte-Sponville, A.	French philospher and writer.
Cupitt, D.	English religious philosopher, lecturer and writer.
Dalai Lama	Spiritual head of Tibet. Nobel Peace Prize
Ferguson, G.	American writer and psychologist.
Geering, L.	Prelate and key New Zealand religious thinker.
Grayling, A.C.	British philosopher and author.
Hanh, T.N.	Renowned vietnamese buddhist monk and zen master.
Jamison, C.	Abbot of a UK Benedictine monastery.
Johnson, C.	Writer on religion and Buddhism.
Keen, S.	American writer and philosopher.
Kierkegaard, S.	Danish philosopher; founder of existentialism.
Lama Surya Das	Leading American Buddhist teacher and scholar.
Lane, J.	English painter, author and educator.
Lee, H.	American novelist and Pulitzer prize winner.
Lennox, A.	Contemporary singer, songwriter and critic.
Levine, S.	American poet, author and spiritual teacher.
Macintyre, A.	Notable moral and political philosopher.
Matthiesen, P.	American novelist and non–fiction writer.
Murphy, M.	American writer on human potential and sport.
Overstreet, H.A	American writer, psychologist and teacher.
Rohe, F.	American writer; eg: "Zen of Running"
Sainsbury, J.	Founder of major supermarket chain.
Selby, J.	Modern American writer and psychologist.
Snunit, M.	Writer.
Trungpa, C.	Buddhist scholar and prolific writer.
Wilber, K.	American philosopher; prolific writer.

Bibliography

In some instances we have been unable to trace or contact the copyright holders. We have, however, given full credit to author and publisher as stated in the book that the quotes are taken from. If notified, the publisher will be pleased to rectify any errors or omissions at the earliest opportunity.

Many of the quotes are now out of copyright and in these instances, where it hasn't been possible to find the source, a short description is given. The list also includes references to books and people who may be of interest to the reader.

Abbey, Edward,   Desert Solitaire, Ballantyne Books, 1981
Adams, John,   The Works Of John Adams, Second President Of The United States, Easton Press, 1992
Aeschylus,   Prometheus Bound, Dover Publications, 1995
Amiel, Henri Frédéric, Amiel's Journal, McMillan & Co, 1918
Aquinas, St Thomas,   1225-1274, Italian scholar, philosopher and theologian
Aristotle,   The Nichomachean Ethics, Dent Everyman, translated by D P Chase, 1949
Arjan Dev, Guru,   1553-1606, Adi Granth (1604)
Augustine, St,   The Confessions, Hendrickson, 2004
Bach, Richard,   Jonathan Livingstone Seagull, Harper Collins, 1994
Bach, Richard,   There's No Such Place As Far Away, Grafton Books, 1980
Bacon, Francis,   The Elements Of The Common Law Of England (Maxims Of The Law), 1597
Bagehot, Walter,   Biographical Studies, Longman, Green & Co, 1902
Barclay, William,   The Gospel Of Matthew, New Daily Study Bible, Saint Andrew Press, 0715207806, 2001
Berdyaev, Nicholas,   The Fate Of Man In A Modern World, SCM Press, 1935
Berger, John,   The White Bird, Chatto & Windus, 1985
Bergson, Henri,   Henri Bergson: Two Sources Of Morality And Religion, Kessinger Publishing, 1932
Berry, Wendell,   Standing On Earth, Golgonooza Press, 1991
Berry, Wendell,   What Are People For?, Rider, 1990
Bhagavad Gita,   c. 500BC, revered Sanskrit Hindu scripture
Bible Societies,   The, New English Bible, in association with Cambridge University Press and Oxford University Press, 1973,
Bierce, Ambrose,   The Devil's Dictionary, Filiquarian Publishing, 2006
Blake, William,   Complete Writings, Oxford University Press, 1979
Bohm, David,   Wholeness And The Implicate Order, Routledge, 1995

Bonhoffer, Dietrich, reprinted with the permission of Scribner, a division of Simon & Schuster, Inc., from Letters And Papers From Prison, revised, enlarged, ed. by Dietrich Bonhoffer, (Translated from the German by R H Fuller, Frank Clark, et al). ©1953, 1967, 1971 by SCM Press Ltd. All rights reserved.

Bradley, General Omar, quoted in Bartlett's Familiar Quotations, Little Brown, 1980

Bronowski, Jacob, The Identity Of Man, The Natural History Press, 1971

Browning, Robert, Paracelsus, J M Dent & Sons, 1898

Buddha, (Prince Gautama Siddhartha, The Enlightened One), c.563-c.483BC, founder of Buddhism

Bulwer-Lytton, Edward Robert, 1831-1891, English poet, diplomat and politician

Bunyan, John, The Pilgrim's Progress, Andrew Elliott, 1865

Butler, Samuel, The Way Of All Flesh, Franklin Watts, 1903

Camus, Albert, Selected Notebooks And Essays, Penguin Books Ltd, 1967

Camus, Albert, The Myth Of Sisyphus, Penguin Books Ltd, 1965

Capra, Fritjof, The Tao Of Physics, Shambhala Publications Inc., Boston, MA. www.shambhala.com, 1975

Capra, Fritjof, T The Turning Point, Wildwood House, 1982

Capra, Fritjof, Uncommon Wisdom, Fontana, 1989

Cargas, William, Encountering Myself, Seabury Press, 1978

Carlyle, Thomas, Sartor Resartus; Lectures On Heroes, Chapman & Hall, 1888

Carpenter, Edward, Towards Democracy, G Allen & Unwin, 1918

Carrel, Alexis, Reflections On Life, Hamish Hamilton, 1952

Carson, Rachel, Silent Spring, Hamish Hamilton, 1963

Chardin, Teilhard de, The Phenomenon Of Man, Perennial, 2002

Cawood, Matt, Take Off Your Shoes, article in Resurgence magazine, issue 240, www.resurgence.org

Chase, Alexander, quoted in International Thesaurus Of Quotations, Penguin, 1976

Chaucer, Geoffrey, The Canterbury Tales, Penguin Classics, 1961

Chinmoy, Sri, Garden Of The Soul, Heath Communications, 1994

Chopra, Deepak, Dispelling The Darkness, article in Resurgence magazine, issue 238, www.resurgence.org

Chuang-Tzu, Inner Chapters, Wildwood House, 1974

Colegate, Isabel, A Pelican In The Wilderness, Harper Collins, 2002

Collins, Cecil, ©Tate, London 2008, extract quoted by permission of Golgonooza Press from Meditations, Pages, Poems From A Sketchbook, 1997

Collis, John Stewart, Living With A Stranger, VAL Publishing, 1987

Colton, Charles Caleb, Lacon, William Tebb, 1866

Compte-Sponville, Andre, from A Short Treatise On The Great Virtues: The Uses Of Philosophy In Everyday Life by Andre Compte-Sponville, published by William Heinemann. Reprinted by permission of The Random House Group, 2003

Confucius,	The Analects, (translated by R Dawson), Oxford University Press, 1993
Conrad, Joseph,	Lord Jim, Claremont Classics, 1994
Coomaraswamy, Ananda,	What Is Civilisation?, Golgonooza Press, 1989
Cortazar, Julio,	The Winners, Pantheon Books, 1965
Cupitt, Don,	The Sea Of Faith, BBC Books, reproduced with the permission of SCM Press, 1984
Dalai Lama,	Four Noble Truths, reprinted by permission of Harper Collins Publishers Ltd, ©Dalai Lama, 1998
Dalai Lama and Howard Cutler,	The Art Of Happiness, Coronet Books, 1999
Darling, Frank Fraser,	Wilderness And Plenty, Ballantyne Books, 1971
Daumal, René,	Mount Analogue, Penguin Books Ltd, 1974
Devall, Bill,	Simple In Means, Rich In Ends, Gibbs Smith, 1988
Devall, Bill and George Sessions,	Deep Ecology, Gibbs Smith, 1985
Dhammapada, The,	The Dhammapada, Penguin Books Ltd, 1973
Dillard, Annie,	Pilgrim At Tinker Creek, Pan Books, 1976
Disraeli, Benjamin,	from a speech in the House of Commons, 11 February 1851
Dogen, Zenji,	1200-1253, Japanese Zen Buddhist Teacher, A Treasury of Knowledge of the True Law (Shobogenzo)
Dostoevsky, Fyodor,	Crime And Punishment, Vintage Classics, 1998
Dostoevsky, Fyodor,	The Brothers Karamazov, W W Norton & Co, 1976
Donne, John,	'To the Countess of Huntingdon', John Donne, The Major Works, Oxford University Press, 2000
Douglas, Norman,	An Almanac, Society of Authors as Literary Representative of the author Norman Douglas, 1945
Dryden, John,	The Hind And The Panther, Pt 111, ln 839, (1687)
Durckheim, Karlfried Graf,	Absolute Living, Arkana, 1990
Durckheim, Karlfried Graf,	The Way Of Transformation, G Allen & Unwin, 1971
Einstein, Albert,	Ideas and Opinions, Crown Publishing (Random House), 1982
Einstein, Albert,	The World as I see it, Watts & Co, ©Rationalist Association (formerly Rationalist Press Association), 1940
Eiseley, Loren,	The Immense Journey, Vintage Books, 1959
Emerson, Ralph Waldo,	Emerson's Essays, J M Dent & Sons, 1955
Emerson, Ralph Waldo,	The Conduct Of Life, 1st World Library, 2004
Empedocles, c.450BC,	Greek philosopher, from his poetic treatise On Nature
Enright, Dennis Joseph (ed),	The Oxford Book Of Death, Oxford University Press, 1983
Epictetus,	1st century AD, Greek Stoic philosopher and moralist
Ferguson, Gail,	Cracking The Intuition Code, Contemporary Books, reproduced with the permission of The McGraw-Hill Companies, 2000

Field, Joanna,	A Life Of One's Own, Chatto & Windus, by permission of Paterson Marsh Ltd on behalf of the Estate of Mrs Marion Milner, 1934
Francis of Assisi, St,	(Francesco di Pietro di Bernardone), c.1181– c.1286, Italian founder of the Franciscan movement
Frankl, Viktor,	Man's Search For Ultimate Meaning, Basic Books, 1975
Fromm, Erich,	Man For Himself, Routledge, Keegan Paul, 1948
Fromm, Erich,	To Have Or To Be, Abacus, 1979
Fromm, Erich,	The Art Of Loving, Harper & Row, 1956
Fromm, Erich,	Zen Buddhism And Psychoanalysis, Harper & Row, 1970
Gandhi, Mahatma,	The Moral And Political Writings Of Mahatma Gandhi, Navajivan Press, 1927
Gandhi, Mahatma,	An Autobiography Or The Story Of My Experiment With The Truth, Navajivan Press, 1948
Gary, Romain,	Promise At Dawn, Harper & Brothers, 1961
Gasset, Ortegay,	Theory Of The Novel, JHU Press, 2000
Geering, Lloyd,	The World To Come, Polebridge Press, 2000
Gibran, Kahlil,	The Prophet, Heinemann, 1980
Gide, André,	Les Nourritures Terrestres, Mercure de France, 1897
Gill, Eric,	A Holy Tradition Of Working, Golgonooza Press, 1983
Goethe, Johann Wolfgang von,	The Practical Wisdom Of Goethe, G Allen & Unwin, 1933
Goldsmith, Edward,	The Way: An Ecological View, Themis Books, 1996
Govinda, Lama Anagarika,	The Way Of The White Clouds, Overlook Press, 2006
Gracián, Baltasar,	A Truthtelling Manual And The Art Of Worldly Wisdom, Charles C Thomas, 1956
Grayling, A C,	The Meaning of Things/Meditations for the Humanist, by permission of Oxford University Press, Inc. and Weidenfeld & Nicholson, a division of The Orion Publishing Group, 2002
Gurdjieff, George Ivanovitch,	All And Everything, Routledge, Kegan Paul, 1949
Gurdjieff, George Ivanovitch,	Meetings With Remarkable Men, Routledge, 1963
Hahn, Thich Nhat,	Love in Action, Reprinted from Love in Action: Writings on Nonviolent Social Change (1993) by Thich Nhat Hanh with permission of Parallax Press, Berkeley, California, www.parallax.org, 1993
Hammarskjöld, Dag,	Markings, Faber & Faber, translated by Leif Sjöberg and W H Auden, 1965
Happold, Frank,	Mysticism, Pelican, 1967
Hardy, Sir Alister,	The Spiritual Nature Of Man, Clarendon Press, 1979
Hawken, Paul,	The Magic Of Findhorn, Souvenir Press, 1976
Hawthorne, Nathaniel,	The Blithdale Romance, Ticknor & Fields, 1865
Hermes, Georg,	1775-1831, German Roman Catholic theologian

Hesse, Herman,   Demian, Helvetica Press Inc, 1971
Hesse, Herman,   My Belief, Panther Books, 1976
Hofmann, Hans,   Search For The Real And Other Essays, The MIT Press, 1967
Hopkins, Gerard Manley, taken from The Letters Of Gerard Manley Hopkins To
                        Robert Bridges, Oxford University Press, 1955
Hokusai,   A Talk About Hokusai, 1896, Lafarge
Hollick Malcolm,   The Science Of Oneness, O Books, 2006
Hugo, Victor Marie,   1802-1885, French novelist, poet and dramatist
Hutcheson, Francis,   An Inquiry Into The Original Of Our Ideas Of Beauty And
                        Virtue, J Darby, 1725
Huxley, Aldous,   The Perennial Philosophy, Chatto & Windus, 1946
Huxley, Sir Julian,   Religion Without Regulation, Watts & Co, ©Rationalist
                        Association (formerly Rationalist Press Association), 1967
Inge, William Ralph,   quoted in Thesaurus of International Quotations, Penguin
                        Books Ltd, 1979
James, Henry,   Partial Portraits, Kessinger Publishing, 2006
James, William,   Essays On Faith And Morals, Meridian Books, 1962
James, William,   The Varieties Of Religious Experience, Collins, 1975
Jamison, Abbott,   Finding Sanctuary, ©Liturgical Press and Weidenfeld &
                        Nicholson, a division of The Orion Publishing Group, 2006
Jeffreys, Richard,   The Story Of My Heart, Longman, Green & Co, 1922
Johnson, Charles,   Proverbs, Canongate, Edinburgh, 1998
Joshu,   The Recorded Sayings Of Zen Master Joshu, Shambhala
                        Publications Inc., Boston, MA. www.shambhala.com, 1998
Jung, Carl,   Man And His Symbols, Pan, 1978
Jung, Carl,   excerpts from Modern Man In Search Of A Soul by C G Jung,
                        reprinted by permission of Houghton Mifflin Harcourt
                        Publishing Company, 1933
Jung, Carl,   Synchronicity, Routledge & Kegan Paul, 1987
Kant, Immanuel,   Immanuel Kant, Groundwork Of The Metaphysics Of Morals,
                        Harper & Row, 1964
Keats, John,   from Ode On A Grecian Urn, st. 5, 1820, from Complete
                        Poems, Penguin Books Ltd, 1976
Keats, John,   Letters Of John Keats by R Giltings, Oxford University Press,
                        1987
Keen, Sam,   To Love And Be Loved, Bantam, 1997
Kierkegaard, Søren,   Fear and Trembling and the Sickness unto Death, Princeton
                        University Press, 1974
Kipling, Rudyard,   Kim, Penguin Books Ltd, 1994
Koestler, Arthur,   extracts from Arrow In The Blue (©1952 Arthur Koestler) are
                        reproduced by permission of PFD (www.pfd.co.uk) on behalf
                        of The Estate of Arthur Koestler, 1952
Krishnamurti, Jiddu,   Krishnamurti, The Impossible Question, Penguin Books Ltd,
                        1978

Krishnamurti, Jiddu,	The Penguin Krishnamurti Reader, Penguin Books Ltd, 1970
Krishnamurti, Jiddu,	The Open Door, The Krishnamurti Foundation Trust, 2003
Krishnamurti, Jiddu,	from a speech in Holland 1929, quoted in Chambers Dictionary of Quotes, Chambers, 1996
Lama Surya Das,	Awakening The Buddha Within, Bantam, reprinted by permission of The Random House Group Ltd, 1997
Lane, John,	The Spirit Of Silence, Green Books, 2006
Lane, John,	Timeless Beauty, Green Books, 2003
Lane, John,	Timeless Simplicity, Green Books, 2001
Lao Tzu,	Tao Te Ching, Wildwood House, 1972
Latimer, Bishop Hugh,	The Second Sermon Preached Before The King's Majesty, 19 April 1549
Lee, Harper,	To Kill A Mockingbird, Pan Books, 1981
Lennox, Annie,	article in Resurgence magazine, issue 240, www.resurgence.org
Leopold, Aldo,	A Sand County Almanac, Oxford University Press, 1981
Lerner, Max,	The Unfinished Country, Simon & Schuster, 1959
Levine, Stephen,	A Gradual Awakening, Rider & Co. reprinted by permission of The Random House Group Ltd, 1980
Lewis, Clive Staples,	The Screwtape Letters by C.S. Lewis © C C S. Lewis Pte. Ltd. 1942
Lewis, Clive Staples,	quoted in The Unquiet Grave by Cyril Connelly, 1945, Hamish Hamilton, © C C S. Lewis Pte. Ltd. 1942
Lincoln, Abraham,	The Collected Works Of Abraham Lincoln, Rutgers University Press, 1953
Lindbergh, Anne Morrow,	excerpt from The Wave Of The Future, ©1940 and renewed 1968 by Anne Morrow Lindbergh, reprinted by permission of Houghton Mifflin Harcourt Publishing Company, 1940
Lovelock, James,	The Ages Of Gaia, Osford, 1989
MacIntyre, Professor Alasdair,	After Virtue, Gerald Duckworth & Co, 2004
McLuhan, T,	Touch The Earth, Abacus, 1978
MacMurray, John,	Freedom In The Modern World, H1992
Main, John,	The Joy Of Being, Darton, Longman & Todd, 1969
Mansfield, Katherine,	Journal Of Katherine Mansfield, Constable & Co, 1927
Marcus Aurelius,	Meditations, Penguin Books Ltd, 1964
Marshall, Robert,	Alaska Wilderness, University of California Press, 1982
Maslow, Abraham H,	Religions, Values And Peak-experiences, Penguin (Compass), 1976
Matthiessen, Peter,	from The Snow Leopard by Peter Matthieson, published by Harvill Press. Reprinted by permission of The Random House Group Ltd, 1989
May, Rollo,	Man's Search For Himself, Delta Publishing, 1973

Mayne, Michael,   The Sunrise Of Wonder, Darton, Longman & Todd, 2008

Melville, Herman, Mardi,   The New American Library of World Literature, 1964

Mencius (Meng-Tzu),   The Book Of Mencius, translated by Lionel Giles, John
                                   Murray, 1942

Mencken, Henry Louis,   quoted in International Thesaurus Of Quotations, 1973,
                                   Penguin Books Ltd

Merton, Thomas,   Contemplation In A World Of Action, G Allen & Unwin,
                                   1974

Merton, Thomas,   Elected Silence, Burns & Oates, 1961

Merton, Thomas,   New Seeds Of Contemplation, Burns & Oates, reproduced by
                                   kind permission of Continuum International Publishing
                                   Group, 1962

Merton, Thomas,   The Wisdom Of The Desert, New Directions, 1960

Milner, Marion,   see Field, Joanna

Moitessier, Bernard,   The Long Way, ©1971 by Editions Arthaud, Translation copy
                                   right 1973 by William Rodarmor, Courtesy of Sheridan
                                   House Inc. 1971

Morris, Desmond,   The Nature Of Happiness, Little Books Ltd, 2004

Mortlock, Colin,   Beyond Adventure, Cicerone Press, 2001

Mortlock, Colin,   The Adventure Alternative, Cicerone Press, 1984

Muir, John,   The Wilderness World Of John Muir, Houghton Mifflin
                                   Harcourt, 1954

Mumford, Lewis,   excerpt from The Conduct Of Life, ©1951 and renewed 1979
                                   by Lewis Mumford, reprinted by permission of Houghton
                                   Mifflin Harcourt Publishing Company and published by
                                   Secker & Warburg. Reprinted by permission of The Random
                                   House Group Ltd, 1951

Murdoch, Iris,   The Sovereignty Of Good, Routledge Classics, 2001

Murphy, Michael and
Rhea White,   The Psychic Side Of Sport, Addison-Wesley, 1978

Naess, Arne,   Ecology, Community And Lifestyle, translated and edited by
                                   D Rothenberg, Cambridge, 1989

Nansen, Fridtjof,   Farthest North, Modern Library, 1999

Native American Wisdom,   words from Native American Wisdom, Running Press, 1993

Niebuhr, Reinhold,   The Nature And Destiny Of Man, Nisbet & Co, 1946

Nietzsche, Friedrich,   The Portable Nietzsche, Viking Press, 1969

Nietzsche, Friedrich,   Thus Spake Zarethustra, Penguin Books Ltd, 1974

Norris, Kathleen,   Hands Full Of Living, Doubleday, Doran & Co, 1981

Noyce, Wilfrid,   The Springs Of Adventure, Heinemann, 1958

Noyce, Wilfrid,   They Survived, John Murray, 1962

O'Donohue, John,   Anam Cara, Bantam, 1998

O'Donohue, John,   Divine Beauty, Bantam, 2004

Orage, A R,   On Love, The Janus Press, 1957

Ouspensky, Peter D,   quoted in A Guide For The Perplexed by E F Schumacher,
                                   published by Jonathan Cape, 1977

Ouspensky, Peter D,   Tertium Organum, Kessinger Publishing, 2004
Passmore, John,   Man's Responsibility For Nature, Duckworth, 1980
Pedlar, Kit,   The Quest For Gain, Granada, 1981
Penn, William,   1644-1718, English Quaker reformer and colonialist, founder
                                  of Pennsylvania
Peterson, Christopher and
Martin Seligman,   Character Strengths And Virtues, Oxford University Press,
                                  2004
Plato,   The Republic, Penguin Books Ltd, 1970
Plato,   The Symposium, Penguin Books Ltd, 1999
Plotinus,   The Enneads, Penguin Books Ltd, 1991
Plotinus,   The Philosophy Of Plotinus, Century Crafts, 1950
Pope, Alexander,   An Essay On Criticism (1711), Kessinger Publishing, 2004
Pound, Ezra,   from Guide To Kulcher 1938, quoted in Chambers Dictionary
                                  Of Quotes, Chambers, 1999
Pulsford, John,   Quiet Hours, James Nesbit & Co, 1857
Radhakrishnan, Sarvepalli,   Eastern Religions And Western Thoughts, Oxford University
                                  Press, India, 1940
Raine, Kathleen,   article in Resurgence magazine, issue 114, This article is
                                  quoted by permission of Golgonooza Press, ©the literary
                                  estate of Kathleen Raine, 2008
Rankin, Aidan,   The Jain Path, O Books, 2006
Rilke, Rainer Maria,   Letters Of Rainer Maria Rilke, W W Norton & Co, 1948
Rinpoche, Guru Sogyal,   The Tibetan Book Of Living And Dying, Rider, 2002
Rohe, Fred,   The Zen Of Running, Random House, US, 1975,
Rolland, Romain,   Some Musicians Of Former Days, Ayer Publishing, 1977
Roszak, Theodore,   Person/Planet, Anchor, 1978
Rousseau, Jean Jacques,   Emile, J M Dent & Sons, 1955
Rousseau, Jean Jacques,   Meditations Of A Solitary Walker, Penguin Books Ltd, 1995
Rousseau, Jean Jacques,   The Social Contract, J M Dent & Sons, 1955
Rumi, Jelaluddin,   The Mathnawi Of Jalalu'ddin Rumi, Gibb Memorial Trust,
                                  1982
Ruskin, John,   The Ethics Of The Dust, George Allen & Co, 1907
Russell, Bertrand,   Education And The Good Life, Liveright Publishing Co,
                                  1954, The Bertrand Russell Peace Foundation
Russell, Bertrand,   Principles Of Social Reconstruction, 1916, G Allen & Unwin,
                                  Routledge. The Bertrand Russell Peace Foundation, 1997
Russell, Bertrand,   Unpopular Essays, Routledge. The Bertrand Russell Peace
                                  Foundation, 1995
Russell, Peter,   The Awakening Earth, Ark Paperbacks, 1985
Rutherford, Mark,   Last Pages From A Journal, Oxford University Press, 1915
Sainsbury, John,   article in Resurgence magazine, issue 243,
                                  www.resurgence.org

Saint-Exupery, Antoine de,   excerpts from Wind, Sand And Stars, ©1939 by Antoine
                              de Saint-Exupery and renewed 1967 by Lewis Galantiere,
                              reprinted by permission of Houghton, Mifflin Harcourt
                              Publishing Company, 1939
Sales, St Francis de,   1567-1622, French prelate and spiritual writer
Saul John Ralston,   The Unconscious Civilization, Penguin Books Ltd, 1998
Schopenhauer, Arthur,   On Human Nature, G Allen & Unwin, 1926
Schubert, Franz Peter,   1797-1828, Austrian composer and musician
Schumacher, Ernst
Friedrich,   A Guide For The Perplexed, Jonathan Cape, 1977
Schumacher, Ernst
Friedrich,   from Small Is Beautiful by E F Schumacher, published by
                              Hutchinson. Reprinted by permission of The Random House
                              Group, Ltd. ©1973 by E F Schumacher. Reprinted by
                              permission of Harper Collins Publishers
Schweitzer, Albert,   A Biography, Syracuse University Press, 2002
Schweitzer, Albert,   Civilization And Ethics, Macmillan Co. reprinted by
                              permission of Mrs Rhena Schweitzer Miller, 1929
Schweitzer, Albert,   My Life And Thought, G Allen & Unwin, 1933
Schweitzer, Albert,   Reverence For Life, Syracuse University Press, 2002
Scott Peck, Morgan,   reprinted with the permission of Simon & Schuster Inc., from
The Road Less Travelled   by M Scott Peck, M.D. ©1978 by M Scott Peck, M.D.
                              All rights reserved
Seaver, George,   Albert Schweitzer, A & C Black, 1947
Seaver, George,   Edward Wilson Of The Antarctic, John Murray, 1938
Seaver, George,   The Faith Of Edward Wilson, John Murray, 1948
Seaver, George,   The Man And His Mind, A & C Black, 1947
Selby, John, Seven Masters,   One Path, 2003, published by Rider. Reprinted by
                              permission of The Random House Group Ltd. ©2003 by John
                              Selby. Reprinted by permission of Harper Collins Publishers
Sheldrake, Rupert,   The Sense Of Being Stared At, And Other Aspects Of The
                              Extended Mind, Arrow Books, 2004
Shepard, Paul,   Nature And Madness, University of Georgia Press, 1982
Smiles, Samuel,   Self-help, S W Partridge & Co, 1912
Smythe, Frank,   The Spirit Of The Hills, Hodder & Stoughton, 1940
Snunit, Michael,   The Soul Bird, Constable & Robinson, 1998
Snyder, Gary,   Turtle Island, New Directions, 1974
Socrates,   Essays On The Philosophy Of Socrates, Oxford University
                              Press, 1992
Steiner, George,   Real Presences, University of Chicago Press, reprinted by
                              permission of Faber & Faber, 1991
Stevenson, Robert Louis,   Travels With A Donkey In The Cevennes, Falcon Press, 1948
Storey, Father Brian,   letter in The Times, 20 June 2005, reproduced by permission
                              of Father Storey

Storr, Anthony,	Solitude, Fontana, 1988
Stravinsky, Igor,	quoted in Thesaurus Of International Quotations, Penguin Books Ltd, 1979
Suzuki, Shunryu,	Studies In Zen Buddhism, Rider, 1955
Suzuki, Shunryu,	from Zen Mind, Beginner's Mind, by Shunryu Suzuki, protected under the terms of the International Copyright Union. Reprinted by arrangement with Shambhala Publications Inc., Boston, MA. www.shambhala.com, 1973
Swedenborg, Emanuel,	Journal Of Dreams, Swedenborg Foundation, 1956
Sykes, William,	The Eternal Vision, Canterbury Press, 2002
Tagore, Rabindranath,	extract taken from Rabindranath Tagore: Of Myself', translated by Devadatta Joardar and Joe Winter. Published by Anvil Press Poetry in 2006
Tennyson, Alfred Lord,	1st Baron Tennyson, 1800-1892, English poet, poet laureate
Thoreau, Henri David,	Walden, J M Dent & Sons, 1934
Thoreau, Henri David,	Works Of Henri David Thoreau, Avenal Books, 1981
Toffler, Alvin,	Future Shock, Pan, 1970
Tolle, Eckhart,	The Power Of Now, Hodder & Stoughton, 2001
Trungpa, Chögyam,	Shambhala, Shambhala Publications Inc., Boston, MA. www.shambhala.com, 1984,
Tschu-Li, Shambhala,	The Sacred Path Of The Warrior, Shambhala Publications Inc., Boston, MA. www.shambhala.com, 1995
Unamuno, Miguel de,	1864-1936, Spanish philosopher and writer
Upanishads, The,	Ten Principal Upanishads, Faber & Faber, 1937
Upanishads, The,	The Upanishads, translated by Juan Mascaro, Penguin Books Ltd, 1973
van der Post, Laurens,	from A Walk With A White Bushman, by Laurens van der Post, published by Chatto & Windus. Reprinted by permission of The Random House Group Ltd, 1986
van der Post, Laurens,	Jung And The Story Of Our Time, Hogarth Press, 1976
Watts, Alan,	Cloud-hidden, Whereabouts Unknown, abridged by Sphere Books, 1977
Weil, Simone,	The Need For Roots, Routledge Classics, 2006
Weil, Simone,	Gravity And Grace, Routledge, 2002
Weil, Simone,	The Need For Roots, Routledge, 2002
Weil, Simone,	Waiting For God, Perennial Classics, 2001
Whitehead, Alfred North,	Adventures of Ideas, Cambridge University Press, 1939
Whitehead, Alfred North,	Science And the Modern World, Free Press, 1967
Whitehead, Alfred North,	The Concept Of Nature, Prometheus Books, 2004
Whitman, Walt,	A Choice Of Whitman's Verse, Faber & Faber, 1968
Wilber, Ken,	A Brief History Of Everything, Gill & Macmillan, 1996
Wilber, Ken,	from Sex, Ecology, Spirituality, by Ken Wilber, ©1995, 2000 by Ken Wilber. Reprinted by arrangement with Shambhala Publications Inc., Boston, MA. www.shambhala.com, 1995

Wilber, Ken,   The Integral Vision, Shambhala Publications Inc., Boston,
                                MA. www.shambhala.com, 2006
Wilcox, Ella,   1850-1919, American writer, poet, mystic Rosicrucian
Wilde, Oscar,   1854-1900, Irish playwright, novelist, essayist, poet and wit
Wordsworth, William,   The Prelude, Oxford University Press, 1969
Wyatt, John,   The Shining Levels, Penguin Books Ltd, 1976
Yanagi, Soetsu,   The Unknown Craftsman, by Soetsu Yanagi, adapted by
                                Bernard Leach, published by Kodansha International Ltd, 1978
Yeats, J B,   Letters To His Son, Faber & Faber, 1944
Yeats, W B,   quoted in Macmillan Treasury Of Relevant Quotations,
                                Macmillan Press, 1979
Yutang, Lin,   The Importance Of Living, William Heinemann Ltd, 1939

Endnotes

Chapter 1

[1] Leader of small expeditions and originally expected to lead the Everest expedition.

[2] See Chapter 14, The Search for Beauty.

Chapter 3

[1] Quoted in The Perennial Philosophy by Bertrand Russell

Chapter 4

[1] see '*The Last Blue Mountain*' by Ralph Barker

[2] The top grades of British rock climbing at that time were Very Severe (VS); Hard Very Severe (HVS); Extremely Severe and Exceptionally Severe (XS)

[3] Cracking the Intuition Code, (1999).

Chapter 5

[1] *Native American Wisdom*, Running Press, (1993).

[2] The Long Way.

Chapter 6

[1] See under the virtue of honesty for situation details.

Chapter 7

[1] By Dr. A. Dimberline.

Chapter 8

[1] *The Gospel of Matthew.*

[2] *'Great Virtues'* by André Comte-Sponville, (2003).

[3] *Small is Beautiful,* (1973).

[4] See Chapter 15 in *"After Virtue" by Prof. A. MacIntyre.*

[5] The origin of the term is that each of the five senses makes a decision then all five come together to form a 'common' (or combined) judgement.

[6] See under Humility

[7] Whilst there should be a progression towards *Self-Reliance*, there is also an inevitable regression in old age, at very least in a physical sense, towards dependence. Life indeed is a circle!

[8] Many philosophers seem to agree that this is the ideal approach to life: *Living in the now.* See Chapter 19.

[9] See Chapter 13.

[10] A method of waterproofing a wooden boat.

[11] On one expedition with another friend a dog joined us for three days!

[12] Far better, of course, is to impel *yourself* ie: self-reliance.

[13] See chapter on Love.

[14] A form of Buddhism devoted to the concept of the gentle warrior.

[15] UN figures show that on 11 September 2001, c.35 000 children died of starvation and related diseases around the globe.

[16] The English were popular in North Norway because of their exploits in the Second World War in this area.

[17] Due for completion in 2010 if sufficient funding is raised.

[18] A term used by the Buddhist Shambhala sect.

[19] *Lancet*, September 2007.

[20] See Chapter 17.

[21] Members of the crow family.

[22] *Cloud Hidden, Wherabouts Unknown.*

Chapter 9

[1] *Partial Portraits.*

Chapter 10

[1] See also the virtue of 'concentration'

[2] Whilst adrenalin is natural, it is still a drug.

[3] *Timeless Beauty.*

[4] Chopra 2005, *Resurgence Magazine.*

[5] In *Seven Masters, One Path.*

[6] In *Awakening the Buddha.*

Chapter 11

[1] Having fearful and timid citizens make it easier for individuals to become 'consumers' and helps make more money. (Resurgence Magazine, number 243, July/August 2007)

[2] From Fear and Trembling Unto Death.

[3] The opening paragraph to the classic *The Tao of Physics*, p.11

[4] See *Gaia* by James Lovelock

[5] See also the later chapter 'Transcendent Experiences'

[6] *Resurgence,* no. 238 September/October 2006

Chapter 12

[1] From the poem *'Stations on the Road to Freedom'*

[2] See *'The Seed And The Sower'* by Van der Post.

[3] See chapter Truth and Living in the Moment

[4] 372 to 289 BC

[5] *The Prophet.*

Chapter 13

[1] See also *'Beyond Adventure'* chapters 5, 6, 7, and bibliography. Whilst I have a whole file of such experiences by other people from ancient to modern times, they are not my own experiences. There is *no* substitute for your own experience.

[2] *Religion, Value and Peak Experiences,* 1964.

[3] See Chapter 17.

[4] Briefly mentioned under *'Unity'* in Chapter 13.

[5] This section taken from *Beyond Adventure*, 2001.

[6] See also chapter 6 in *Beyond Adventure'*, 2001.

[7] National Parks, for example, are often seen in this way, at least by users, and sometimes by the planners.

[8] See the book of that name bv Aldous Huxley.

Chapter 14

[1] *Freedom in the Modern World.*

Chapter 15

[1] *The Great Northern Diver.*

Chapter 16

[1] The difference between experiencing something practically as distinct from reading about it.

[2] See Chapter 18.

Chapter 17

[1] *Seven Masters, One Path,* (2003)

[2] See *'The Last Blue Mountain'* by Ralph Barker, (1959)

[3] *The Road Less Travelled,* (1979)

[4] From a Greek myth—a beautiful youth who fell in love with his own reflection and pined away.

[5] *Arrow in the Blue,* (1952).

[6] See *Beyond Adventure,* pp. 62-3.

[7] This transcendental experience is what Maslow would term a *Nadir* experience, the opposite of a peak experience. Later reflection on this moment indicated that our unconscious must store the future as well as the past!

[8] Apart from bulls and fast torrents she had to cross!

[9] The Brothers Karamazov (1927)

[10] *The Phenomenon Of Man*

Chapter 18

[1] Both were sent a copy of the manuscript on the recommendation of young friends of mine.

[2] Both have become good friends.

[3] *A Gradual Awakening,* (1980)

[4] I have tried to avoid using the word 'mind' as it raises many ambiguities and arguments as to its meaning.

[5] As they are both involved in teaching in wild Nature they also give me great hope for the future, especially if they are typical of the younger generation involved in education out of doors.

[6] *'The Soul Bird'* by Michael Snunit, (1998)

Chapter 19
[1] *The Zen of Running,* (1974).

Chapter 20
[1] See W. Noyce. *To the Unknown Mountain.*

[2] Grade II described as "fairly frequent rapids…"; Grade III includes "difficult raft channels" (from the international grading system of rivers according to difficulty).

[3] An eddy is an area of water either stationary or moving upstream.

[4] An expedition of 200 miles; 17545 metres of ascent; 21 cols and passes; 600 flowers identified.

Chapter 22
[1] With the exception of those genuinely excused on medical grounds.

[2] Ibid.

[3] By self, I mean in all positive senses. Physical, mental, emotional and spiritual. I do *not* include *egotistic* self.

Chapter 23
[1] Albert Schweitzer, by G. Seaver.

[2] The Faith of Edward Wilson, by George Seaver.

[3] Ibid

[4] From a talk about Hokusai by J. Lafarge (1896)

Index

action, reflection 136
adventure
        instinct for, in young people 9, 11
        need for, in civilisation 238
        in wild Nature for young people 251
aggressiveness, road rage, yob anger 86
alpine-flower photography, Annette 232
altruism 77–8
anti-social adventure, murder, mayhem self-discipline as curb 72
versus natural adventure 11
Aristotle, on virtues 28
arrogance 35, 103
awareness and unawareness 59
        and ignorance 55
        and reflection 50
        of environment, self and others 55–7
meeting with storm petrel 56–7
awe and wonder, sense of 18, 137

Bach, Johann Sebastian, music and purity 190–91
balance in nature, greed of mankind 161
beauty
        and love 206
        night sky 138
        red sunset 56
        search for 181–3, 186
        truth and 43
        wildness and adventure 14, 184–5
beliefs and values 42
'blame culture' modern, money for lawyers 94
books, importance of 247
British, attitude to being 237
butterflies 161
camping in Glacier Bay, Alaska, black and grizzly bears 22
certainty and uncertainty 157
Chasing Rainbows 214, 216
Christian heritage, abandonment of 46
civilised society, characteristics of 11
civility, less of, in modern life 62
classical music, beauty of 189–90

climbing, needs enthusiasm, determination, patience
        physical, mental, emotional involvement 32–3
        Lakeland hill at dawn 246
        self-discipline and 33
        sense of freedom 32
        Trivor, Karakoram Himalayas, snow and ice climbing 227
closed minds and prejudice, modern age feature 91
coasteering solo 203
coastguard and safety harness 236
College of Education, Ambleside, Lake District 10
compassion, quotations 64–5
compassion or indifference 63
complexity as vice 47
computer games, virtual reality
versus reality of physical involvement in natural environment 10
concentration 75–6
Confucius 130–31
connectedness 48, 58
'conscientious objector', to war 166
conscious and unconscious 55, 147
consumerism as modern god 106
corruption, endemic in life 142
cosmic awareness 199
courage and cowardice 113, 237
courage and determination 67
courage in climbing 34
creativity 98, 100
cult of individual without responsibilities 89, 241, 251

danger of solo kayaking
comparison with salmon doing it 230
virtues needed to survive it 229–30
danger of white water kayaking 221
dangerous game of conkers 236
Darwin, Charles Theory of Natural Selection,self-reliance 73
death, thoughts on 208
death of wife, Annette 48–9, 199–200
decline in our civilisation 240–41
destruction
        of humans and life forms by humans 251
        of wild Nature 242
        wisdom of minimal 30
determination and irresolution 66
devastation of natural world 104

disaster of modern world,money, status and power 251

Eagle flower, rare in wild 175
early retirement, 1992
Head of Outdoor Education, Ambleside, 14
earth from outer space 197
eco-centred actions, need for 91, 242
egocentricity of modern world 21
Einstein. Albert, on ideals 43
Emerson, Ralph Waldo, 'Self-Reliance' 73
empathy, with natural world and with others 79–80
energy in Nature 159–60
ethics and Christian heritage 46
Everest climbing, comments on 4, 5
evil, human capacity for 169
expedition to Arctic Circle, kayaking 98–9
experience
        of wild Nature, our society's need for 240–42
        Exxon Valdez oil spill, Alaskan coastline 93, 204

fashion statement in society: four-wheel drive vehicles 169
fear and anxiety 22, 156
fear as major block 71
Field Studies 8, 9
fishing incident off Alaska 63
forgiveness and condemnation 93–4
Four Cardinal Virtues 46
freedom and self-discipline 167
freedom to work out life's journey, for every individual, 30
friendliness in climbers 34, 81, 82
friendship 213
        with non-human world, dog 82–3

Gardom's Edge, Derbyshire, climbing 3
'gentleman' concept, disappearance of 86
geography field trip experience in Scotland 3, 4
global warming 178
God, Truth and Beauty 195
goodness
        of mankind, intrinsic 168–9
        in wild nature 168–9
gratitude and ingratitude 88, 232

Hahn, Kurt, founder of Outward Bound, on apathy 112

Hammarskjöld, Dag, journey to inner self 144
Health and Safety Executive 236
heroes, bogus, set up by society 149
heroes, true,
   Buddhist monks march in Rangoon 148
   Dalai Lama, Nelson Mandela, Mahatma Gandhi 149
   personal list 150
homosapiens, a joke 251
honesty 47, 142
   foundation virtue 49, 50, 54
   unity with Nature, solo kayaking in Alaska 53–4
   with oneself and other people climbing 51–3
hospital visit, courage of Annette 113–14
human body, importance of 18
human potential for evil 140
Hume, Cardinal Basil 104, 141
humility, importance of 103
'humorous' sketches on television 117
humour 116
   when climbing 33

illness and death of wife, Annette 206–7
importance of everything in Nature 242
indifference or compassion 64
indiscipline, vice of 72
individual, cult of, modern world emphasis on 58, 77
individual fulfilment, aim of living 32
individuation, Carl Jung 29
ingratitude 89
inner and outer self 145
inspiration of Annette 223
interaction with wild Nature, beginning of wisdom 130
international adventure off Scotland 93
intolerance about religion 91
intuition, messages from unconscious 24, 128

Jainist religion, minimum destruction of Nature 102
Jillot, Bernard, climber 34
Jung, Carl, collective unconscious 146
justice and injustice 95
Kant, Immanuel 24
kayak expedition to Alaska, solo 22–23
kayak trip on Wye, Wales
   gratitude for surviving 89
   upriver journey 227–8

kayaking from Cumbria to Isle of Man by night, 56
Keble College interview 4
kindness 43, 84
Koestler, Arthur, on beauty 183
Korea, computer games supersede sport 10–11

Lakeland fells, high view, beauty 196
life forms in natural world 159
life of Annette 222
link to other humans 29
living in the moment 219
lizard on rock in Spanish Pyrenees, empathy 79
love, what it is 211–12
love 201
        for Annette 207
        of beauty in wild Nature, experience crossing Irish Sea 205–6
        of climbing 202
        of human beings, Oxford Outdoor Centre 204
        of self, and forgiveness 204
        of wild nature 15, 203, 204

Mahatma Gandhi 112, 141
        gentleness 86
        on morality 142
        on tolerance 92
Mahler, Gustav
        hut in the mountains 188
        theme music of 'Death in Venice' 187
materialism of modern world 21, 44, 106
maturity 29
meat eating 169
migration of life forms
        godwits' flight to New Zealand 138
        osprey solo flight, tracked 138
minimal destruction 186
modern world separateness from Nature 178
moral substitute for war, war within humans 168
morality 142
motivation behind actions, crucialness of 48
mountain flowers 14
music 187–92
        comfort of, in bereavement 188
        of wild Nature
        cry of loon 191
        lark song 192

mystery and God 193–5
mystery and religion 200

National Association for Outdoor Education 10, 91
Native American Indian tribes
love of nature, before coming of white man 28
man belongs to the earth 58, 65
respect for Nature 104
natural world, sense of sacred 139
Nature
        affinity with 28
        aliveness and importance of 15
        attitude of minimal destruction to 49
        importance of everything in it 35
        justice to 96
        man out of balance with 161, 252
        residing in unconscious mind 175
        wisdoms from 153
New Zealand, invitation to lecture, success of 15
Nietszche, Friedrich 146, 221
Northern Lights in Arctic Norway 139, 196
Noyce, Wilfrid, Everest climber 34
        climbing the Matterhorn 111

ocean, experience with wild nature 23
osprey flight, tracked, New York to South America 73–4
Outdoor Education, as part of education for young people 10, 236–7
Outer Hebrides, kayak navigation 137
Outward Bound concept, 'impelled into experience' 84
Outward Bound movement, for character and fitness training 43–4

paddling skill 174
patience 66–70
personal values framework 42
politeness and rudeness 48
pollution of rivers in New Zealand 106
pollution of wild Nature 106, 251
purity and impurity 106
Pyrenean climb with Annette 231, 232

quotations, use of 214–5

raven, 'conversation' with 176–7
respect 61, 62

of mountains 33

towards Nature 62

responsibility and irresponsibility 101

Risk and Reformation Advisory Council 236

risk assessments in education 236–7

rock climbing, fear in 19

romantic love and friendship 21, 202, 203

rude behaviour, characterised on TV 89

Russell, Bertrand, on vitality as important virtue 112, 155

Schweitzer, Albert 112

example of altruism 77

Scott expedition to Antarctic 148

sea birds, love of, meeting with storm petrel 56–7

sea kayaking and spiritual awarenesss 197

Second World War, aims of fighting 29

self, sense of wonder about 139

self-centredness 79, 136, 227

self-discipline 71–2

self-knowledge 18–25

self-reliance 73, 74

self-respect in mountain environment 61

separateness in modern world 21

Seven Deadly Sins 46

simplicity and complexity, less is more 109, 110

smiles 81–2

solitude as oneness 179

solitude in nature, heightened awareness of 15

spirit of place 199

spiritual aspect of being human, heart, soul, conscience 20

spiritual involvement in climbing 32

spiritual sense, natural religious sense 138

spirituality and wild Nature 199

sport, increase in bad behaviour 168

St Paul, nine elements of love 210

Sun, earth's need for 198

terns, extent of annual migration

respect and compassion for 49

tolerance and intolerance 91

transcendent experiences, unity 172–9

transcendental intuitions 215

truth, search for 50, 141, 143

truth, seeker after, unpopularity of this 5

truth and beauty 43

uncertainty 155
unconscious, elemental importance of, Carl Jung 24, 25
unity between conscious and unconscious self 163–4
unity with nature 178
universal love 216
unkindness 84
unselfishness, as Warden of Woodlands Outdoor Centre 34

vegetation in Alaska, protection of 54
vices and virtues 33, 46, 48
virtue
        Annette 208–9
        importance of, historic quotations 44–5, 49
        life of young climber 34
vitality and apathy 111
vitality and determination 66–7

war, moral substitute for 167
war and courage 168
Western society, materialism of 28
white water canoeing 8, 9
wife, Annette, as spiritual presence 38
wild flowers 113, 139, 175–6, 221
wild Nature 188
        as church and sacred 196, 198
        in individuals 242
        love of 176
        in our unconscious 23
wild places, sanity of 109
wilderness challenges, and individual fulfilment 225
wisdom, what it is, 127–35, 151
wisdoms from nature, five pillars 154
Woodlands Outdoor Centre, Glasbury on Wye, South Wales job as Warden 8

young people's courage, impressed by 10

Comments on the Book
(pre-publication)

"It's quite possible that 'The Spirit of Adventure' will be the most important book you will ever read. If not, it should be. A bold statement, but one I believe to be true. Why? Because it deals with the most fundamental questions facing anyone who breathes: how best should I live my life? During a lifetime of outdoor education and adventure, in which the author has been forced to confront his own fears and frailties, he has discovered an inner journey that has proved to be as exciting but even more profound than any physical challenge. Drawing on his own wide-ranging experiences, and the wisdom of others, he has created a guidebook that shows a route to Everyman's soul."

Kev Reynolds (Travel Writer)

"A stimulating and fascinating read...it raises lots of questions. but I see that positively as good texts should do that...I really did enjoy reading this and am sure that many will gain a lot from it."

Geoff Cohen (Climber and Statistician)

"It is an honour to read Colin's thoughts which he delivers with honesty and humour. You don't have to agree with everything he writes but you should definitely read this book!"

Heather Rhodes (Outdoor Instructor – New Zealand)

"Many thanks for letting me read your book. It is an extraordinary testimony to the character and, in particular, the intellectual honesty of an unusually gifted individual. It will be received by all who are able to share even a little of your quite exceptional experience and application."

John Cook CBE (Climber and Education Administrator)

" It was a privilege to share your thoughts based on a lifetimes reflections...if reading your book can encourage reflection earlier in an active life, it could aid the process of becoming even more mature in the way that you describe...I agree wholeheartedly with your statement: 'The major task in life is to bring my unconscious into my conscious state as much as I can.'."

Monica Baynes (Psychotherapist - retired)

"This book is an extension of Beyond Adventure. It probes the depths of humanism and leaves a few wounds on those who falter along the way. Humanity will have come of age when its values are followed without the need for laws to enforce them. This book is a pathway to that end."

Ray Goldring (Outdoor Instructor, Consultant and Auditor)

"I admire your ability to sustain such clear, logical trains of thought and express such complex issues with a high degree of clarity and somehow maintain an honest, clearly personal view and state it simply."

Marian Armstrong (Tutor, Librarian – retired)

"A wonderful collection of reflective thoughts with a huge potential for productive influence…I have found your writing fascinating and thought provoking."

Max Biden (Climber and Accountant)

"The Spirit of Adventure, through a unique combination of reflection on personal experience and historical wisdom, challenges one to question how we live our lives today. The wisdom contained within needs to be read NOW."

Ross Morton (Manager OBNZ)

"Inspirational and deeply thought provoking: a framework and guide for the adventure that is life."

Andrew Dimberline (Teacher)

"I loved the way this book actually felt like a journey whilst I was reading it…sort of walking through seminal paths of your life, but also sharing the writing/editing/reflecting activities that accompanied the writing of the book…I believe your approach helps avoid a didactic/preachy vibe."

Jillian Cooke – Canada

"The Spirit of Adventure is a book full of hope and wisdom. Mortlock's voice is clear, true and burning with message. It is beyond important that it is sent echoing through schools, factories, hospitals and streets alike, to be recognised as the healing and revolutionary piece of writing it has the potential to be."

Eleanor Forster (Outdoor Instructor - Scotland)

"This has to be one of the best, most resonant and most important writings I have ever read. It could just change the course of the lemmings that humans have become and if this can only reach enough teachers, youth leaders, ordinary folk and (heaven help us) politicians, there may be a sea of change. Brilliant! AJM (Annette) would be beaming!"

Margaret Ellis (English teacher – retired; Archaeologist and Cave Guide)